THE CITY THAT DOES NOT AGE

The history of Sofia

BISTRA JOHNSON

Copyright © Bistra Johnson 2016

ISBN: 978-0-9556875-3-2

The right of Bistra Johnson to be identified as the Author of this Work has been asserted by her in accordance with the Copyright, Designs and Patents Act 1988

Cover design © Bistra Johnson

All rights reserved. No part of this publication may be reproduced, stored in a retrieval system, or transmitted in any form or by any means, electronic, mechanical, photocopying, recording or otherwise without the prior permission in writing of the publisher.

DEDICATION

To the memory of my late father, Jordan, who was due to co-write this book, but instead, I was left to carry the torch all by myself. I cannot fill his shoes, but I did my best and hope my readers will be indulgent and overlook its flaws

CONTENTS

Acknoweledgements **7**
1. **At a Crossroads of Civilisations**, Preface **8**
2. **Prologue** **13**
3. **Antiquity And Roman Times** **16**
   - Ancient Beginnings – The Thracian City of Serdonpolis **16**
   - Macedonian Invasion **19**
   - A Roman Provincial Capital **20**
   - The Roman Emperors Who Shaped the City of Serdica **29**
     I.   Early Days – a Golden Age **29**
     II. Religious Tolerance – the Edict of Serdica and the Edict of Milan **33**
     III. Serdica is my Rome **35**
     IV. The Council of Sardica 342/343 AD **38**
     V.   Constantius vs Vetranio **40**
4. **The Middle Ages** **43**
   - Barbarian Invasions **43**
     I.   The Goths, the Visigoths and the Empire. The end of antiquity **43**
     II.   Persecution of paganism **45**
     III. Attila the Hun **47**
     IV.   Anthemius triumphs at Sardica **48**
     V.   Zeno and the Ostrogoths **50**
     VI.   Justinian I the Great **53**
     VII. Germanus, Justinian's Heir Apparent, based in Sardica **55**
     VIII. Maurice's Balkan campaigns & Final Decline **56**
   - Bulgaria vs the Empire **59**
     I.   The Scull of Nicephorus **59**
     II. The Building Fervour of Omurtag & Malamir **62**
     III. The Miracles of St. John of Rila **63**
     IV. Basil, the Bulgar-Slayer **65**
   - The Time of the Crusades **69**

- I. *Pechenegs* **69**
- II. *Crusaders* **72**
- III. *Manuel I Komnenos vs the Serbs and the Hungarians* **74**
- IV. *Gregory Anthiochos on the 'hardships" of Sardica* **77**
- V. *The Magyars and the Holy Relics of a Bulgarian Saint* **80**
- VI. *Barbarossa and his Crusaders in Straliz* **81**
- VII. *The Treasures of Boyana Church* **83**

5. A Trip in Time But Not in Space, Interlude   **87**
6. Ottoman Times   92

- ❖ The Shishman Royal Dynasty and the Ottoman Invasion **92**
- ❖ The Fall of Sofia **94**
- ❖ The Ill-Fated Crusade of King Wladyslaw of Varna and John Hunyadi **99**
- ❖ Ottoman Military Campaigns in the West and the Black Death **103**
- ❖ Patron-Saints Make Their Appearance in Sofia **105**
- ❖ The Return of the Black Death and Various Other Events **106**
- ❖ Sofia, a Favoured Stopover for Travellers **108**
- ❖ The Catholic Presence in Sofia **113**
- ❖ Evliya Chelebi's Sojourn in Sofia **116**
- ❖ The Habsburg Wars **119**
- ❖ An English Lady Goes to Sofia's Hammam **121**
- ❖ The Archives Speak Out **122**
- ❖ Sofia from the Memoirs of a French Aristocrat **124**
- ❖ Another Frenchman in Sofia **126**
- ❖ The Impressions of a British Travel Writer **128**
- ❖ Education **131**

7. Earthquakes, Interlude   **134**
8. Decline & the Road to Independence 136

❖ Sofia Loses its Status in an Administrative Shuffle **136**
❖ The Hanging of Levski, Bulgarian National Hero and a Revolutionary **139**
❖ April Uprising – the Aftermath and the Battle for Sofia **141**

9. After the Liberation   **147**

❖ The Rebirth of the City   **147**
❖ The Intelligentsia   **174**

10. Sofia Enters the 20th Century   **184**

❖ A Time of Renewal   **184**
  I. How the city acquired its Coat of Arms   **184**
  II. The most Iconic Buildings of the Capital   **185**
  III. A New World of Technological Developments   **194**
❖ Foreign Visitors to the Capital   **197**

11. Wars, Terrorist Attacks and Civil Unrest in the First Half of the 20th Century   **204**

❖ WWI   **205**
❖ The Coup d'Etat of 9th June 1923   **209**
❖ The Terrorist Attack at St. Nedelia Church 1925   **210**
❖ The Coup d'Etat of 19th May 1934   **212**
❖ WWII, Bombardments and the Aftermath   **213**
❖ The Coup d'Etat of 9th September 1944 and the Red Army in Sofia   **217**

12. Post-War Period & the Beginning of the New Millennium   **218**

Conclusion   **228**
Bibliography   **230**
Index   **236**

ACKNOWLEDGMENTS

I would like to express my gratitude to my husband, Mark, who saw me through this book; who was extremely supportive, patiently read every chapter as they came out, mused over, listened, made suggestions, assisted in the editing, proofreading and put up with me the whole time when it was in the making.

Thanks to my late architect father, Jordan, for the inspiration he gave me, for his invaluable help and encouragement and for all the materials from his rich archive that he put at my disposal

I want to thank my mother, Antoinette, who believed in me, supported me and encouraged me through some of my darkest hours.

Thanks to all my family and friends, especially my sons, Danny and Tony, who were in my thoughts while I was working on my book.

Last but not least: I am thankful for the indifference and rejection that I have met with from different quarters, because it strengthened my resilience, helped me to build up my courage and to overcome any doubts I might have had.

AT A CROSSROADS OF CIVILISATIONS

PREFACE

The bronze statue of St. Sofia is striking, standing on a high pedestal at the central square Nezavisimost and looking to the east. She wears a long and very revealing black dress blown by the wind, which leaves nothing to the imagination, and sports a golden crown sitting neatly on her elaborate hairdo. Her arms are outstretched and she holds a laurel wreath in her right hand; an owl is perched on her left arm – Nike and Athens rolled into one. Her youthful golden face seems rather unimpressed, perhaps because of the huge building site, lying just below.

St. Sofia is not even looking at it, but straight ahead towards a future that only she can see. The past is embodied by a tiny church, huddled half buried on a small mound amongst the havoc wreaked by diggers, cranes and various other excavating machines. The church is old and is erected on top of the even older remains of an ancient crypt. Built in the 11th century, St.Petka of the Saddlers has miraculously survived to this day despite being frequently threatened with destruction. As the name suggests, it was connected with the Guild of the Saddlers who resided in this area during the medieval period and who had chosen St. Petka (Paraskeva), a Christian martyr from the time of Diocletian (beginning of the 4th century AD), as their patron saint.

The current Orthodox priest has been researching the history of the church and has a few stories to tell. He speaks about a temple existing there as early as the 4th century, at any rate there is the crypt beneath the edifice that dates from that period. He also talks about his personal connection with the church - his grandfather was part of the demolition team that was commissioned to pull it down in the first years of the communist regime. However, the night before, his grandfather had a dream: standing in front of the temple, he heard a voice from above, telling him that he might insert a stone, but not remove one...Most of the others had had the same dream. One man though disregarded the admonition and raised his pick intending to get on with the work, but then he suddenly froze and was unable to move. He stood like a wax figure for a couple of hours, his mates being powerless to help him. Thanks to this heavenly intervention the church was saved and granted the status of a national monument. It takes a leap of faith to accept this story, but the fact is that the church is still there.

Urban legends aside, in fact, sometime in the 70s, St. Petka Church narrowly escaped demolition once again. It was at the time of another "modernising" of the city centre. A pedestrian underpass had been envisaged there and the question of demolishing the church arose yet again.

The well known Bulgarian archaeologist Magdalina Stancheva, in an interview, recalls that St. Petka at the time was a sorry sight. It stuck out at about 70 cm (28 inches) above street level, its roof gone. Pencho Kubadinski, the Minister of Building and Architecture, had called a meeting to discuss the project. Magdalena Stancheva, although a bit intimidated by all the influential people present, declared: *"This church in the city centre has not been destroyed even by the Turks, now we are about to destroy it. It is a testimony that whatever else, it was allowed to have a church in the city centre ... between two huge mosques."* Pencho Kubadinski was obviously impressed by this statement. Despite the difficulties, the church was preserved and restored. Magdalina Stancheva goes on to say that she has shown many a foreign visitor around the city centre and pointing to the tiny church would ask them: *"Tell me, is there another capital that has sliced its centre so that all traffic is disrupted, to keep an old monument?"* She then added: *"If it was not for this church, this square would look different."*

Indeed, thanks to that timely intervention, the tiny church was not just saved from destruction, but has become a focal point. It hasn't changed much since then, well, almost, with just a little nod to the current trend. On the facade is displayed a modern stylized image of the saint, depicted as a handsome, pious looking woman, glancing somewhat sideways at the glamorous newcomer, the statue of St. Sofia. There is a certain connection between the two ladies, although they don't look alike. Both seem a bit out of place and not sure what to make of their surroundings, although both are supposed to represent the transition - old meets new, so to speak. The models who posed for the respective artists, no doubt still roam the streets of the capital, rather pleased with themselves – their youthful images will remain in the heart of the city long after they are gone.

Meant as a New Age symbol of the city that "grows but does not age", the statue of St. Sofia was erected there at the dawn of the new Millennium to replace the marble statue of Lenin that used to be in the same spot during the communist era. But who is she exactly? The busy inhabitants of the city are a bit confused: "the city's patron, but not a religious saint" (whatever a religious saint is),"a goddess protector of the city", "the goddess of wisdom"? Wait a second! Surely the goddess of wisdom, according to the Greek mythology, is Athens and she's given her name to the Greek capital; the Romans called her Minerva. Where does Sofia come in this equation? And if a saint – where is the halo, if she wasn't a queen, why does she have a crown?

In order to find out, we have to go back in time again, back to that pre-Christian period, when pagan religions were battling for domination. Patron saint in fact is the Christian substitute for a tutelary deity, meaning a guardian, a protector, as Pallas Athena is the patron goddess of Athens. But lots of cities in antiquity opted for a goddess like Tyche (meaning "luck" in Greek), who determines the fate and prosperity of the city, its destiny in short. The Romans called her Fortuna.

Cities in the Hellenistic era would come up with their own version of Tyche, identifiable by the so called "mural crown" she wears, that is a crown that represents the city walls. Her image appears on coins from that period and even later, until the time when Christianity became the official religion of the Roman Empire. Julia Domna, the wife of the Roman Emperor Septimius Severus for example, was represented on a coin from Serdica precisely in the guise of Tyche with her mural crown. Serdica was the name of Sofia in Roman times, so the city later used a stylized version of this image for its coat of arms.

Later legends, such as the one recounted by Captain Edmund

Spencer, the English 19th century travel writer, attribute somewhat divine origins to Sofia (as is the case with so many other cities). A certain celestial dweller fell in love with a mortal girl, a beauty known as Serdicé. For her, he left behind his heavenly abode, took her for a little flight and hovered for a bit in the skies, in Superman fashion, before deciding to settle in the beautiful plain that they had spotted from above. The city they founded there was named after Serdicé (which sounds very much like the Slav word for "heart"), although later on it took on the name of the magnificent church, St. Sofia.

This much is true - the name of the city really comes from the name of the oldest Christian basilica, St. Sofia (Sveta Sofia) located in its centre, about a kilometre or so away from the statue, which is looking in that direction. There was a Christian martyr St. Sofia; frescos within the church represent St. Sofia with her daughters: Faith, Hope and Love (Charity). Her day, according to the Eastern Orthodox Church, is celebrated on September 17th and so accordingly, the city of Sofia also celebrates on the same day. Nevertheless this is a misconception; in fact the church is named Hagia Sophia, which means Holy Wisdom in Greek.

Hagia Sophia is a remarkable church, although very different from her glamorous and world renowned counterpart - The Hagia Sophia of Constantinople/Istanbul in neighbouring Turkey. And yet they date from about the same time – the time of the Byzantine Emperor Justinian the Great (6th century AD). Justinian, who had rebuilt the Hagia Sofia church in Constantinople, had also rebuilt its namesake in Serdica, but completed in a very different style. And yet it has unmistakably the looks of a Byzantine basilica – an imposing, yet simple, red brick building of eternal beauty that the vagaries of time have spared to this day. One quirky peculiarity – it hasn't got a bell tower – and you have to look for the bell itself, because it's not to be found where you might expect it! Why? Read on to find out, it will all be revealed in the end!

The legend says that Justinian had a sickly daughter who was advised to come here and take the waters this city is so famous for. Miraculously the maiden recovered quickly and delighted, Justinian built the church and named it after her...It's doubtful that there is any truth in this story. Justinian didn't have any children and although his wife Theodora had a niece with that name who later married Justinian's nephew Justin and became Empress in her turn, it's unlikely that she ever set foot in the Balkan city. But the hot mineral springs and their healing properties had been renowned since Antiquity.

So there you have it. Most great cities are founded on the sea coast or along a big river. Sofia is founded around thermal mineral water springs at the foothills of a mountain. Sofia plain is so vast and fertile that it is not surprising that settlers were flocking here since ancient times. The oldest settlements discovered on its territory date from the first part of the Neolithic – 4th century BC. Balneotherapy and spas must have come into fashion about then... Sofia boasts 8 types of mineral water from about forty something mineral sources around the Sofia plain, with varying temperatures between 45-60°C and a combined flow of about 550 l/sec; sufficient to treat about 100 000 people per day...And yet, there are no more mineral baths in the city today; just water fountains where people come to fill their bottles!

The splendid building dating from the beginning of the 20th century, that used to house the Central Mineral Baths, is finally restored, but is to be turned into... a museum of Sofia, with a spa-centre to go with it! How well such an unlikely pair is going to function, is anybody's guess. On one side the design team involved with the Museum part, maintains that there are too many spa-centres but not enough museums to preserve the city history. For example an exhibition space, dedicated to the architects who designed the building itself, is so important, because if it wasn't for them, all the debate wouldn't be taking place in the first instance. There are also some priceless objects waiting to be put on display, such as the carriage of Marie-Antoinette from the French Government and a Grandfather clock from Queen Victoria, both given to King Ferdinand as wedding presents, or one of the first motor cars that took to the streets of Sofia. Their opponents, who are for using the building for the purposes it was built for at the outset, underline that displaying museum exhibits above water conduits is asking for trouble. But it seems that the project is going ahead regardless of the objections. Violeta Vasilchina, an art critic, in a long and winding article, which one can't quite make head or tail of, waxes lyrical about the Mineral Baths building. She sees its *"cheerful image completed as a persuasive-paradoxical synthesis between a temple, a hammam and a public palace, pragmatically, symbolically and aesthetically well thought with the expression of all its components – festive decoration, reinforced concrete construction, its ceramic magnificence, harmonious interiors, acoustics, the sophisticated appearance of the lady after her bath, wearing her bath gown..."* So you may seek this persuasive-paradoxical synthesis for yourselves and if you are convinced, well, good for you!

But now, while the diggers are still busy with their messy work, let's take this opportunity to go down to this ancient world they have opened for us and investigate the site, this is the moment to do it, to go back in time, as far back as possible and take a really good look. What was it like to live in that city?

PROLOGUE

"On the Balkan peninsula, the disintegration has now reached its height. It is in everyone's interest that a more complete and more stable crystallisation should take place. If ever it is to get out of the domain of dreams, it is enough to look at a map to see that the centre of gravity of the future edifice should be neither in Bucharest, neither in Belgrade, neither in Thessalonica, even less in Athens. Geometry places it, and the Bulgarians know it well, in a position central in a different way, in Sofia."

Louis de Launay

It might come as a surprise, but this quote, contemporary as it seems, dates actually from the beginning of the 20th century – more than 100 years ago. The author, a French writer, biographer and a poet (not to mention his geology engineering degree, *Ecole des Mines de Paris*) in a book about Bulgaria, analyses the position of its capital, Sofia. For a Bulgarian person, this may be stating the obvious, but it's not so obvious for the rest of the world.

To put it in a nutshell, Sofia is situated in the middle of the Balkan Peninsula. And it is this location that determined its destiny.

Time Line

- Ancient Beginnings – known today as Sofia, the city was founded at the foothills of Mount Vitosha amidst numerous hot and cold mineral springs
- Thracian Times – it was then known as Serdonpolis; it survived the Macedonian invasion of 342 BC
- Roman Province from 29 BC – favoured by emperors – Serdica
- Byzantine Times – Sardica, since the 4th century (part of the Eastern Roman Empire)
- Barbarian invasions: Visigoth incursion (376-382 AD); Attila the Hun and the sack of Sardica in 443
- Middle Ages: Through road for pilgrims, merchants, Crusaders (11th – 14th century); known as: Triaditsa / Straliz/Stralizia/Sternes/Atralza/Hesternit/Scereducy/Sofia
    i. A Bulgarian City – Sredetz – 9th- 10th; 13th-14th c.
    ii. Byzantium Strikes Back - 11th century - Triaditsa
- Ottoman Invasion –14th century - Sofya/Sofia, capital of provincial backwater (Roumelia) until 19th century
- Liberation – Sofia, capital of the new Bulgarian state
- Sofia in the 20th Century – 20th Century Wars
- The New Millennium – time of changes

As we can see the city has had quite a chequered history. And it has seen it all during its lifetime, which spans about 7000 years or so. The town has been known under various names, and its inhabitants have not always been the Bulgarians. In fact, its status as a capital of Bulgaria is relatively recent – only since the Liberation from Ottoman rule in 1879 (we don't count a very brief period just before it was invaded by the Ottoman Turks).

Nevertheless Sofia/Serdica had gained and retained its

significance throughout the centuries despite the vagaries of time. It couldn't be otherwise, a major road went through it, linking Constantinople with Singidunum (now Belgrade) and Central Europe. This road dates from Roman times, although it was built following older Thracian roads. The Romans knew the importance of a good infrastructure and were quick to construct roads, usually by improving on existing local ones, in the newly conquered territories. That was done not just in order to establish the Roman way of life, but first and foremost for military purposes. As with many other Roman roads, the reports referring to the use of the thoroughfare at Sofia/Serdica concern armies marching along it. After that administration takes its place and only then is commercial use and the needs of private travelers thought of.The major road at Sofia/Serdica became known later as *Via Militaris* or *Via Diagonalis*, but was also referred to as *Via Traiana* (after 1600) or even, erroneously, *Via Singidunum*. Another road that went through Serdica, connected Bononia (now Vidin) on the Danube with Thessaloniki.

The overall distance between Singidunum and Constantinople is 924 km. In olden times it took about 10 days to get from Singidunum to Serdica and 13 from there to Constantinople, or 23 days all together. Well, in those far away days people travelled either on foot, either, if they were well off – on horseback or in a horse-drawn carriage. *"After that, at the place where Bulgaria starts from, rises a fortress called Bulgarian Belagrava [Belgrade], to be distinguished from another town of the same name in Hungary. From there, within a one-day trip, after crossing a river [Morava] one reaches the mean small town of Brunduzium [Branichevo, next to the present-day town of Kostolats in Serbia].... After a five-day trip, there came the first and not big town of Nish on the same side of Greece. The towns of Nish, Hesternit [Sofia], Philippopolis [Plovdiv] and Adrianople [Edirne] are at a four-day distance from each other, and from the latter town to Constantinople it takes five days,"* states Odo of Deuil, a knight who took part in the Second Crusade (1147–1149).

Nearly 500 years later, now part of the Ottoman Empire, the

city had not lost its significance: *"Sofia is one of the biggest crossroads in Turkey, as one has to pass from there on his way to Constantinople, Venice, Dubrovnik and Hungary..."* – from a travelogue about the mission of Louis de Ei, Baron de Kormanen (1621).

So it is the geographical position of Sofia in the middle of the Balkan Peninsula at the crossroads between East and West, North and South (respectively Asia Minor/ Middle East and Europe, The Baltic and the Aegean), that determined its fate and still continues to do so. On one hand it assured its growth, but on the other, it made it the target of various conflicting interests, trying to take advantage of its strategic importance. It is however surprising that in this day and age, the importance of Sofia is so overlooked and its epic past is all but ignored outside its boundaries.

ANTIQUITY - THRACIAN AND ROMAN TIMES

ANCIENT BEGINNINGS – THE THRACIAN CITY OF SERDONPOLIS

SERDICA - SREDETS - SOFIA since ancient times was growing at the foot of three hills: Slatina to the east, Koniovitsa to the west and the most beautiful of them all, Lozenets to the south. The centuries old oak forests, vineyards and cherry trees in its meadows explain why since the Dawn of Time, since the times of the tribe of the ancient Serdi it was honoured as a holy hill. On its west slope were the caves and catacombs of the oldest Christians from the Serdi tribe.

The Monastery Of The Holy Trinity Has Risen To Face A New Golgotha, by Architect J. Tangarov, Coordinator of the Friends of Sofia Committee

Despite the advances of archaeology and the data recorded by history, the ancient past still remains something of a mystery – tantalising and yet quite reluctant to yield its secrets. Very little is known about the first inhabitants of this area. They left us some artefacts to inform us of their presence and awaken our curiosity. So we know that they really existed. There is plenty of archaeological evidence to illustrate this. Walking the streets of the city of Sofia we actually walk above the remains of human habitation that go back millennia. That underground world is full of secrets, waiting to be discovered.

A human settlement existed on the territory of the Bulgarian capital since early Neolithic times, the first half of the 6th millennium BC, to be precise, according to the archaeologists. The remains of three more settlements from the Eneolithic period were also discovered; one, dating from the 4th millennium BC (Stancheva, 1958, Georgiev, 1959) – is situated exactly underneath the centre of the modern city, just at the east side of what was going to be the city wall of the future Roman metropolis and what is now Alexander Battenberg Square.

But what can we find out about all this in the history books? The Greek historian Thucydides (ii. 96) in the 5th century BC informs us that: *"...Treres and Tilataei, who dwelt on the northern slope of Mount Scomius (present day Vitosha), and extended towards the west as far as the river Oscius (present day Iskar)..."* And in The Cambridge Ancient History we find that: *"In the place of the vanished Treres and Tilataei we find the Serdi for whom there is no evidence before the first century BC. It has for long being supposed on convincing linguistic and archeological grounds that this tribe was of Celtic origin."* Who on earth were the *Treres* and the *Tilataei*? Even the *Serdi* appear rather elusive, especially when certain sources claim that they were of Thracian origin, while others, like the one above, assert that they were Celts. And the *"convincing linguistic and archaeological"* proof is quite intangible.

The 6th – 5th century BC was exactly the time of Darius I, known as the Great, who ruled the Persian Empire at its peak. During his campaign in the Balkans he led an army, consisting of various Thracian tribes from Asia Minor, including *Serdi* (*Sardi*), some of whom stayed on and mixed with the local Thracians. Hence the similarity of the names – Sardis was the capital of ancient Lidia and the fabulously rich King Croesus, conquered by Cyrus, a predecessor of Darius. But we'll leave the experts to argue the point while we get on with our story.

First of all, let's say a few more words about the actual site of this settlement. We already mentioned the mountain and the mineral springs, as being the main attractions. But there is more. Sofia plain is extensive, rich, sheltered by the mountains around it. In old geological times it has been the bottom of a lake, thus the natural terracing, favouring agriculture. At about 550m (1804 feet) above sea level, it measures 75km x 16km (46.6 miles x 9.94 miles) and is strategically positioned at the crossroads of the diagonal connecting Europe and Asia (northwest – southeast) and the axis from north – south; from the Baltic to the Aegean Sea.

The big mountain that dominates the city is Vitosha, but it's been known through history under different names – the ancients refer to it as *Scombrus*, *Scomius* or *Scopius*. Thucydides for example states that the *Strymon* river (now known as Struma) springs from the mount of *Scomius* (II 96), which agrees with the report of Aristotle (Meteorol. I. 13. Cf. Plin.IV.10), only the latter calls it *Scombrus*, while Pliny the Elder refers to it as *Scopius*.

The town of the *Serdi*, Serdonpolis, would've been a thriving centre in Thracian times, amongst all the other settlements in the vast Sofia plain. The ancient city was located close to the abundant healing thermal springs in the very heart of the present day Sofia. Somewhere there would've been the indispensable *Nymphaeum* (a monument consecrated to the nymphs).

Archaeological finds show that Serdonpolis had a regular street grid plan, that is, the streets run at right angles with each other, forming a grid. The residence of the ruler, well fortified, was built apart, in the highest spot of this vicinity, not far from where the basilica St. Sofia is situated today. Such a plan is not unlike the plan of Seuthopolis, the Thracian city of Seuthes III, ruler of the Odrysian kingdom. There must have been strong connections between the two cities. The archaeological data proves that they maintained a trading relationship, but Serdonpolis also had commercial links with places located as far away as the Aegean Sea. The fortunes of Serdonpolis would've been changing depending on the fortunes of the Thracian tribe that inhabited it. It saw of course the somewhat meteoric rise to fame of the neighbouring Macedonian kingdom, 4th century BC.

MACEDONIAN INVASION

Philip the Macedon invaded Thrace in 342 BC and so, for a period of time, Serdonpolis was under Macedonian rule. In fact the ancient sources contain very few details about Philip's campaign; apparently he had large forces with him and fought several battles. A tithe was levied on the Thracians, but they were left semi-autonomous, under the rule of their own kings, who were subordinate to Philip. However, as Thrace had become an administrative division of Philip's fiefdom, a *Strategus* of Thrace was appointed. There is a reference to Philippopolis, supposedly founded by Philip in the place of the Thracian fortified settlement Eumolpias.

Serdonpolis is not specifically mentioned and one could only speculate as to whether Philip had ever stayed in that city. It's known (from the Greek historian Justin) that on his way back from his successful Scythian campaigns, Philip was confronted by the *Triballi* (a Thracian tribe), who claimed a share of his booty, as a toll for passing through their lands. But the Macedonian leader would not have any of this; during the ensuing battle, Philip was wounded in the hip, in such a way, that his horse was killed and it was thought that he had lost his life too. Panic spread among the troops and in the ensuing pandemonium, the whole booty went missing, as if accursed, all but causing the Macedonian downfall. Philip's itinerary is not known and so localising the place of this, for him disastrous battle, is just conjecture. However, it is likely that he had been crossing the Sofia plain at the time, so the battle might've taken place there. Thus no soaking in the hot thermal pools for Philip, if ever this idea had crossed his mind! Instead he would've had to attend to his wound and find another horse.

It's not surprising that various legends are doing the rounds, like the one claiming that Philip went up mount *Skombrus / Scomius* (Vitosha) in the mistaken belief that he would be able to see the White Sea (the Aegean) from the top, or in a different version, it was Alexander the Great himself who decided to conquer the mountain and went for it with 12 of his soldiers but after a week of fruitless efforts, he gave up the idea of getting to the highest point, Black Peak (Cherni Vrah). Perhaps his tutor, the great Aristotle, might have told him about it and had encouraged him to do some exploration on his behalf? Alexander's campaign in the Balkans occurred in the spring of 335 BC. If we let our imagination loose, we might be able to picture him taking the waters and enjoying the local specialities before pressing on for his rendezvous with immortality i.e. eternal fame. Indulging in a strenuous excursion up mount *Skombros,* in the midst of a challenging military campaign, is taking it a bit too far though.

The above stories might appear very far-fetched, but actually there is some truth there; Livy, the Roman historian, does mention such an expedition of Philip the Macedon, but not up Mount *Scombros*; the mountain in question was in fact the *Haemus* / Balkan; ancient authors state that a fine view is to be had from the highest peaks, offering a 360°panorama that includes the Danube, the *Euxine* (Black Sea), the Alps (presumably the Julian Alps) and the Adriatic. No doubt that's what Philip was hoping to see when he set off on his excursion up the mountain. It took him three days but the weather deteriorated and he descended without seeing anything of great interest. Even if he did have more clement weather on his side and a pair of very powerful binoculars, it's still doubtful that he would've seen any of the above features from such a distance. But then geography has considerably advanced since those times.

A ROMAN PROVINCIAL CAPITAL

Our time travel in the city of Sofia itself can actually take us back only as far as the Roman era; the further back in time we go – the scarcer the information to be found – in the end we can only rely on the archaeological evidence to fit the pieces together.

Unfortunately, despite its ancient beginnings, the first written documents in existence, referring to the city, are the Roman records of their military campaigns in Thrace – it is cited in most sources that *"the town is first mentioned under the name of Serdonpolis in connection with the campaigns of the Roman general Marcus Licinius Crassus in 29 BC. "* Indeed, Crassus did march against the Thracian tribes *Bastarnae* in Moesia in 29 BC. First of all he torched *Segetic* (Serdic) settlements in the plains before defeating the *Bastarnae,* led by King Dellon (no relation to the actor!). In 28 BC the *Bastarnae* were causing problems again and Crassus returned to deal with them, routed also the *Meldi* and the *Serdi* and left an *Odrysian* tribe, friendly towards Rome, in the conquered lands. The question though is whether those tribes were Thracian or Celtic, as certain contemporary authors suggest? Isn't it all rather confusing? We had first the *Treres* and the *Tilataei,* supplanted by the *Serdi,* then, there were all those other tribes that Crassus had to fight or to negotiate with. The name *Meldi,* being of Celtic origin – apparently a tribe with such a name inhabited the valley of the River Marne in Gaul/France - led some historians to deduce that the entire people inhabiting this area at the time were Celts! At any rate, it appears that Crassus left his allies, the *Odrysians,* in the place of the vanquished *Meldi* and *Serdi!* Did they remain there though and for how long? This is not clear - there is no archaeological or written evidence to work with - and that's why it is pointless speculating on the origin of the first inhabitants of this city, which as we will see, has always been such a melting pot of cultures, coming from every possible direction.

But anyway, whatever happened to that indigenous population? Were they entirely decimated or driven away? *Serdi* or *Odrysians*, it appears that some of them at least remained. They would've accepted the new rule, but would've kept their customs. At least, the archaeological finds testify that the name of the city which was to become eventually Sofia, was at that time Serdonpolis, the city of the *Serdi (Sardi or Serdonese)*.

Jordan Tangarov, a prominent Bulgarian architect, offers an interesting hypothesis, based on the architectural parallel between Serdica/Sardica and Sardis, the capital of ancient Lydia (located in Asia Minor, today in Turkey). The Persian Emperor Darius I the Great (whose predecessor Cyrus II, as we already said, had taken the city of Sardis in the 6th century BC) did come to Thrace and some of his troops remained there; were they the mysterious Serdi/Sardi who founded Serdonpolis? Interestingly, apart from the similarity in the names, also intriguing is that the forums of the two cities, Sardis and Sardica should be built at about the same time (during the reign of the Roman Emperor Hadrian), judging by the similarity in the use of two levels of columns in both cases, as documented by architect Sava Bobchev.

During the recent construction of the Europe Warehouse and Trade centre in Sofia, a Thracian tumulus from the Roman period was discovered (so much for the theory that the *Serdi* were Celts). This unique archaeological site was investigated by a Bulgarian archaeological team and they discovered that as far as burials were concerned, the Thracians, living in the 3rd century Roman Serdica, hadn't deviated from their traditions.

According to Daniela Agre, the leader of the archaeological team, there have been two funerals in that particular tumulus, despite its modest dimensions: one body cremated and the other laid to rest. The cremation must've been that of a wealthy woman who had been burnt on a funeral pyre in the centre of the tumulus. A small cosmetic box, bronze fibulas and earrings and various other trinkets leave no doubt about her sex. The ashes were put into a ceramic vessel, placed near the dead body of a male, presumably killed during a battle, judging by the state of his remains (damaged scull, severed legs).

Herodotus, the father of history, wrote that there was a custom in some Thracian tribes to have one of the wives of the deceased (in those times the Thracians were polygamous) to accompany him on his journey to the afterlife. That appeared to have been a great privilege and seemingly the wives often quarreled as to who the chosen one was to be. By the looks of it, he was spot on and what is more this ritual was still current in the 3rd century AD! By then the Thracians had become Roman citizens and some of them got wealthy too. This is not surprising, for they would've participated in the rise of the mighty Empire. There is enough epigraphic evidence from the Roman era, to permit us to have a glimpse into their life. Before the 4th century the inscriptions on the monuments are mainly in Greek (100 against only 14 in Latin), which comes as no surprise, for notwithstanding the fact that Serdica is already a Roman city at that time, the main language there still remains Greek. Later on the trend is reversed, Latin becomes predominant.

The first person to study this "stone archive" was a certain Count Marcili. Passing through Sofia while journeying in Bulgaria, he wrote down the Greek and Latin inscriptions he found. He published his notes in 1744. From the official inscriptions left by the local authorities, it becomes clear that the name of the city was Serdonpolis – the city of the Serdi, called even *Lamprotati Serdonpolis* – the brightest city of the Serdi, the City of Light! There are numerous inscriptions with the name of the city spelled either as Sardica or Serdice. The people, who wrote them, either in Greek or in Latin, were using the letters A or E at their own discretion in their effort to transcribe more correctly the Thracian name of the city. From the inscriptions found we can assess the ethnic background of the Serdicans – it appears that they were quite a mix and of course they change over time. Between the 1st and 3rd century the citizens of Serdica are predominantly Thracians, mixed with some immigrants from other provinces and some high-ranking Romans in positions of authority.

First of all there are the Thracian names – everybody initially had just one name in the eastern world, and Thrace is no exception; Didza, Mukadzenis, Mukas, were some of them and their profession was also added as an additional reference. More numerous were the people with two names – proper name plus father's name; there is for example Deidis Didzu – Deidis, the son of Didza. This custom also comes from the east and is common not just in Thrace, but also in Greece and in Asia Minor. But gradually, much as would be expected, the Roman way becomes prevalent. Three names were becoming the norm, with some additional references to complete the picture. Newly-fledged Roman citizens from the Praetorian Guard, for example, would take the first two names of the ruling emperor (calling themselves "his sons"), would keep their Thracian name as a third name and would also include their home town. So we have M(arcus)

Aur(elius) M(arci) f(ilius) Mestrius d(omo) Serdica which means Marcus Aurelius (after the Emperor of the same name) Marci (his Thracian name) son of Mestrius from Serdica ; M. Aur. M. f Vellicio d Ulpia Serdica (Marcus Aurelius Marci son of Vellicio from Ulpia Serdica) etc. Some of the names found are rather a "mix and match" and they are the ones that are predominant in Serdica. For example - Aurelius Didza Lukiu – where the first name is the Roman Emperor's, followed by a Thracian one, Didza, and ending with another Roman one, taken in that particular form so as to indicate: Aurelius Didza, son of Lucius. In other cases there is a fusion of Roman and Greek (Asclepiades, son of Guy) or Roman and Thracian name (Aurelius, son of Mestrius). So far we spoke only of male names; in fact inscriptions connected with women are very rare. The Greek names of the followers of Cybele and Attis (the Phrygian Great Mother Goddess and her lover) are preserved and also various other names from gravestones.

    Here is the place to say a few words about graveyards, vast cemetery worlds, just outside the city walls, so before entering the "city of the living", the traveler passes by the "city of the dead". Morbid? Well, not exactly; it appears that in antiquity people in general and the Thracians in particular, were unafraid of death and saw it as a sort of threshold to the afterlife. Accordingly lots of the headstones bore inscriptions, containing greetings for the traveler, something which disappeared after the 4th century with the advent of Christianity. A significant number of tombstones, or rather monuments, were erected while the person they were intended for, was still alive. Mostly people opted for tombstones (*stella*); however some "show-offs" went for more elaborate options. The first Serdican *archon* (high official) for example, had a chapel with an altar built for him, while he was still alive. The widow of Epeptos, a Thracian, had a burial chamber built for both of them, which, after her own demise, was to be buried under a mound, according to the Thracian custom. Often the tombstone inscriptions contain the explicit instruction not to have anybody else buried in the same grave, but the age of the deceased is rarely indicated there.

Wherever it does occur, it shows that people then did not live long.

While early on, Crassus had troubles with the Thracian tribes, the period which started at the time of Emperor Augustus (27 BC) and lasted till the death of Emperor Marcus Aurelius (180 AD), about 200 years, was a real golden age for the Roman Empire, known as *Pax Romana*. And indeed peace and prosperity then reigned across the whole Empire, trade was flourishing and communications apparently were better than ever before or even afterwards. The elaborate network of Roman roads was imprinted forever on the face of the once Imperial territories. *"The main lines of land communication between the eastern and western empires, especially important after the founding of Constantinople, ran to the north of the Dalmatia through the Drave and Save valleys via Serdica and Sirmium,"* states Penny MacGeorge in her Late Roman Warlords. To be sure, the important road from Aquileia (an important ancient Roman city in Italy at the head of the Adriatic) to Constantinople went by Siscia (Sissek), Sirmium (Mitrovic), Serdica (Sofia), Philippopolis (Plovdiv) and Adrianople (Edirne), a total distance of 1128 Roman miles (1037 miles/1669 km).

It was precisely the Roman era that determined the fate of Serdica and left a lasting legacy. With its incorporation into such a great Empire, the importance of the city grew accordingly. The Romans didn't waste much time before rebuilding it. Emperor after emperor, each one would want to leave his own mark on it. "Rome wasn't built in a day" as they say. Neither was Serdica; it was nevertheless transformed little by little into a flourishing metropolis, fit for emperors.

But what did the Serdicans think about this extensive rebuilding fervour? Did they just take it in their stride, the same way their descendants today get on with their lives amidst the chaos, the dust and the noise that are causing such pandemonium at the very heart of the city? Roman Serdica would've looked like a building site most of the time – perhaps not so different from what we see now; where there is extensive excavation work going on in connection with the tunnels for the metro line; same place, different time.

The Roman city is exactly there, underneath the modern city centre. Walk down the steps of the underground pedestrian crossing, situated in front of the Presidential residence and you will be walking back in time. You will be stepping across the centuries onto the *Decumanus Maximus*, the stone Roman road at the Eastern gate of the city of Serdica. Interestingly, this gate was also uncovered in 1969 during building works in the city centre – another pedestrian underpass was to be constructed there. It was again Pencho Kubadinski, the Minister of Building and Architecture - neither a civil engineer nor an architect - who nevertheless got involved in preserving the Eastern Gate. According to Hristo Genchev, who is an architect, a group from GLAVPROEKT, the Institute of Architecture and Town Planning, signed a petition and handed it to the minister. Then again, Magdalina Stancheva, the well known archaeologist, recounts that she met Kubadinski at the building site, pointed to the two towers of the Eastern Gate and the city wall, just uncovered below their feet and asked him: *"Comrade Kubadinski, do you see this gate? It's through this gate that Khan Krum entered Serdica. Who dares to destroy this monument? We always talk about Serdica. But we do not say that the Bulgarian Khan who has conquered Serdica, has entered the city exactly here. Even if nothing else is deemed important enough to be preserved - and the fortress is much older than the time of Khan Krum – just because of the fact that the Bulgarian Khan has entered here to conquer Serdica ... it must be preserved. "* Stancheva then explains that she knew about Kubadinski's fascination with anything related to the ancient Bulgars and their khans. According to her, he had said to the foreman, responsible for the works: *"Look here, young man. You take care of the construction works, but Stancheva will take care of the historical remains. You shouldn't meddle there."*

Furthermore Kubadinski himself supervised the advancement of the project and at one point had the plans changed because the Eastern Gate was not shown to its advantage. Apparently he thought it would look like wallpaper, just outlined on the wall of the passageway, so he had the bright idea to have a third access to the underpass, traced in such a way, as to allow the pedestrians to pass through the gate itself. His plan was carried out and so the 20th century Sofianites were able once again to enter Roman Serdica through the Eastern Gate and to walk down *Decumanus Maximus*.

Decumanus Maximus is the east-west orientated thoroughfare in any Roman city. In the middle of the city (*groma*) it crosses *Cardo Maximus*, the main north-south thoroughfare, which was the main shopping street. In Serdica this intersection is located just where the church St.Petka of the Saddlers today withstands the persistent assault of the excavators. There was, and still is, the heart of the city. The central square (Roman forum), the City Council (*bouleuterion*), the Council of Elders (*gerousia*) and various temples are all here.

We must say a few words about the Rotunda St. George, just off *Decumanus Maximus,* now dwarfed by the huge buildings of the Communist era. Unlike the above mentioned edifices, it has survived almost unscathed the vagaries of time and is considered the oldest building in the city (4th century AD). It can be seen behind the hotel Balkan (previously Sheraton) in the midst of a whole complex of Roman ruins, not as fortunate to escape destruction. Dating from the time of the Roman Emperors Galerius and Constantine the Great, it is believed that the Rotunda was built on the site of an ancient pagan temple and was intended for public use, but the experts still can't agree on what the initial purpose of this edifice might have been. It is unlikely for it to have been a *martyrium* (a structure built over the tomb of a Christian martyr), as some suggest; surely there would've been some notion as to the identity of the martyr in question. Other hypotheses go even as far as to suggest that the Rotunda served as an Imperial residence, or that it was built as a church in the first instance, formed part of the Episcopal Palace and was possibly used during the ecclesiastical Council of Serdica, that we'll talk about a bit later.

The eminent archaeologist and historian Bogdan Filov has provided evidence in his study (Sofia St. George's Church, published in 1933 and republished in 2005) that the Rotunda was, in fact, one of the several public baths of the city; at any rate the *caldarium,* the hot baths. Unfortunately his hypothesis was rejected when the Communists came to power, as Filov who had become a Prime Minister, and after the demise of King Boris III, a regent for the young Simeon II, was seen as an "enemy of the people" and executed in 1945. All his academic work has since been denigrated and all but forgotten. His detractors discarded his theory about the Rotunda on the grounds that the *hypocaust* - the under-floor system (from Greek, meaning "heating from beneath"), was supposedly too high (1.00 - 1.20 m), while a height of 70 – 80 cm was required for the baths. This hypocaust, they said, served for ventilation and drainage of the floor; furthermore they denied the existence of furnaces (*praefurnium*), sources of the hot air that circulated under the floor, indispensable for the baths, although the furnaces are still there for everyone to see. Although Filov's work on St. George was published again after the political changes and some present day experts, such as Ventzislav Dinchev, concur with him, certain sources, lots of them on the Internet, still reject his theory and maintain that the Rotunda was initially intended as a *martyrium*. At any rate, the function of the Rotunda must've changed with the advent of Christianity, for since that time it has been used as a *baptisterium* – baptistery and a church.

There is also another building underneath the present day St. Nedelia Church that has caused a lot of ink to flow. In the beginning of the 20th century, eminent scholars like Alexander Rashenov and Bogdan Filov again, had stated that those remains were of the Roman Imperial Baths. However, later on, during the Communist era, experts like Magdalina Stancheva amongst others, opted for a *praetorium* instead. According to the Merriam Webster Dictionary the Latin term *praetorium* could mean one of the following: 1) *a* : an ancient Roman general's tent in a camp or *b* : a council of war held in such a tent and 2) *a* : the official residence of an ancient Roman governor or *b* : a splendid countryseat or a palatial residence especially in ancient Rome Obviously number 1 is not applicable here. As for number 2, there are various considerations, which make it an unlikely candidate.

In 1985 a swimming pool of generous proportions was discovered there (its width - 8.40 m, its length - more than 16 m). Floor and wall heating system (*hypocaust*) was employed to maintain ambient temperature, which suggests that the water used was probably not more than 30^0C (not thermal mineral water, as is the case with other baths nearby). The professors of architecture Boyadjiev and Tangarov concur with the conclusions of their predecessors Rashenov and Filov. Later on another expert, Ventzislav Dinchev also confirms this, writing about the swimming pool in a *"balneae"*, i.e. Roman baths. However, the building underneath St. Nedelia Church is still referred to as *praetorium* in many sources. But now let's walk down one of those boulevards - Boulevard Todor Alexandrov or Boulevard Marie Louise - for we will be literally walking either above *Decumanus Maximus* or above *Cardo Maximus* respectively, and think about all the Roman Emperors who have been here and have left their mark on the city.

THE ROMAN EMPERORS WHO SHAPED THE CITY OF SERDICA

EARLY DAYS - A GOLDEN AGE

Emperor Trajan (13th Emperor, 98 AD – 117 AD) grants a city status to the town (*municipium* - centre of an administrative region), named after him Ulpia Serdica (his full name being Marcus Ulpius Traianus), and lays the foundations for its classical urban structure in the 1st century AD. However the fortified wall wasn't finished till about 176 - 180 A.D. during the joint rule of Marcus Aurelius (the 16th Emperor) and his son, Lucius Aurelius Commodus (18th Emperor). Inscriptions on the four gates are known to have read: „*Good luck! The greatest and divine* emperors Caesars Marcus Aurelius Antonius Augustus Germanic Sarmatic, father of the Fatherland, Pontifex Maximus, and Licius Aurelius Commodus Augustus Germanic Sarmatic, gave the fortress walls to the city of Serdonpolis when the Governor of Thrace was Aselius Aemilius, the Emperor's representative as strategus, appointed as a future consul".

Yet the Cambridge Ancient History (2005 edition) informs us that: *"Situated in a remote high plain near the headwaters of the river Oescus (Iskur) in northwest Thrace, Serdica was a place of little importance until it was chosen as metropolis of Aurelian's New Dacia and was then for a few years the favourite residence of Constantine, a native of the area."* Aurelian's rule started in 270 AD. The city, if truth be told, had already acquired more than just a *"little importance"* a hundred years earlier, in the times of Marcus Aurelius who, according to the same source *"built at his own expense – the formula was explicit in this case – the walls of Philippopolis and Serdica."* The walls in question – in Serdica – were significant at any rate: 8-9 m high and 2.2 m thick, made of brick with solid stone, 2m high foundations with round turrets every 50-60 m. The fortress formed a pentagon, enclosing an area of about 164 000 m². Later on, when this area became insufficient for the rising population, the city expanded outside the town walls. In the 2nd-3rd century a theatre was built outside the town walls approximately halfway between the Eastern Gate and the site of St. Sofia basilica. It must've been finished at the time of the Emperors Caracalla and Geta (joint 22nd Emperors, 209 AD – 211 AD), because coins with their images were discovered at the site. The theatre was in use until 269 AD – 270 AD when it most certainly suffered damage during the invasions of the Barbarians, notably the Goths who set this unprotected part of the city on fire. It seems that 100 years later the theatre was reconstructed - and transformed into a large amphitheatre! That makes it a rather unique find! The remains were discovered in 2004 by chance while building a new hotel, which, no surprise, was named Arena di Serdica and those remains can be seen – what's left of them - in the basement of the building.

The Cambridge Ancient History also states that *"under Gallienus the defences of cities affected by inroads across the lower Danube were repaired at Serdica, Montana and Philippopolis."* That must have happened then between 253 – 268 AD, before the reign of Aurelian (who became an Emperor in 270 AD). But there are other inconsistencies in the Cambridge Ancient History, notably concerning the minting activity in Serdica. *"After having put an end to the breakaway Gallic and Palmyrene regimes, Aurelian reduces the number of mints in Gaul to just one (at Lyon), moves the mint from Milan to Ticinum (Pavia), adds a mint at Serdica, another in Syria (perhaps at Tripolis) and for a short while another one in the Balkans. The reformed coinage is therefore produced at eight mints – Lyon, Rome, Ticinum, Siscis, Serdica, Cyzicus, Antioch and Tripolis – comprising 39 officinae."* Alaric Watson in his work "Aurelian and the 3rd Century" also states that *"on his arrival in the Balkans in the summer of 271, Aurelian set a mint at Serdica on the main Milan to Byzantium road."*

Now most other sources state that Gallienus (41st Emperor, 218 AD – 268 AD) was the one who established the mint at Serdica. However, coins, struck in Serdica, according to the numismatic evidence, date as early as the time of Marcus Aurelius (16th Emperor, 161 AD - 180 AD); in fact there are various Serdican coins in existence, depicting not just him, but also his co-emperor Lucius Verus (161 - 169 AD) and his wife, Empress Faustina Minor (the Younger). That means that the mint in Serdica already existed for 100 years before Aurelian! This mint activity seemingly continued till Caracalla's death (217 AD) and even later; there is a coin, for example, dating from the reign of Emperor Elagabalus (218 – 222 AD) and, after a rather puzzling interruption, was resumed at the time of Gallienus (253 AD).

After that, in the years 267 – 269 AD, Goths and other barbarians invaded the Balkans. It appears to have been a large scale and long-term invasion, or possibly more than just one incursion. Sources are extremely confused on the dating of these invasions, and also of the aggressors and their objectives, to say nothing of modern day historians, who are very uncertain about the whole period.

Then, in September 270, Aurelian was proclaimed emperor by the legions (44th Emperor). Aurelian's short reign reunited a fragmented Empire while saving Rome from the barbarian invasions that had reached even Italy itself. That earned him the title *RESTITUTOR ORBIS*, "Restorer of the World", which appears on many coins, mostly from Serdica.

Aurelian was born in Serdica to *"an obscure provincial family"*. He had rapidly come up through the ranks, serving Emperor Claudius II Gothicus. Incredible as it might sound, during his brief rule, Aurelian shot to stardom very quickly, so much so that, judging from Latin inscriptions found in Italy, Spain and North Africa, he was worshipped as a god, *"deus"* during his lifetime! Although other emperors before him desired to be addressed like that – Domitian, for example; no written records refer to anyone before Aurelian, as God and Ruler.

Then there is the numismatic evidence. The mint in Serdica, *"the most innovative of Aurelian's mints, towards the end of his reign"* (Alaric Watson, "Aurelian and the 3rd century") came up with two remarkable issues, very rare today, bearing the designation *DEO ET DOMINO AURELIANO*. In fact the title *Dominus* was not deemed appropriate for an emperor in those times, as it was reserved for slaves, addressing their master, and *Deus* was even less so, because it was meant for immortal gods only. Even deified emperors had to be content only with *Divus* – divine. And yet on one of these coins from Serdica we see on the obverse the bust of Aurelian, *DEO ET DOMINO NATO AVRELIANO AVG* ("born god and lord") while on the reverse he is presented as holding a sceptre and receiving a laurel wreath from a female figure, presumably the goddess of Victory. The other coin is very similar, but bears the designation *IMP DEO ET DOMINO AVRELIANO AVG*. On some other coins from the mint in Serdica he is portrayed on the reverse receiving a globe from Jupiter – with the legend *IOVI CONSER* (Jupiter the Protector). There are also coins from Serdica where he appears along with *SOLI INVICTO*, "the Invincible Sun" on the reverse (Sol standing, right hand raised, holding a globe, usually treading down upon one of two captives) and it is known that he attributed his victories to the Sun-god and attempted to establish him as the main divinity of the Roman Pantheon, following the principle "one god, one Empire", an idea later taken on by Constantine the Great.

The story goes that Aurelian confronted a group of rebellious soldiers and, lifting his imperial cloak with his right hand, he stated that god alone can bestow the purple and it was for god alone to determine the length of his rule and not even 50 such mutinies could change this divine destiny. Sadly his rule was cut short when he, ironically, like so many other emperors, was killed by his own praetorian guard in 275 AD. But before it came to that, Aurelian had already managed to effectively end the so called "crisis of the 3rd century". In 272 AD he decided to abandon the province of Dacia, on the north side of the Danube, as too difficult and expensive to defend. He then reorganised a new province of Dacia south of the Danube, within the former Moesia, called Dacia Aureliana, with Serdica as the capital. This was later divided into Dacia Ripensis with its capital at Ratiaria (on the Danube) and Dacia Mediterranea with Serdica as the civil and ecclesiastical metropolis. Some maintain that all this was done during the time of Aurelian, while others say it was done later, during the rule of his successor, Diocletian (51st Emperor, 284 AD – 305 AD). The restructuring of the antique theatre into an amphitheatre, only recently discovered in Sofia that we spoke about earlier, was started during the time of Diocletian. It's been used for military parades, gladiator games and fights with wild animals, all this for the entertainment of the public; "*Bread and circuses,*" as the Roman satirist and poet Juvenal said.

RELIGIOUS TOLERANCE – THE EDICT OF SERDICA AND THE EDICT OF MILAN

The successor of Diocletian, Galerius, (53rd Emperor, AD 305-311) was born in Serdica. At the time of his rise to power the city had already been expanding for a century and a half and had become a significant political and economic centre. At the time of his death, in 311, Serdica became the city where Christianity was recognized as an official religion. Galerius had been suffering for some time from an incurable disease – whether he was a victim of Fournier gangrene, genital ulcer or bowel cancer, it's not clear, but it must have been something horrific, because according to contemporary chroniclers, Eusebius and Lactantius: *"The stench was so foul, as to pervade not only the palace, but even the whole city..."* Was that the city of Serdica? It's implied, but it's not certain. Then again, it seems that the ailing emperor was taken there towards the end. Previously known for his fierce persecution of Christians, it appears that in the final stages of his disease, Galerius had a change of heart, or else, his co-ruler and friend, Licinius (59th Emperor) managed to coerce him. It's known that Licinius was present at his deathbed at the end of April 311 and the dying emperor entrusted his wife and bastard son to him; it seems that's when the Edict of Toleration towards Christians was drafted.

A law to that effect was duly issued in June 311 AD at Serdica, which is now referred to as the Edict of Serdica. For the first time in the history of the Empire, the Christians were *"legally granted the right of professing their faith and practicing their cult; they were also permitted to re-establish their meetings and their church buildings"* (J.F. Knipfing – "The edict of Galerius 311 AD – re-considered"). Nevertheless there wasn't unanimity on the issue between Galerius successors - Licinius, Constantine and Maximinus. The co-rulers were in fierce competition for the lion's share of the great Empire that they couldn't hold together. At one point though Constantine, who sought alliance with Licinius, gave him his half sister, Constantia, in marriage, celebrated in Milan in the year 313 and then the two co-rulers issued jointly the so-called Edict of Milan, which expressed not only official toleration for the Christians, but also established the means for restitution of the property confiscated during the Persecution and exempted Christian clergy from municipal civic duties.

"SERDICA IS MY ROME"

Constantine the Great (57th Emperor, 306 AD - 337 AD) is considered as the first Roman Emperor to convert to Christianity, although he only did so at the very end of his life. He was born in Naissus (present day Nis) and understandably had a preference for the region. At the time, Serdica, as we already said, was for awhile his favoured residence. He spent long periods of time there between 316 and 330 AD. Constantine even considered moving his capital there permanently. Sometime in 317 AD -318 AD his architects managed to realize a sumptuous extension of Galerius' palace although in size and majesty it wasn't on a par with the magnificent palace of his predecessor, Diocletian, in Spalato.

However, Constantine had another, larger residence at his disposal; just outside Serdica, in present day Kostinbrod, near another mineral spring, the *Palatium Scretisca,* his country seat. It was extensive, and according to archaeologists, a most impressive example of late Roman residential peristyle architecture, realised on two levels with magnificent porticos and interior courtyard, this residence is probably the biggest one on the Balkans. There were distinct areas within this enormous complex, including a throne room, dining room, baths, a rotunda (possibly serving for religious purposes), necropolis. Sadly, the once splendid palace is now left to rack and ruin; weeds and scrub are growing abundantly in the crevices of the walls of Constantine's imperial abode. Forgotten, like the Sleeping Beauty's castle, it awaits to be rediscovered and restored to its former glory. The horse changing station, mentioned in the contemporary road guide, *Hinerarium Burdigalense (333),* as *Mutatio Scretisca* (one of many on the well-known *Via Militaris* / Military Road from Western Europe to Constantinople), was at an easy distance (1 km) from the palace. Constantine would've been found regularly on this stretch of road, making the rounds of his fiefdom. The next stage of this itinerary was *Civitas Serdica*, the city of Serdica. Doubtless, the emperor was overseeing the works he had commissioned and considering what other improvements he could make.

In Serdica he had the amphitheatre extended and renovated. The size of the arena was 43 m x 60.5 m (141 feet x 198 feet) that is 10 m less than the one in the Coliseum in Rome, but still of considerable size. A stone tablet was discovered near the structure depicting a gladiator fighting with wild beasts – a billboard of its time. Entertainment was not in short supply then.

Constantine must have had a rather good time in Serdica, for it is said that he called it "My Rome". According to the 12th century Byzantine chronicler Zonaras, Constantine was keen to have a city named after him. The story goes that the emperor had first tried to establish his city at Serdica, then in Sigaeum in the Troad (Troy, now in Turkey), but eagles seized the ropes of the builders and dropped them on the site of Byzantium. Due to this divine intervention, Byzantium was chosen for the honour to bear Constantine's name. *"The idea seems to have flashed across the mind of Constantine of choosing some Illyrian town, Sardica or his favorite Naissus; but, notwithstanding the prepossessions which as a native he naturally felt for those regions, he could hardly entertain the idea seriously. Their distance from the sea, their situation not readily approachable, even with good roads, put Sardica and Naissus at once away from the number of possible capitals; but it is interesting that there was just a chance that the capital of modern Bulgaria—Sofia is the old Sardica— might have been made the capital of the Roman Empire, and called Constantinople."* A history of the later Roman Empire from Arcadius to Irene, 395 AD to 800 A.D. (1889) by Bury, John. B.

"Not readily approachable"? Sardica, situated at one of the most strategic crossroads in the very centre of the peninsula, not readily approachable! Let's not forget that *Via Militaris* (also known as *Via Diagonalis*), connected by other roads to *Via Egnatia*, linking Western and Central Europe with the Middle East and Asia, is intersected at Sardica by another important artery – the one from North to South, connecting the Baltic Sea with the Aegean. But perhaps Mr. Bury didn't know the area well! As a native, Constantine was familiar with it, and from his point of view - it was convenient, strategically placed, close to his home city,

Naissus (Niš) - just about 100 miles away, and also, he obviously liked it – it must have been quite a place in his time!

The amphitheatre would've been just finished, offering even more entertainment, there were the mineral baths that Serdica was so renowned for, a lively commercial centre and let's not forget the splendid palace Constantine had in the very centre! Whatever he thought, the fact is that he spent a lot of time there and clearly felt quite at home. It was at Serdica that Constantine and Licinius, his rival and co-Emperor, reached an agreement in 317 AD, according to which Licinius ceded most of Europe to Constantine and re-established his capital at Nicomedia, while Constantine based himself in Serdica and Sirmium. A treaty was signed at Serdica on 1st March 317 AD. Constantine's sons Crispus and Flavius Claudius Constantinus (Constantine II) were proclaimed Caesars, as was Licinius junior. Seven years later Constantine finally eliminated Licinius and became the sole Emperor. It was after that victory that Constantine decided to establish his capital in Byzantium and accordingly the city was renamed Constantinople. Serdica still retained its importance though.

Constantine, as we said, did not convert to Christianity until the end of his life. However, thanks to him the Edict of Milan (finalizing the Edict of Serdica, 311 AD) was signed in 313 AD, proclaiming religious tolerance throughout the Empire and so Christianity was officially legalised in the Roman Empire. With Christianity on the rise (although not the one and only official religion of the Empire till the time of Emperor Theodosius, 380 AD), Christian churches were built in the city of Serdica, albeit the majority were erected outside the town walls. *Intra-muros* large basilicas were erected along the western walls and later on (5th – 6th century AD) some public buildings were converted into Christian temples. The Rotunda St. George that we mentioned earlier underwent exactly such a transformation. It was the churches *extra-muros* that were mushrooming. One was built just outside the Eastern Gate and another one further to the east – in fact it stood in the same place where Hagia Sofia basilica is today, that is, at the highest spot in the vicinity, not very far from the amphitheater, mentioned earlier, which had been the scene of many a Christian martyrdom. It's possible that there is a connection there and that the edifice was intended to be a *martyrium* (a chapel built at a spot associated with a Christian martyr) or a funeral chapel and, in fact, a silver reliquary was found there at some later time. It was a modest church then, with a magnificent tessellated floor (entirely preserved to this day), and surrounded by an extensive Christian Necropolis.

The richer citizens had villas just outside Serdica; the vestiges of a few of them have been discovered in some districts of the city. At one stage though, they had to fortify them, due to frequent barbaric invasions. Presumably it happened at the end of the 3rd and the beginning of the 4th century AD when the town wall was also rebuilt and strengthened and more turrets were added. For example, some work was done on the town wall at the Northern Gate of the city. It was effectively rebuilt and reinforced, using mixed masonry (*opus mixtum*) – successive layers of river stone and 4 brick rows. The base is 2 m thick. The round turrets and gateways are preserved and their interior side broadens the wall by stairs. At some places there are side exits (*poternae*).

At about that time Serdica changed its name somewhat to become Sardica; presumably it sounded better to the predominantly Greek-speaking Byzantines.

THE COUNCIL OF SARDICA (342/343 AD)

This is the ill-fated ecclesiastical Council (or Synod) of 342/3 AD which deserves a few more words to be said about it.

Constantine II (60th Emperor, 337 AD – 340 AD), Constantius II (61st Emperor, 337 AD – 361 AD) and Constans (62nd Emperor, 337 AD –350 AD), the sons and heirs of Constantine the Great divided the Empire amongst themselves, according to his wish, but discord soon set in. Constans, the youngest son of Constantine the Great, ended up ruling two thirds of the vast Empire (the western part of it) after the death of his eldest brother

Constantine II and was based in Rome. His other brother, Constantius, ruled the eastern part of the Empire and was based in Constantinople. So – two Emperors, two capitals and a Christian church disintegrating rapidly even before being properly established.

As we can imagine, the brothers did not get on tremendously well. The respective branches of the Christian church did not get on any better. West vs East, Latin vs Greek, locked in bitter strife, two parts of the same empire, unwilling to cooperate. The religious issues then often reflected in political and military matters. Regarding religion, Constans, the youngest son, ruler of the West, supported the Nicene Orthodoxy (Nicene Creed, formulated at the Council of Nicaea, 325 AD, deals with the relationship between God, the Father, the Son and the Holy Ghost) against Arianism (deemed heretical at the same Council of Nicaea), which was backed by his brother Constantius, ruler of the East. So, reconciliation between the two sides was badly needed. The initiative of this meeting was actually Pope Julius' (337 AD – 352 AD), but it was up to the Emperors to organise it. Constantius was too busy with a Persian war and left his brother to get on with it. Accordingly Constans decided to convene a council at Sardica.

Sardica, the city to host this big event, belonged ecclesiastically to the Patriarchate of Rome and was in the territory of Constans, but was just across the border from Constantius, a sort of "halfway house" between the two camps. No doubt a lot of effort went into organising such a big event. Obviously, it attracted a lot more people to the city than just the 170 participants who attended the Council. The preparations were in all probability not on such a large scale as, say, the Olympic Games we know today, but nonetheless, they would've involved a lot of planning and funding. And, although Pope Julius had acceded to the calling of this council by the two co-rulers, he let them do the hard work and reverted to the old custom of sending two priests and a deacon to represent him.

There were 96 Western bishops, so the Eastern bishops,

feeling outnumbered, decided to stick together and opted for shared lodgings. They were not pleased to see the participation of Athanasius, Marcellus of Ancyra and Asclepas who had been excommunicated from the Eastern Synods, and they refused point blank to sit with their Western counterparts (who wouldn't hear of changing the Nicene Creed), despite some attempts made by Ossius of Cordova to reach a compromise. Thus this futile attempt to unify the church ended up in tears. The Western and the Eastern bishops quarreled; the Eastern bishops stomped off in a huff and withdrew to Philippopolis (today Plovdiv), ostensibly to celebrate Constantius' victory against the Persians, and there they held an alternative Council, and came up with a new creed, which was signed and dated as if issued in Sardica. The "Westerners" in meantime passed a censure on the "Easterners" for leaving and some of them were deposed and excommunicated. The Nicene Creed was left as it was. Hence each faction issued separate statements, which further widened the gap that separated them and put an end to any hope of reconciliation. That's why we can say that the Council of Sardica was, to put it bluntly, a fiasco.

In the aftermath of the Council of Sardica, the Western and the Eastern Church entered a period of "Cold War", which lasted till the final schism in 1054. But there was more to worry about than mere theological issues. The old empire was declining and unable to protect its borders against the frequent invasions of the barbarians, attracted by its wealth.

CONSTANTIUS VS VETRANIO

Fate wasn't very favourable towards Constans. Only a few years after the Council of Sardica, deeply unpopular with his troops, he had to run for his life, pursued by one of his own commanders, a certain Magnentius. He tried to reach Spain, but was killed on the way, leaving his rival in the driving seat. His brother, Constantius was busy at the time in the east, so he couldn't do a lot to rectify the matter. Magnentius tried to win the important legions on the Danube to his cause, but they decided to proclaim their own candidate, Vetranio, Constans' *magister peditum* ("Master of the Foot", the supreme commander of the infantry) in March 350 AD. Some sources (Philostorgius, 3.22), point to Constantia, the sister of Constans and Constantius (later known as St. Constance), as being instrumental in convincing Vetranio, probably believing him to be trustworthy, to join forces with her brother against the usurper. At any rate Vetranio was proclaimed an emperor and even had some coins minted with his image on them. Was this a stratagem to keep Magnentius at bay? It seems that once on the imperial throne, Vetranio envisaged to remain there for five years at least and even hoped for ten, obviously not just to keep it warm for Constantius! At least this is what the numismatic evidence indicates.

While professing loyalty in letters to Constantius, he doesn't appear to have been trustworthy after all; but then Vetranio was trying to obtain money and military aid from Constantine's son, promising to fight the usurper. Constantius obliged, but must've been rather disappointed with the results, or lack of them. To top it all, Vetranio even backed Magnentius in trying to convince Constantius to form a triarchy with the two of them, a proposition declined by Constantius. Moreover, Vetranio put a garrison at the Trajan Gate (known also as Succi), the fortified mountain pass on the road to Sardica (34 miles/55 km from the city); to control such a stronghold, meant to control *Via Militaris* and to be able to block Constantius' advance. If Constantius had any doubts about Vetranio's integrity, this move would've exposed the general for what he was. Even so, Constantius was in luck as one of Vetranio's junior officers, Gomoarius, turned traitor and joined him (for which he was later promoted to the high rank of *magister equitum* - "Master of the Horse", the supreme commander of the cavalry). At any rate Constantius had enough troops at his disposal and was determined to keep what was rightfully his, with or without Gomoarius' help.

Gibbon in his Decline and Fall describes the moment when Vetranio and Constantius eventually met, a crucial encounter that took place exactly at Sardica. Sardica plain was certainly quite vast and the meeting of the two large armies would've been a momentous event! It seems that Constantius was eloquent enough and managed to win over the troops led by Vetranio – after all, the last son of Constantine the Great was the rightful heir and successor! *"...the plain of Sardica resounded with the universal acclamation of "Away with these upstart usurpers! Long life and victory to the son of Constantine! Under his banners alone we will fight and conquer."*

The shout of thousands, their menacing gestures, the fierce clashing of their arms, astonished and subdued the courage of Vetranio, who stood, amidst the defection of his followers, in anxious and silent suspense. Instead of embracing the last refuge of generous despair, he tamely submitted to his fate; and taking the diadem from his head, in the view of both armies fell prostrate at the feet of his conqueror. Constantius used his victory with prudence and moderation; and raising from the ground the aged suppliant, whom he affected to style by the endearing name of Father, he gave him his hand to descend from the throne."

While Vetranio went on to retire honourably, Constantius led more campaigns at the Danube frontiers in the late 350s and restored stability to those regions after the troubles caused by Magnentius' revolt. However, the end of his reign was all but peaceful. Having difficulties in managing the whole empire on his own, he promoted Julian, a cousin of his, to the rank of Caesar and married him off to his last surviving sister, Helen. But Julian, one might've guessed it, wanted to wear the purple, which led to a war. Here, we meet Gomoarius again; this time it's him, holding the Trajan Gate to stop Julius's advance. But Constantius' time was up. He died before the outbreak of a civil war, declaring Julian as his successor.

THE MIDDLE AGES

BARBARIAN INVASIONS

THE GOTHS, THE VISIGOTHS AND THE EMPIRE. THE END OF ANTIQUITY

And then the Huns arrived out of the blue and wreaked havoc across Europe. The Huns were nomads from the steps of central Asia, but their origins are shrouded in mystery. In the 4th century they started their march westwards, destroying everything on the way. Panic swept through Europe. But the worst was yet to come. In the beginning the Huns were not particularly organized and each tribe followed their respective leader. They destroyed the empire of the Goths and took over, while the Visigoths ran southwards and coerced the Byzantines - Emperor Valens - to let them stay in Moesia. Soon they were fighting them and pillaging Thrace on the way. Emperor Valens was unable to stop them and perished in the battle of Adrianople (Edirne) in 378 AD.

It seems that the residents of Adrianople didn't realise right away that their Emperor had lost his life. According to the account of an anonymous Greek solder, as recorded by the Roman historian Ammianus Marcellinus, when the assailants lifted the siege of Adrianople to pillage elsewhere, the citizens of Adrianople *"set out at midnight and avoiding the public highways and devising every effort for increasing their speed, hastened with the valuables which they were carrying still safe, through wooded and pathless places, some to Philippopolis and from there to Serdica, others to Macedonia, in the hope of finding Valens in those regions (for it was wholly unknown to them that he had fallen in the midst of the storms of battle, or at any rate had taken refuge in a hut, where it was thought that he had been burned to death)"*. (Ammianus Marcellinus, Rerum Gestarum John C. Rolfe, Ph.D., Litt.D., Ed). We might as well ask why the refugees from Adrianople chose to run to Serdica and Macedonia, rather than retreat to Constantinople, better fortified and at an easy distance? Even if they believed their emperor to be elsewhere, surely the more reasonable decision would've been to get to the capital and wait till things calmed down instead of going after him into the unknown. Unfortunately Marcellinus just reports the facts, but doesn't give any explanations.

The nephew of Valens, Gratian who was coming to the rescue, but arrived too late, became de facto the sole ruler of the Roman Empire. The following year, no doubt feeling overwhelmed, he appointed Theodosius I (later to be recognised by the Eastern Orthodox Church as St. Theodosius) to rule "Thrace and the East" as his co-emperor, while he went to settle affairs in western Gaul.

Sozomen, the historian of the Christian Church, is the only one to record the transfer of territorial jurisdiction that went along with Theodosius's ascension to the imperial throne, notably that the prefecture of Illyricum, until then in the Western Empire, with its dioceses of Pannonia, Dacia and Macedonia, was now under the rule of the new Eastern Emperor, along with the provinces that Valens had ruled. At that period the praetorian prefecture had become the highest level of administrative division - the prefects functioned as chief ministers of the state; and since the emperor was present, it was also the unit of imperial military command. Traditionally in this period, the praetorian prefect of Illyricum resided in Sardica. Therefore the city's importance increased. It was a standard Roman practice not to appoint a lower official when the superior resided in the district, so Theodosius was not too bothered to rush and appoint someone as long as he was engaged in the area.

At any rate, these were troubled times for Illyricum, with barbarian incursions becoming more and more prevalent. The chronology of events is very unclear, but anyway Sardica suffered a lot during this period. The basilica St. Sofia was destroyed during the 6 years of Visigoth plundering (376-382). After their withdrawal it was rebuilt again as a burial church, with partly preserved tessellated floor, symbol of the ancient Roman tradition. The Rotunda St. George also suffered during those raids and wasn't reconstructed until a lot later. Theodosius, apparently in an effort to restore communications, had work done on the road linking Sardica and Philippopolis, as some recovered milestones and inscriptions testify. Theodosius was the last emperor to rule over both the west and the east empire (after the demise of Gratian). The end of his reign is seen as the end of antiquity as well.

PERSECUTION OF PAGANISM

The persecution of paganism started in the late 4th century AD – precisely during the reign of Theodosius I the Great (379 AD – 395 AD), the last, 67th Emperor, to rule over both the eastern and the western parts of the Roman Empire. He promoted the Nicene Christianity as the only legitimate Imperial religion and ended state support for the traditional Roman religion (i.e. the cult of innumerable deities). Despite Pagan pleas for tolerance, Theodosius authorised and/or participated in the destruction of temples, holy sites, images and objects of piety throughout the Empire. Serdica did not escape from this predicament either. The temples dedicated to the various gods of the Roman Pantheon were demolished or else turned into Christian churches.

The Rotunda St. George might initially have been built as a pagan temple (3rd century AD) and later turned into a baptistery (a building housing the baptismal font, baptism being of major importance for those who converted to the new religion). However, as already explained, the experts say today that the edifice was originally one of the many public baths the city was so famous for.

Here we should say that St. Nicolas, alias Santa Claus, when Bishop of Myra in the 4th century, was the one who ordered the destruction of pagan temples, notably the world renowned temple of Artemis. Interestingly this momentous event has been depicted in a fresco of the medieval Boyana Church in Sofia. Four people are presented in the mural – the Bishop himself, in his Episcopal robes with his hand raised in a sign of admonishment; two workmen are setting the destruction of a beautiful statue of Aphrodite with Paris' apple in one hand; the two appear as if frozen in their endeavour, while the half-naked goddess on her high pedestal appears unscathed and indestructible. The unknown author of the fresco clearly had some sympathy with the patroness of love, despite his Christian beliefs.

In more recent years, during the building of a bank in the very centre of the city, on the site of St. Spas Church, destroyed in the war, an interesting discovery was made. An area was unearthed, where numerous statues of diverse sizes and provenance had apparently been gathered together and smashed to smithereens with hammers in a destructive frenzy. The edifice where they've been piled-up, undoubtedly a pagan temple, was also demolished at about the same time. A house was built in its place and a Christian basilica nearby. However, some parts, mainly hands and feet, managed to escape the annihilation; from them it is possible to deduce the identity of the deities that they had belonged to: Apollo, Athens, Dionysius, Aphrodite, Tykhe (the goddess of Fortune) etc. The temple was possibly dedicated to Athens, Tykhe and Heracles (with the latter especially favoured by the soldiers). The torso of a small naked Venus had also miraculously survived the attack, and also that of Athens, dressed in a long *chiton* (an undergarment) tightened around the waist and wrapped in a *himation* (a cloak) – the goddess of wisdom had been spared in the city of the Holy Wisdom.

Despite the fanatical destruction, certain artefacts have survived to this day, either by chance, either because pagan worshipers were determined to preserve them. Another example, a golden plated bronze head of Apollo, only recently discovered, is a masterpiece which would've belonged to a statue on a scale larger than human size and would've been placed either in a temple dedicated to the god (2nd century AD) or in the forum.

The amphitheatre of Serdica must've also fallen into disuse during this period, because Emperor Theodosius in his religious zeal prohibited the gladiator games. Theatre plays were not allowed either. Also, let's not forget that, earlier on, Christians had been martyred in this place, an uncomfortable fact to say the least. So the structure slowly fell into decay; first the arena was gradually covered with soil, then the seats in the amphitheatre were buried in their turn.

It was the end of antiquity.

ATTILA THE HUN

St. Sofia, only recently restored after the withdrawal of the Visigoths was to be destroyed again when Sardica was sacked by Attila the Hun (443 and 447/448 AD). The Byzantine Emperor Theodosius II was no match for the "Scourge of God", as Attila was known, but tried to beat him at the game of diplomacy at least. *"The Byzantine court was insulted by five or six successive embassies,"* Gibbon tells us in "Decline and Fall"; *"The Imperial treasury was exhausted,"* while *"the Barbarian monarch was flattered"*.

It was during this period that Attila announced his intention to come as far as Sardica and meet any of the emperor's representatives there. This was nothing less than adding insult to injury. It was Attila himself who had pillaged the city and reduced it to ashes. Not exactly the most auspicious place to meet and discuss treaties! So the council of Theodosius declined the proposal on the grounds of *"the desolate and ruined condition of Sardica"*. It was Maximinus, a high ranking imperial official who had the dubious honour to lead the embassy to Attila's court near Naissus (Nis) in 448. His friend, the historian Priscus seized the opportunity to meet the Barbarian king and decided to go with him; they were accompanied by the latest two ambassadors of Attila, who were leaving the Byzantine court and an interpreter. Priscus left a comprehensive record of this mission and we owe to him an interesting narrative of their stay at Sardica.

Arriving in Sardica, thirteen days away from Constantinople for a fast traveller, Maximinus found for himself that, what he was told about the state of the city wasn't exaggerated; no roof remaining to sleep under, so he had to pitch his tents amongst the ruins, as if they were in the wilderness. Next Maximinus and

Priscus had to play the role of the hosts *"as the remains of Sardica were still included within the limits of the empire"*, and to offer a dinner to the others: the interpreter Vigilius and the two ambassadors of the Huns, Orestes, a noble subject of the Pannonian province, and Edicon, a valiant chieftain of the tribe of the Scyrri.

Little did the Byzantines know that these two were to come to fame later on, for the most fabulous destiny was awaiting their sons: the two servants of Attila were to become the proud fathers, respectively, of the last Roman emperor of the West and of the first Barbarian King of Italy. But that night at Sardica neither Maximinus nor Priscus had any inkling of those future developments. *"They provided, with the assistance of the provincials, a sufficient number of sheep and oxen, and invited the Huns to a splendid, or, at least, a plentiful supper."* But the reception didn't go smoothly. The dinner party degenerated into a spat between Attila's envoys and their Byzantine hosts. The Byzantines, waxing lyrical about their great emperor and their equally great empire, irritated the representatives of the Hun, who were understandably singing his praises. The interpreter Vigilius showed very little discernment, vehemently rejecting any intimation that the emperor Theodosius might be anything less than divine. Maximinus and Priscus had trouble diverting the conversation to appease the angry opponents. Finally they offered rich gifts to the Barbarians – silk robes and Indian pearls, which were well appreciated.

ANTHEMIUS TRIUMPHS AT SARDICA

After Attila's demise the Huns gradually lost their hegemony, though they were still causing trouble. In the winter of 466/467 a gang of Huns, led by a certain Hormidac, crossed the frozen Danube river, stormed into Dacia and wreaked havoc in the whole province. Anthemius, a distinguished general, was sent by the Byzantine Emperor Leo the Thracian (Leo I) to neutralize them.

Anthemius managed to entice them away from the Danube plain into the mountains around Sardica, where their cavalry was of little use. The Huns, under assault, found refuge in Sardica itself. We owe the minutiae of this siege not to a historian, but to a certain Apollinaris Sidonius, a poet who wrote a flattering panegyric (Carmen 2) in honour of Anthemius, who had meanwhile become the Roman Emperor of the West - just a few months after that victory. Interestingly Apollinaris Sidonius himself went on to become a saint. What he tells us puts a slightly different emphasis on the whole story and despite his apparent desire to please his emperor, there is no reason not to believe him as far as the narrative goes.

In verse 270 he describes how the Huns cross the frozen *Pister* (the Danube) on their chariots, leaving on the ice the imprints of their wheels and arrive to devastate the fields of the Dacians (the local population – the province being known as Dacia). *"Straight against them didst thou go as they roamed through the Dacian fields; thou didst attack and vanquish and hem them in; and soon as Serdica beheld thee with thine encampment laid out, thou didst straitly besiege them."* The city's fortifications, recently repaired after Attila's destructive actions were apparently strong enough to withstand a siege when manned by such a garrison, but the trouble was that the Huns arrived with very little food supplies in their chariots; while pillaging the Danube plain, they had shown more interest in gold and valuable goods, and it was their greed that caused their downfall.

Anthemius's army also lacked provisions. But his troops, it seems, were prepared to put up with it and stayed put. *"The town marvelled at thee as thou didst tarry thus for long within the rampart* (the circumvallation – a line of fortifications built by the attackers around the besieged city), *because thy soldiers went not forth into the fields in regular or stealthy raids. Though oft they lacked corn and always wine, they lacked not discipline."* So at least the locals were left in peace during this curious war, as one historian calls it. Facing starvation, the Huns were forced to accept open battle – and they found an unlikely ally, that of one of Anthemius' senior officers, who, no doubt tempted by the riches of the enemy, opted to side with them; the traitor was about to join the Huns with the cavalry he commanded, leaving his position undefended and at their mercy.

However the best-laid plans of mice and men often go awry, as they say. When the two armies came face to face, the traitor who hadn't counted on the loyalty of his troops to Anthemius, attempted to retreat before the enemy, while Anthemius stood his ground, fighting on foot. Realizing what was going on, inspired by the gallantry of their general, the cavalry swiftly turned round and took their original position at the flanks, which had been left bare. Here Sidonius waxes lyrical about the greatness of the general – not to forget that this panegyric was written at the time of Anthemius's ascension to the imperial throne and it was important to be in his good books.

So despite the treachery, the general led his troops to victory, then rooted the traitor out, who managed to flee to Hormidac. However Hormidac and his band also had to hide back in the city. But their situation had become untenable and the Huns were obliged to sue for peace. Anthemius was intransigent: *"The price for this peace,* he reportedly said, *is the head of the traitor."* Hormidac and co complied without much ado. This is how Anthemius saved Sardica from complete destruction. Hormidac and his mates, a sorry group, headed back towards the Danube without their booty, without their chariots, without their horses, but lucky to be alive.

ZENO AND THE OSTROGOTHS

In 467/468 AD Emperor Leo I appointed his son-in-law Zeno as *magister militum per Thracias*, Master of the Soldiers in Thrace, in order to drive back the Huns, now led by the son of Attila, Denzig (Densegich). But Aspar, the Master of the Soldiers of the East, saw Zeno as a rival and bribed his guard, who were to assassinate him. However Zeno got wind of the plot and managed to escape to Sardica. Meanwhile Emperor Leo elevated Aspar's son Patricius to the rank of Kaisar (Caesar) and betrothed him to his other daughter, Leontia. Zeno was determined to get rid of his rival. He managed to have Aspar assassinated in 471 AD. In retaliation the commander of the Thracian Goths, Theodoric Strabo ("Squinter"; strabismus - cross-eyed, from Greek, *strabismos*), who was related to Aspar, led a revolt to avenge him. They say Strabo was defeated by Zeno and Basiliscus; however it seems he was able to dictate terms: to obtain the properties left by Aspar, an agreement to settle his Thracian Goths in Thrace and to receive the rank of *magister militum*. These terms being rejected by Leo, Strabo went on a campaign against the cities in Thrace.

It doesn't seem that Sardica suffered in these raids, the cities attacked were Philippopolis and Arcadiopolis. Eventually Strabo did sign a peace treaty with Leo in 473 AD; the Goths were paid an annual tribute of 2000 pounds of gold, their independence was recognised and Strabo got his *magister militum* title. Meanwhile, also in 473 AD, Zeno was promoted to *magister militum* of the Eastern Empire, taking Aspar's place. Furthermore Leo I elevated his 5 year-old grandson, son of his daughter Aelia Ariadne and Zeno, as co-emperor under the name of Leo II. Leo I conveniently died soon afterwards (January 474 AD), so young Leo II became the sole emperor with Zeno acting as regent. However, before the year was over, the child was also dead, and rumour had it that Zeno had poisoned him, to get the throne for himself. In the meantime Zeno had to deal with Strabo, who had rebelled against him after the death of Leo. But it was not easy. Basiliscus used the mayhem to install himself on the throne and remained there for the next couple of years till Zeno finally managed to overthrow him.

While this was going on, the Western Roman Empire was drawing its last breath, having succumbed to the barbarians (the Germanic tribe Heruli). Their leader Odoacer became the Ruler-King of Italy, and Zeno couldn't do anything about it. He had more pressing matters to deal with, troubles closer to home, in Thrace. He was still having problems with Theodoric Strabo, the leader of the Thracian Ostrogoths, but also with his namesake, Theodoric Amal (the Great). For years Thrace was the stage for an epic drama in which Zeno and the two Theodorics were the main protagonists. He tried to set them against each other, without much success; then having tried all sorts of different stratagems he decided to pay Strabo off and give him back his old title. But then Zeno convinced the Bulgars to attack Strabo and his army in their own camp. Strabo defeated them in 480/481 AD, but died soon afterwards. After his death, his namesake, Theodoric the Great, took on the leadership of all the Ostrogoths and became Zeno's bête noir, causing even more trouble in the Balkans. No doubt Sardica would've also suffered the wrath of the Ostrogoths during this period, although it seems that they were mostly ravaging Macedonia.

Year 479 AD: Theodoric Amal raids Macedonia and threatens Thessalonica. Emperor Zeno is in negotiations with him, *"but the emperor had really nothing to offer worth the Ostrogoth's acceptance. A settlement on the Pantalian plain, a bleak upland among the Balkans, about 40 miles south of Sardica and a payment of 200 pounds weight of gold, as subsistence money for the people, till they should have had time to till the land and reap their first harvest, this was all that Zeno offered to the chief, who already, in imagination saw the rich cities of the Adriatic lying defenseless at his feet."* (Theodoric the Goth - Barbarian Champion of Civilisation by Thomas Hodgkin).

It's clear that Theodoric turned down this proposal, fortunately for the Sardicans who would've had to put up with those troublesome Barbarians as neighbours. It's not clear though where exactly was situated that "bleak upland" settlement, 40 miles south of Sardica, offered to the Ostrogoths – what if it was Borovets, which has now become such a renowned ski resort? Another question we might ask is why they were not given something more suitable – surely that would've been more advantageous for the Empire and would've ended a lengthy and costly conflict.

The following years saw Theodoric pursue the politic of intermittent war and peace with the Empire. According to the 6th century chronicler Marcellinus, in 483 AD, much to the consternation of many in Constantinople, Theodoric had obtained the position of a consul, the much coveted title of *magister militum* and the temporary responsibility for *Dacia Ripensis* and Lower *Moesia*. But in 487 AD, Theodoric *"never satisfied by the favours of Zeno made a hostile advance with a large force of his own as far as the royal city..."* By that time Zeno had had enough. In order to get rid of the tiresome Ostrogoth, in 488 AD Zeno managed to persuade him to go to Italy and fight Odoacer, which is what he did, with great success, becoming in turn King of Italy, based in Ravenna.

JUSTINIAN I THE GREAT

Justinian I the Great, was a Byzantine Emperor from 527 AD to 565 AD. In The history of the Decline and Fall of the Roman empire, Edward Gibbon tells us that he was *"born near the ruins of Sardica (modern Sofia) of an obscure race of barbarians, the inhabitants of a wild and desolate country, to which the names of Dardania, of Dacia and of Bulgaria have been successively applied"*. He pursues: *"the names of these Dardanian peasants are Gothic, and almost English: Justinian is a translation of upravda, (upright); his father Sabatius (in Graeco-barbarous language Stipes) was styled in his village Istock, (Stock;) his mother Bigleniza was softened into Vigilantia"*. Now, for those who know Slavonic languages, it's pretty obvious that those names are Slavonic, no doubt about that. *"Upravda"* might sound like "upright" in English, in Bulgarian it means "just". And anyway, why is it so improbable for him to be of Slavic origin? Only because it didn't suit later historians?

Interestingly, Saint Dimitry of Rostov writes in the 17th century that *"St Justinian, the Byzantine emperor was a Slav. He was born in the village of Vedriani near Sredets in Bulgaria."* According to many, his inclusion in the Orthodox Church Calendar as Saint Tsar Justinian - Upravda, celebrated on 14th November, is most likely due to his Slavonic roots. It makes sense.

In any case the citizens of the Roman Empire saw themselves as Romans whatever their ethnic background was. Latin was the official language of the Empire till 620 AD when it was supplanted by Greek. So the Romans became *Romaioi* (Ρωμαῖοι), and gradually the Empire was perceived as Greek. The name Byzantium doesn't appear till much later as part of an effort by 16th century historians to distinguish between different periods during the existence of the Empire.

The 17th century Catholic bishop Ivan Tomko Mrnavić (Marnavich), who wrote a biography of Justinian in Latin, translated from an earlier Slavonic original, states that *"gradually, with time, the name of Sardica was changed to its present day name, which comes from Justinian's church."* That is true, during the reign of Justinian, the old church of St. Sofia in the city centre, was reconstructed to become the basilica we know today and the city wall was also rebuilt.

We are not going to go into lengthy speculations here as to whether the controversial work of Mrnavić „*Vita Justiniani"*, was a forgery, as some suggest, or not. The original was apparently written by Justinian's teacher, Bogomil (Grace Theophilus). This MS was lost (not surprising, bearing in mind that the Ottomans, who had invaded the Peninsula, had no interest in preserving the Byzantine and Bulgarian cultural heritage); but it doesn't mean the original didn't exist; and it doesn't signify that the translation of Mrnavić is a forgery, as a certain Mr Bryce, who had discovered the Latin MS in the Barberini library in Rome, suggests. Moreover the argument that *"no Slavonic MS of the age of Justinian could possibly exist"* is unfounded. The Cyrillic alphabet may not have been invented at the time, yet the Slav people (or whatever they were then called – Illyrians, Thracians or Dardanians) who inhabited the area, would use another alphabet (Greek or Latin), to write things down. The Thracians did use the Greek alphabet, as various inscriptions found in Thrace testify.

But to get back to the enigmatic Bogomil – later on he was to become the Bishop of Sardica under the name Domnio. The church "St. Sophia", he wrote, was built in his, Domnio's, honour and accordingly, after his death he was buried there. This version of events is less romantic than the other one, according to which the church was built to commemorate the visit of Justinian's daughter Sophia, who was restored to health when she stayed for a time to take the waters in Sardica. Justinian did not have a daughter though and there is nothing else at all to support such a theory. Whatever the origins of Justinian were, it is clear that he deemed Sardica important enough to put so much effort into rebuilding it and re-establishing it as an important administrative and commercial centre in the Byzantine Empire.

In the Middle Ages Sofia remained for the most part a Byzantine city, a stronghold for more than 200 years in a predominantly Slav territory. But the young Bulgarian State, founded to the south of the Danube and recognised by the Byzantine Empire in the year 681 AD, had started to expand and understandably clashes between Bulgarians and Byzantines multiplied with time.

GERMANUS, JUSTINIAN'S HEIR APPARENT BASED IN SARDICA

Germanus, a distinguished general, was a cousin of Justinian the Great and the most influential of his relatives. He was seen as his heir apparent, although this was never officially stated. In 550 AD Justinian appointed his cousin as Commander in Chief of an expedition to Italy. Germanus was based in Sardica and from there started to muster an army. His sojourn most certainly explains the name of a village in the vicinity of Sofia. To this day it is known as German. A popular commander, Germanus attracted a huge following. In order to appease the Ostrogoths, he married Matasuntha, the granddaughter of Theodoric the Great (King of the Germanic Ostrogoths and Ruler of Italy). Justinian was favourable to this marriage which was making Germanus the successor of both the East Roman and Goth realms.

While this was going on, Sclavenes (Slavs) went on the rampage in the south, and the city of Thessalonica found itself in danger. Justinian dispatched Germanus to go there and deal with them. The general duly obeyed and when that was accomplished, he returned to Sardica.

In the autumn of 550 AD the army was all ready to march on Italy and Germanus even issued orders for departure in two days, when all of a sudden, he fell ill and died soon afterwards, quashing all the grandiose plans. Germanus did not even live to see the birth of his son, who bore his name. Sadly, his demise put an end to any hopes of reconciliation between Goths and Romans in Italy and entailed many more long years of carnage and turmoil.

MAURICE'S BALKAN CAMPAIGNS AND FINAL DECLINE

The end of the 6th and the beginning of the 7th century were marked by unrest on the peninsula, due to incursions coming from the north - Avars, Slavs and Bulgars were causing a lot of problems and keeping Emperor Maurice busy. He was fighting a losing battle though. The Barbarians were inevitably to become a permanent presence in his back yard.

Sardica must've had its fair share of it, although little is known about the fate of the city in those troubled times. There is archaeological evidence that its walls, strengthened by Emperor Tiberius I Constantine, Maurice's predecessor, had withstood the Avaro-Slav and Bulgar assaults and were still in use until well into the high Middle Ages. Other structures also resisted these incursions; several public and private buildings within the city walls and St. Sofia church, located outside the walls. The road network also endured.

Surprising as it might appear, despite the upheaval, the imperial infrastructure was largely maintained. An inscription from Sardica for example, dated to 580 AD, specifies repairs to *"an aqueduct under a certain Julianus, bearing the rank of candidates"* and a number of similar local inscriptions from the 5th and 6th centuries from across the Empire indicate that such maintenance work was carried out on a regular basis ("Warfare, State and Society in the Byzantine World, 565-1204" by John Haldon).

However, despite this, there seems to have occurred at that time a decline in the standard of many major public roads, due perhaps to a shift in priorities in the allocation of resources. Already in the late 4th and early 5th century, there is regret about the poor state of many roads (as stated in *Codex Theodosianus*, a compilation of the laws of the Roman Empire). It is said that in the last years of the 6th century the Roman/Byzantine general Comentiolus supposedly had to rely on an elderly man to find the military road (*Via Militaris*) passing through the so called Trajan's Gate, a fortified mountain pass (the fortification originally built by Emperor Trajan and named *Stipon*, is situated near present day Ihtiman, in the province of Sofia, Bulgaria). It's also known that in the autumn of 599 AD the same commander Comentiolus, who must've been appointed as military commander for Thrace, reopened the said Trajan's Gate. Apparently this pass on the road to Sardica had not been used by the Romans/Byzantines for decades. Why? How did they get from Constantinople to Sardica? Even if this story is exaggerated, it indicates what contemporaries thought about the road system in the region.

The period 612 AD – 626 AD is a time of renewed raids by Avars and Slavs, taking advantage of the reduced number of Roman troops on the Balkans. Sardica was taken along with the cities of Naissus and Justiniana Prima in 615 AD (or according to other sources in 617 AD). For how long did it remain in the hands of the assailants? It's impossible to say.

According to the "Miracles of Saint Demetrius" (written presumably towards the end of the 6th possibly the beginning of the 7th century), ca 618 AD *"the inhabitants of Naissus and Sardica who have had occasion to experience the Slavs besieging art on the walls of their respective cities, have found refuge within the walls of Thessalonica which enjoyed God's protection"*. It's likely that not just the city dwellers, but also the local peasants sought refuge in the south, as both cities were captured by the Avars; presumably whole tribes of Romanized Thraco-Illyrians were running away for dear life (the tribes mentioned in the Miracles, the Sagoudats and the Rynchinians or Valacho- Rynchinians, are in fact Slavic).

But then Thessalonica itself was besieged by the Barbarians. The escapees from Naissus and Sardica were terrified, saying that they had jumped out of the frying pan and into the fire and that they were all about to die along with the Thessalonians. Whether the ghost of St. Demetrius, the patron saint of the town, really appeared on the city walls and sent the assailants to flight, is a question of faith; presumably some gold, offered by the Thessalonians would've been a more decisive factor in the turn of events. The fact remains that the city was able to resist the barbaric incursions and a great number of refugees found sanctuary there, while the Barbarians eventually gave up and left. How many of the refugees stayed on and how many returned to their homeland later on, once things had settled down, it is impossible to say.

Meanwhile Heraclius, the new Emperor, had other fish to fry; the Persians were on his doorstep! Interestingly, precisely Heraclius is responsible for introducing the Greek language as the official language of the Empire. Latin was becoming redundant! But new languages were starting to spread with the arrival of the "Barbarians". Slavs, Avars, Bulgars were overrunning the Balkans and there was no stopping them. The Slavic tongue was becoming one of the most prominent languages spoken there.

Byzantium was gradually losing its grip on the Peninsula. Heraclius and his successors, threatened from all sides, were helplessly witnessing the disintegration of the great Empire. The cities of the Balkans were undergoing a transformation: from the prosperous antique polis, to the fortified medieval *castrum*.

Sardica was no exception. As we know, it had been fortified from very early on and apparently, when dark clouds gathered on the horizon, the rich abandoned their flourishing villas out of town to find a refuge inside, behind the city walls. The amphitheatre, or what was left of it, was used intermittently in those times as a seasonal military camp, a stable, a warehouse, and, as various invaders came and went, as a refuge for the assailants. The villas of the affluent citizens would've been plundered, wrecked, set on fire. A whole way of life was coming to an end, but the city kept its importance despite the turmoil. Nevertheless to find itself on the fringes of the once prospering Empire, exposed and unprotected, was an unsettling situation; it would've meant that the city had to fend for itself and could not rely on help from outside.

Sardica had disappeared altogether from the Byzantine radar at the time when some of its residents are reported to have taken refuge in Thessalonica and was not mentioned for the next 200 years, until 809, when it was taken by the Bulgarian Ruler Krum. Sardica might have not been represented in the Church Councils of 680, 692 or 787, yet circumstantial evidence points to the existence of a Christian population that had been taking care of the basilica St. Sofia.

In the meantime, while the Empire was declining, the Bulgars were establishing themselves to the south of the river Danube where they had founded a new Bulgarian state, recognised by the Byzantine Empire in 681 AD. They were here to stay. Soon afterwards the new Emperor Leo III (717 – June 741) became indebted to them for helping him to deal with the Arabs who had laid siege to Constantinople. Afterwards Leo started on a series of reforms, most importantly iconoclasm; the destruction of icons, issuing various edicts against the worship of images. Not all his subjects were impressed with this, notably the people of the Balkan and Italian provinces. How much the icons in the Sardican churches suffered as a result of this politic, is difficult to say. Probably not that much, for it would've been up to the local governors to enforce such politics. Being on the periphery of the Empire might have been, in this instance at least, a blessing in disguise.

In 732 AD, the city of Sardica, so far under the jurisdiction of the Bishop of Rome along with the rest of the Peninsula, was assigned to the jurisdiction of the Patriarch of Constantinople by the Emperor.

BULGARIA VS THE EMPIRE

THE SKULL OF NICEPHORUS

Sardica encountered the Bulgarians for the first time in March 809 when Krum (Crumnus, Kroum), their leader, besieged the city.

The fortifications were too solid to breach, but somehow, with cunning, he managed to get into the city. According to Theophanes the Confessor, a contemporary Byzantine monk and historian (who, let's not forget, was far from impressed with Krum and the Bulgarians), the 6000 strong garrison was massacred, along with an unspecified number of civilians, and the fortress dismantled. The trouble with Theophanes' chronicle (*Chronographia*) is that he neither explains when this Byzantine garrison was stationed at Sardica, nor whether the city's residents were recent arrivals or were the indigenous population who had survived the Barbarian incursions. The Byzantine chronicler turned saint is also very unclear about the exact turn of events. He states that Krum captured Sardica by *"negotiations and deceit"* and afterwards had soldiers and civilians put to death. At any rate the Bulgarian Ruler, who did not intend to occupy the city, withdrew subsequently to his capital in the east.

The Byzantine Emperor Nicephorus on hearing the news, declared he would spend his Easter in Krum's capital Pliska, which he allegedly did, although Theophanes casts doubt on this feat. Present day historians (like Bury) dismiss Theophanes' objections on the basis that he strongly disapproved of Nicephorus. Whatever the truth, Nicephorus did afterwards march towards Sardica. Once there, he had some trouble trying to persuade the soldiers to rebuild the fortress. The troops had not been paid yet and refused point blank to do the heavy work of the masons. This was nothing short of mutiny. They are reported to have torn down the commanders' tent and to have shouted curses at the Emperor. Theophanes, who apparently quotes an eyewitness account, maintains that Nicephorus managed to prevail, calming down the mutineers with oaths and promises, and was afterwards able to return to Constantinople and to punish the ringleaders with whipping, tonsure and exile.

But there is a sting in the tail. It seems that a few Byzantine officers had survived Krum's massacre after all, which contradicts the previous assertion that the whole garrison was massacred. Anyway, they appeared in front of the Emperor, who was not willing to let them go without punishment; presumably he suspected them of having dealings with the enemy; so they fled and found refuge with Krum (again according to Theophanes). It is strange that they were not so afraid of that "terrible barbarian", although, allegedly, he had just slaughtered their mates at Sardica! One of those, who had to flee from the wrath of Nicephorus, a certain Euthymius (or Eumathius), was an expert in weaponry and warfare, obviously a very useful recruit to the Bulgarian army!

The fortress of Sardica was to be rebuilt at some later time. Archaeologists (notably Stancheva, 1976) believe that a section of its western walls, which had to be fixed and restored with new material by the Bulgarians in the 9th and early 10th century, had been previously damaged significantly by Krum's forces. So much so, that for a time, the fortress must have been rendered useless for the Byzantine forces.

Sardica must've been taken again in 811 or even earlier, though the exact time of the city's annexation to the Bulgarian Kingdom is unclear. There is an enigmatic inscription, known as the First Inscription of Hamberly, dating from 813 and discovered near the village of Malamirovo, in the region of Yambol. It states that: *"...his brother did not forget him and came out [to war] and God gave [allowed] him and he ravaged these places and fortresses Sardica, Develtus, Constancia, Versinikia, Adrianople. These strong fortresses he took..."* So it seems that this mysterious brother of Krum might've been the one who eventually took control of Sardica. But we shall never know for certain. However, whether Sardica was or was not in Bulgarian hands in the summer of 811, the time of Nicephorus' last offensive, is neither here nor there. Its destiny had already become intrinsically linked with the Bulgarian state and its ups and downs.

So Nicephorus went for Krum's capital Pliska again – perhaps in retaliation for the loss of Sardica, perhaps because he wanted to finish with Krum once and for all. So, although Krum sent an embassy to sue for peace, the Emperor, *"blinded by his evil thinking and by the encouragement of his advisors"* (Theophanes), destroyed the city and mercilessly killed civilians, including women and children. It seemed that Pliska had to pay the price for Sardica. By a strange twist of fate, some thousand years later Sardica or Sofia as it became known, was to become the capital of the Third Bulgarian Kingdom. Pliska gradually lost its importance and was left to rack and ruin.

Back in July 811 Krum sent an embassy to beg for peace once again, saying: *'Lo, thou hast conquered. Take what thou wilt and depart in peace.'* The Emperor was unrelenting. But his luck had run out. Going after Krum into the mountains, he fell into a trap set up by the Bulgarians in a mountain pass and there he perished together with his great army. Very few were able to escape, Krum's revenge was complete. It is said (Theophanes again) that the Bulgarian monarch had the skull of his enemy lined with silver and it served him as a chalice when he drank with his men.

THE BUILDING FERVOUR OF OMURTAG AND MALAMIR

"Even if a man lives well, he dies and another one comes to existence. May the one who comes later, upon seeing this inscription remember the one who did it. And the name is Omurtag, kanasubigi. May God grant him to live to 100 years of age." (inscription in Greek, found in a church in the city of Turnovo)

It was Omurtag, Krum's successor who established a lasting peace with the Byzantine Empire. His reign (814 – 831) must have come as a bit of a respite in an otherwise tumultuous era. The peace treaty, signed in the winter of 815/816, was a 30-year peace agreement between Omurtag and Emperor Leo V. The Byzantine records of this treaty have not been preserved, but Omurtag, pleased with the results of his diplomatic endeavours, had the conditions inscribed in Greek on a marble column in his palace at Pliska. Now this column is knocked down and broken, but parts of the inscription are still visible. According to the terms agreed, it appears that Serdica and Philippopolis were left – at least formally, in Byzantine hands. However it seems that these cities were deserted by the Byzantines and later on were again incorporated into the Bulgarian territory.

Known as the Builder, Omurtag undertook a vast construction programme across his lands. His son Malamir pursued his projects. Sardica benefited greatly from their endeavours. Archaeological evidence shows that important building work had been carried out during this period. The town walls were repaired, as were the gateways and the pavement of the streets. Ancient buildings were restored, including the governor's residence, where even the baths were renewed.

The archaeological discoveries also reveal that the population of the city in the beginning of the 9th century was predominantly Slav - Bulgarian, the two cultures already merging into one. As a result the name of the city is transformed to become Sredets which in the Bulgarian language signifies "centre", for during the reign of Omurtag the boundaries of his kingdom had been significantly changed, thus placing Sardica very much in the middle of it. All that said, there was still a significant population of Roman descent remaining in the city.

Meanwhile the commercial traffic continued to flow. The city, let's not forget, was located on a major road (that now crossed through a considerable part of Bulgarian territory) from Western Europe to Byzantium and was still bursting with activity, seeing the coming and going of merchants, transporting goods to and from Constantinople.

Omurtag is known for his persecution of Christians, although it must be said that his reasons appear to be more political than religious – that is opposition to the Byzantine influence, which was connected with the new religion. At least the old churches in Sardica/ Sredets, notably St. Sophia and St. George, remained unscathed throughout his reign. At any rate Bulgaria was not to remain a pagan state for very long.

THE MIRACLES OF ST. JOHN OF RILA

It was King Boris I of Bulgaria, who, it is said in the history books, not only converted the whole country to Christianity and adopted it as the official religion in 865, but also introduced a new alphabet, the Cyrillic, more suited to the Slavic languages. In fact, a significant part of his subjects must've already been Christian. There has been a considerable Christian population living in these lands ever since the advent of Christianity, which was brought to the Balkans by the apostles Paul and Andrew in the 1st century AD. It appears that the first saint associated with Serdica/Sardica lived at the time of the Antonine Dynasty, that is in the 2nd century. Known as St. Potitus/Potito, this Serdica-born saint was never particularly recognised in his native land, but very much venerated in Italy where he was allegedly put to death for his faith by Emperor Antoninus Pius; not so pious after all!

At the time of King Boris, who resided in his capital city of Pliska, Sardica would venerate its own, locally born and bred patron-saint, John of Rila (876 – 946). He lived in the city, known then under its Bulgarian name, Sredets, and stayed for a while in a monastery on Mount Vitosha. He was a healer and, people believed, a miracle-maker. He spent his later life as a hermit in the mountain of Rila, away from the vanities of the world. There he founded the Rila Monastery, which was to become the most important one in the Bulgarian lands.

After his death, John was buried in Rila Mountain, but according to legend the saint appeared to his pupils in a dream and asked them to unearth his body and move it to Sredets. It's known that King Peter I of Bulgaria ordered the transfer of the remains to Sredets so they could be venerated in that city.

A monastery was later built there to accommodate the relics of the saint, which hadn't suffered from their stay underground; the legends say that they were emanating a sweet smell – the odour of sanctity – and had retained the healing properties that the holy man was so well-known for. People flocked to Sredets to worship the saint and his fame was spreading far and wide. Initially a patron-saint of Sredets, John of Rila soon became the patron-saint of all Bulgarians, something they badly needed.

BASIL, THE BULGAR-SLAYER

Since 927 the Bulgarian Orthodox Church had become autocephalous, that is, independent from Constantinople, one of the earliest churches to be established in the world. That came about as a result of Bulgaria's two decisive victories over the Byzantines; at Acheloos (near the present-day city of Pomorie) and Katasyrtai (near Constantinople); the autonomous Bulgarian Archbishopric was declared as autocephalous and elevated to the rank of Patriarchate at an ecclesiastical and national council held in 919. Then in 927 Bulgaria and the Byzantine Empire signed a peace treaty that concluded a 20-year-long war between them, and the Patriarchate of Constantinople recognised the autocephalous status of the Bulgarian Orthodox Church and acknowledged its patriarchal dignity.

Sometime in 970 – 971 (or 972) the Bulgarian Patriarch Damian (in some sources Gabriel-Germanus), had to move the seat of the Church to Sredets, because the capital-city, Veliki Preslav, was burned and a large part of eastern Bulgaria was occupied by the Byzantines.

The Bulgarian King Boris II was held hostage in Constantinople and so the country was ruled at the time by the four sons of the late Count (*Comita*) Nicola, who had been the governor of Sredets. The four brothers were given biblical names: David, Moses, Aaron and Samuel. It was Aaron who had become the governor of Sredets in his father's stead, and the city itself - a temporary capital of Bulgaria. It seems that with moving the seat of the church there, Damian gave, in a way a certain legitimacy to the brothers' claim to rule the Bulgarian state, for although Boris II was still alive, a great part of his kingdom was overrun by his captors. What is known of the Byzantium – Bulgarian relations comes mainly from the rather confusing accounts of the Byzantine historian John Scylitzes, who chose not to record the events that happened in the interval 971 - 986 in chronological order; so it is difficult to establish the actual chain of events.

Following the old maxim "divide and rule", it appears that the Byzantines were trying to set their enemies (i.e. the four brothers) against each other. Despite letting King Boris II and his brother Roman escape, the status quo had remained unchanged; although the 4 brothers had pledged loyalty to the lawful heirs of the throne, it was they, who ruled the country. When David and Moses perished in battles, the Byzantine Emperor, Basil II, tried to win to his side the elder of the two brothers, Aaron, still alive and governor of Sredets, offering him an advantageous peace treaty. Aaron accepted, on the condition to have Basil's sister, Anne, for a wife. Basil agreed and sent a bishop with the bride-to-be. But Aaron realised that Basil was trying to dupe him, the woman who presented herself to the Bulgarian noble, was not the one she claimed to be. Infuriated, Aaron had the bishop put to death and the peace process fell through. It is said that his younger brother Samuel became aware of his dealings with the enemy and had him and his entire family executed for treason in June 976 (or 987?). Only one of his sons, Ivan Vladislav, was spared, thanks to the entreaty of his cousin, Samuel's son Gavril Radomir. 39 years later Ivan Vladislav repaid him the favour by treacherously killing him in order to secure the Bulgarian throne for himself.

However, in 986 it seems that Aaron was still alive for he was there to defend Sredets when Emperor Basil II, laid a siege to it with an army of 30 000, while Samuel and his troops were hiding in the Mount of Vitosha. The Byzantine generals were making a meal out of it; the siege engines were rendered almost inoperable, the cavalry men were frequently getting themselves massacred by the Bulgarians while foraging around, there was a lack of provisions; all this was making Basil more and more irritable as it was bad for his prestige. The fortress remained impregnable and after 20 days or so, he decided to give up and retreat to Thrace; but doing so, the Byzantine army fell into an ambush, set by Samuel's troops and suffered one of its worst defeats ever at the Battle of the Trajan's Gate (a mountain pass, just outside Sofia), on 17th August 986. It appears that Samuel was the only one ever to defeat Basil in battle. This is what John Kyriotes Geometres, the Byzantine writer, had to say, very poetically, on the Battle of Trajan's Gate:

"Even if the sun would have come down, I would have never thought that the Moesian arrows were stronger than the Avzonian spears. ... And when you, Phaethon, descend to the earth with your gold-shining chariot, tell the great soul of the Caesar: The Danube took the crown of Rome. The arrows of the Moesians broke the spears of the Avzonians" (here Moesian = Bulgarian, Avzonian = Roman/Byzantine, Phaeton = Sun, Danube = Bulgaria)

Victory, this time at least, was on the side of Samuel, and Sredets was left in peace for the next 20 years. But a second war started between the Byzantines and the Bulgarians in 996 and dragged on and off for years. Gradually the Bulgarian Empire was reduced to a part of Macedonia, Albania and the mountains around Sredets.

In 1014 Basil returned to Bulgaria, determined to settle his scores with Samuel who had become King of Bulgaria in 997. They fought a decisive battle at Kleidion and this time Basil won, achieving notoriety and a nickname - the Bulgar-Slayer (*Bulgaroktonos*). John Scylitzes, the Byzantine historian, reckoned that in the aftermath of the battle he blinded about 15 000 captives and ordered every group of one hundred to be led back to their king by a one-eyed man. At their sight, the king, a broken man, suffered a heart attack and died a few days later. From that moment on, the fate of the Bulgarian Kingdom was sealed. It was soon to become a Byzantine province.

Krakra of Pernik, the legendary governor of the fortress of Pernik, an outpost of Sredets, fought valiantly in a losing battle to defend them both, and didn't surrender the keys till well after the demise of the last Bulgarian king. But by 1018 the whole of Bulgaria fell under Byzantine rule and Sofia remained a Byzantine city for the next 168 years (until 1194 when it was retaken by the Bulgarian King Ivan Asen).

The city, that had been known as Sredets for the Bulgarians, meanwhile had managed to change its name again – according to some sources it was probably because the Byzantines had found the name 'Sredets' unpronounceable, and turned it to Sraditza and Triaditza/Triaditsa, instead of reverting to the initial name of Sardica.

A Bulgarian journalist even goes as far as to state that Basil II himself came up with the name Triaditsa, which according to her meant "within the mountains" ("The Capital's changing face", by Velina Nacheva, 'The Sofia Echo', 16 Sept 2004). In fact it appears that Triaditsa had been used interchangeably with Sardica since earlier times and there is even speculation that it might derive from the Holy Trinity (Hagia Triada/Agia Triada/Αγία Τριάδα in Greek, Sveta Troitsa/ Света Троица in Bulgarian) i.e. from a church bearing that name. According to Leo the Deacon, the Byzantine historian, who wrote about the Byzantine military expansion in the 10th century, the name Triaditsa (or Tralitsa) is connected with the Holy Trinity and the effort of the Byzantine authorities to get rid of the Bulgarian name.

Whatever the case may be, in 1020 Basil issued a *sigillion* (an official document /act that bears a seal) which outlined the ecclesiastical structure of the province; the rights and possessions concerning the autocephalous Archbishop of Bulgaria, who would now be based in Ohrid, as part of the Archbishopric centred there. It also confirmed the *suffragan* (subordinate) status of sees in Macedonia, Eastern Bulgaria and Sirmium; one of the sees listed is Triaditsa (Sardica).

In 1040 Triaditsa witnessed the abortive uprising of Peter Delian, who claimed to be the grandson of King Samuel, but nothing came out of it. The Byzantine chronicler Kekaumenos talks about a certain Botko, presumably the governor of Triaditsa, as the leader who, in support of Peter Delian, must've made his last stand at the Boyana fortress, (now a district of Sofia), in an attempt to stop the Byzantine army led by Michael IV the Paphlagonian, coming from Thessaloniki; despite his heroic leadership and the gallant determination of his troops, who came out *"as if ashamed to remain in the fortress"* in order to fight an open battle with a much superior enemy, they were swept aside by the elite Imperial forces, who invaded the city and swiftly put to the sword any resistance. It's doubtful that even if those *"illustrious warriors"* had stayed inside the stronghold, as Kekaumenos suggests they should've done, the outcome would've been any different – maybe just a more prolonged agony. If they came out of the fortress, presumably they were desperate, if they lacked provisions for example, they might not have had any other choice.

However Triaditsa, again in the Byzantine fold, kept its status as the centre of a military and administrative region named *Thema* (Theme) *Bulgaria*. The regional governor resided here and also the Byzantine Archbishop. The church services were held in Greek and Greek signs appeared in the churches. Christianity was spreading quickly in Europe and when the Hungarian rulers accepted it as their state religion in 975 AD, an overland route was re-opened (known in Roman times as Via Diagonalis/via Militaris), going down the Danube and across the Balkans to Constantinople, a lot more convenient for the pilgrims from Western Europe than the sea route they were obliged to take before. Dangerous during the wars between Bulgaria and the Byzantine Empire, this route had again become the main thoroughfare since it was incorporated once more within the imperial borders.

The situation of Triaditsa on this major crossroad was both a blessing and a curse. Trade was flourishing, merchants were passing back and forth to Constantinople, pilgrims would stop over on their way to the Holy Places. But, on the other hand, the city often found itself the prize possession of various aggressors. During this period the city, somewhat on the periphery of the Empire, suffered firstly from the attacks of the Pechenegs, and later from the three out of the eight crusades that passed through it.

THE TIME OF THE CRUSADES

PECHENEGS

The Pechenegs had crossed the Danube when the river was frozen, as the Huns had done in earlier times, and were wreaking havoc in much the same way. Some of them, under the leadership of a certain Kegen, entered Byzantine service, but the following winter, which was unusually cold, brought another contingent of Pechenegs led by Tyrach who started to raid the Imperial territory. With the help of Kegen the Byzantines defeated the newcomers. Things calmed down when negotiations opened with the Emperor Constntine IX Monomachos in Serdica. Instead of having them killed or deported, the Emperor had Tyrach's Pechenegs disarmed, baptized and settled in the under-populated hills northwest of Serdica, presumably hoping to use them as mercenaries. Whether the residents of Serdica approved of these arrangements or not, is not clear. The army definitely disliked the idea, judging by the rebellion of the western tagmata (professional military forces) soon afterwards. At any rate there is no further mention neither of Kegen's, nor of Tyrach's Pechenegs.

However, a new round of fighting with the Pechenegs takes place in the summer of 1059 during an unexpected conflict with Hungary. King Andrew I of Hungary advanced into Byzantine territory towards the city of Serdica. Some Pecheneg squads, taking advantage of the situation, joined the Hungarians, breaking the peace with the Byzantines. The Byzantine Emperor Isaac I Komnenos (or Comnenus) responded with a mighty counterattack which drove the Hungarians out and forced them to accept peace terms, after which he dealt successfully with the troublesome Pechenegs in September 1059.

It's possible that parts of the Theme Bulgaria were restructured in that same year of 1059 to form a separate province, the Duchy of Serdica, based in that city, as a measure against Hungary. The appointment of a new Duke presumably meant more troops in the region.

In 1066 Romanos Diogenes was appointed Duke of Serdica by Emperor Constantine X. The Byzantine historian Zonaras reports that Romanos was victorious against the Pechenegs in 1067:
"He killed a lot of them in battle and he took quite a few prisoners, whom he sent to the Emperor, along with the heads of their mates who had been killed. For this deed he was given the title Vestarchēs and the Emperor wrote to him: "This title is not awarded as a gift, Diogenes, but as a recompense for your

courage." However, other contemporary chroniclers reveal that he was involved in a conspiracy against the emperor: *"Romanos (IV) asked Konstantinos X to be made Vestarches, but was told that he would have to show some deeds in order to be thus rewarded. Romanos went to Serdica, where he was appointed Doux, defeated some Pechenegs and sent their heads to the Emperor who then bestowed the dignity. He decided to use his position at Serdica to make a bid to seize power via the Sauromatai (Hungarians), who knew him from when he had fought against them while ruling the cities of the Istros (Danube). He sent them letters to that effect."*

But things did not go to plan, due to the betrayal of his accomplice: *"Discovery of plots of Romanos Diogenes with Hungarians & his banishment to an island: Romanos Diogenes in Serdica saw that the Empire was overwhelmed by enemies because of its rulers' incompetence. He was incensed and planned to seize power, not for its own sake, but in order to redress the fortunes of the Romans. He was encouraged to seek power by his Armenian advisor, who persuaded him to send his own men as envoys to the Hungarians, whom Romanos planned to use in his rebellion. He wanted to bring to his side some of their commanders and citizens. Realising that Romanos' plot enjoyed little support, the Armenian turned hostile and accused him to the locals in the cities of the Danube of intending to betray them and deliver them to the Hungarians. Thus he set them up against Romanos. He attacked him, found him alone and arrested him, and carried him in chains to Constantinople to stand trial for his deeds. The Empress Eudokia found him guilty of conspiracy and out of clemency for a time confined him to an island."*
The Empress must've taken quire a fancy to the dashing young man, for despite this setback, Romanos Diogenes married the widowed Eudokia at a later time and was in turn crowned Emperor (1068 – 1071). But that is a different story.

As for the Duchy of Serdica, according to historians, the office of Duke of Serdica did not concern the command of the city – Serdica was apparently the centre of a new military and administrative unit in 1067. The Byzantine historian Kekaumenos believed the Theme of Serdica to have extended as far as Vidin on the Danube in the early 12th century, given that in 1114 its Duke fought with the Cumans in that region.

The Byzantine Emperors Isaac I Komnenos and Alexius I Komnenos (or Comnenus) both used the city as a military base for their campaigns against the Pechenegs in 1059 and 1079 respectively. Such bases were used as transit stations for the movement of troops, as camps for field armies, for the training of troops and for the preparation of armies for the harshness of campaigns.

CRUSADERS

The first one, led by Godfrey of Bouillon (1096 – 1099), came, as a starving mass that pillaged everything on their way. During the second (1147 – 1149) and the third (1189 – 1192) Crusade, the local population from the city and its environs escaped into the mountains to avoid the heavily armed knights, something, which proved to be a wise move. The poor citizens of Sardica/Triaditsa had a really rough time during this period.

The first company actually was the so called "People's Crusade" (also known as "Pauper's Crusade", "Peasant's Crusade" or "Popular Crusade"). Peter the Hermit, a charismatic monk from Amiens, France, inspired the masses, promising them freedom and eternal salvation and, it is said, riding a donkey, led some 40 000 Crusaders, mostly peasants, including women and children. Most were inexperienced in warfare, though there were a few skilled knights amongst them, like Walter Sans-Avoir (Gautier Sans-Avoir for the French). The poor people had gone through some rather tough times, due to drought, famine, plague, not to mention an outbreak of ergotism, ergot poisoning, known also as St. Anthony's Fire (caused by fungi growing on rye, barley or other cereals); a pilgrimage must've appeared as a bright idea and Jerusalem – as the Promised Land. Peter and his followers set off from Cologne, Germany on the 12th April 1096, well ahead of the main body of the Crusade; however they were beaten to it by another group of French knights, led by Walter Sans-Avoir who preceded them down the old Roman Via Diagonalis/Via Militaris.

The French knights had various problems en route and, feeling not very welcome, they helped themselves to whatever came their way. When they reached Stralicia (Sardica) however, *"a beautiful city of Dacia Mediterranea"*, the locals who had got wind of their arrival, set up a market, so the Crusaders were able to buy what was needed (instead of pillaging the countryside as they had done before) and the governor kindly offered them escorts to take them safely to Constantinople (without causing more trouble).

After various tribulations Peter the Hermit also reached Stralicia in mid July and there he was met by a Byzantine envoy, come all the way from Constantinople (about 400 miles) with the sole purpose to escort him to the Imperial city. They were to receive supplies and to continue on their way without breaking their journey for more than three days.

In the meantime the four main crusading armies set off at the appointed time in August 1096. This campaign later became known as the Princes Crusade. The armies took different routes to get to Constantinople, Godfrey of Bouillon followed Walter Sans-Avoir and Peter the Hermit down Via Diagonalis, a route that, at least legend says, was also taken by his ancestor Charlemagne, on a pilgrimage to Jerusalem. As those preceding him had done, he was escorted by a Byzantine envoy, who had met him between Nis and Belgrade, and on reaching Stralicia (Sterniz), he was able to replenish his supplies and continued on his way to Constantinople.

Odo of Deuil was a historian and participant of the Second Crusade (1147–1149). In his narrative of the Crusade, entitled *De profectione Ludovici VII in Orientem* (On Louis VII's journey to the East), he describes the journey of the army through the Bulgarian lands: *"The towns of Nish, Hesternit [Sofia], Philippopolis [Plovdiv] and Adrianople [Edirne] are at a four-day distance from each other, and from the latter town to Constantinople it takes five days. The area between them is plain and abounds in settlements, fortresses and riches whatever. To the right and to the left there are mountains, and they are so close that they surround a wide, fertile and nice plain..."* Oto of Deuil goes on to say that the Duke of Serdica was very hospitable when Louis VII and his people arrived in the city: *"He was always well received by Greek priests; but as he passed through Serdica, the Doux was also very attentive, staying near him and ministering to his needs; thus he kept the townspeople safe and also the pilgrims comfortable; Louis shared the generosity of the Doux with his army, rich and poor ."* (Odo of Deuil 45)

The Byzantines watched the progress of the Crusaders with suspicion. They did not trust the Barbarians and thought that Conrad III, the King of Germany, who led the German contingent, was very arrogant. The contemporary Byzantine historian, John Kinnamos (Cinnamus), recounts that when the Crusaders approached Serdica, they were met there by a couple of Byzantine dignitaries, who came to welcome them and offer them provisions: *"Basileios Tzintziloukes, chartoularios and military commander met the Crusaders at Serdica (Sofia) to welcome them appropriately and provide them with necessities in association with Michael Palaiologos"* (commander in Italy under Manuel I); (Kinnamos 70.3-16). He goes on to say that while they were crossing the more mountainous regions between the Danube and Sardica, the Crusaders behaved themselves, but when they entered the plains, which followed, they started to show a hostile attitude towards those who brought them provisions and to rob them, and even kill them, if they resisted and put up a fight, while Conrad showed very little concern about it all. *"When the Crusaders were beyond Sardika (Sofia) he disregarded increasing complaints at their bad behaviour, or ascribed the problem to the folly of the mob."* (Kinnamos 70.20-71.5)

MANUEL I KOMNENOS VS THE SERBS AND THE HUNGARIANS

The Byzantine Emperor at the time, Manuel I Komnenos (or Comnenus), must have breathed a sigh of relief when he finally saw Conrad's army ferried across to Damalis on the Asian shore of the Bosphoros. John Kinnamos (or Cinnamus), the historian and military secretary to Emperor Manuel I, who accompanied him on his campaigns, describes in a very straightforward manner *"the deeds of the emperor and purple-born lord Manuel I Komnenos"* (after finishing with *"the feats of the late emperor and purple-born lord John Komnenos",* his father).

Apparently, Emperor Manuel was a regular visitor to the city of Sardica. There is evidence that he took full advantage of the thermal waters that the city was so renowned for. It should be noted too that there was a major military base at Sardica at the time of the Komnenian (Comnenian) dynasty; used as a transit and concentration point for the armies and for the training of troops; a very convenient halfway house when the Emperor had to deal with his western neighbours, Serbs and Hungarians, who were causing him problems every now and then, but also for meeting envoys coming from West Europe.

Interestingly, after a successful campaign against the Serbs who had rebelled and invaded his territory in 1149, he sent his prisoners to settle as soldiers-farmers (*stratiotai*) around Sardica and other Byzantine cities. This was in fact the usual practice in Comnenian Byzantium – grants of land to be made to soldiers on condition of hereditary military service.

Later on, in 1161, Manuel Komnenos again arrives in Sardica to keep an eye on the dynastic strife in Hungary that he is hoping to take advantage of. John Kinnamos informs us that *"his child* [his daughter Maria] *was still fighting off sickness, when the Emperor, concerned by the events in the West, abandoned his domestic affairs and went on his way. And in fact there were rumours that the German ruler Frederick raised his whole nation and advanced towards the Roman territory"* [that is Byzantium]. The ruler in question is Barbarossa, the Holy Roman Emperor, successor to the late Conrad, the Crusader.

A couple of years later, in 1163, the city of Serdica is the meeting place where Manuel Komnenos receives the dethroned Hungarian King, Stephen IV, who is asking for his help against his own nephew, Stephen III, to get back the crown. The outcome is a war with Hungary, but peace is concluded by the end of the year. Manuel renounces his support for the opponents of Stephen III. In exchange Stephen III agrees to send his younger brother, Béla, to Constantinople, to be betrothed to Manuel's own daughter, Maria Comnena. Manuel couldn't wait to lay his hands on Béla's lands, which he had been coveting for some time, so he deemed such a marriage very advantageous. He even made his daughter Maria and Béla, who assumed the name Alexius, his heirs and granted Béla- Alexius the title of *Despot*, which had previously been applied only to the Emperor himself.

However, when Manuel's second wife, Maria of Antioch, finally produced a male heir in 1169, Manuel swiftly had the engagement between Béla-Alexius and Maria Comnena annulled. He also stripped Béla-Alexius of his title of *Despot* and gave him the lesser title of *Kaiser*. Afterwards Béla is married off to Agnes-Anna of Antioch, the Emperor's sister-in-law. So Béla who was to be the son-in-law did, in fact, end-up as brother-in-law to Manuel Komnenos.

As we can see, at the time of all these events, Sardica/Sardike appears very much as the place where Emperor Manuel receives ambassadors and dignitaries from the West. For example, in 1166, the Duke of Austria, Henry II *"came with his wife Theodora and Otto to Sardike, in order to reconcile Frederick and Manuel and achieve a truce in the war with Hungary, thus hiding Frederick's warlike preparations behind a pretence of peace"* (Kinnamos 261.12-262.13). It is a question of mediation between Frederick Barbarossa and Emperor Manuel I. The Duke also arranged some more personal affairs at the same time - the marriage between his daughter, Agnes of Austria and King Stephen III of Hungary was decided on: *"during the return of her father Henry from his peace mission to Sardike, he persuaded Stephanos of Hungary to marry her"* (Kinnamos 262.16-19).

It appears that Frederick and Manuel still needed a mediator some 6 years later, in 1172, for John Kinnamos informs us that the Emperor *"was visited by Henry the Lion of Saxony who tried to dispel his mutual suspicion with Frederick; faced a Serbian revolt (inspired by Venice) and confusion in Hungary after the death of Stephanos; marched to Sardike"* (Kinnamos 286.13-21).

Indeed, Manuel Komnenos is in Sardica, concerned about the newest developments – the Serbs contemplating a revolt (again) and the death of King Stephen III of Hungary who had just died childless, when he received an embassy from the Hungarians who were claiming Béla, the brother of the late Stephen III and the rightful heir, as their King. Manuel must have been rather pleased with the prospect. Thus, in response to the Hungarian demands, Manuel sent Béla and his wife on their way to Hungary with sufficient amounts of money befitting their new status, but not before he had received Béla's pledge never to turn his arms against Byzantium during the reign of Manuel or his young son.

GREGORY ANTIOCHOS ON THE "HARDSHIPS" OF SARDICA

Meanwhile life in the city of Sardica went on. In 1173 a certain Gregory Antiochos, a Byzantine author from Constantinople, sends two letters – one of them from Triaditsa/Sardica (still a Byzantine city, although seen as a provincial one). In this first letter, addressed to his mentor and friend, Eustathios of Thessalonica, he is lamenting his lot – far from his homeland, his father, his friends, his books, he feels very sorry for himself, and enumerates all the hardships he has to *"endure in Sardica"*.

He is most unhappy with the climate and with the disproportion of the four seasons: "*It seems*, he grumbles, *that only this part of the universe is not bestowed with summer, autumn and spring, but just winter – the hardest and most difficult time of the year; at the time when we have the height of summer at home, you find there chill, frost and ice and the winter cold is hellish.*" He goes on and on about the fog, and the humidity, and the clouds, and the rain, and the snow; and about the one and only harvest they reap per year, while in other places, they are able to harvest twice a year.

It's possible that there might've been a mini ice age at that time, because another historian, Niketas Choniates states that after the sun turned toward winter, the road from Philippopolis to Sardica became impassable – the cold froze the rivers, snow covered the earth, filled the ravines and blocked the doors of the houses...Antiochos says that the locals are always wearing cloaks and sheepskin coats and their heads are covered with felt hats. Sardica, according to him, *"is located in a place with harsh climate, which is unsuitable either for vegetable gardens, nor for orchards or indeed for growing vines and to expect to have big clusters of grapes from thickly lined vines. And it seems to me, that the foot of Demeter had never trodden here when she went around the world in search of her daughter and bestowed her bounties onto the tribes on her way, neither Dionysus shook here his thyrsus, wound with vine together with clusters of grapes, while dancing in frenzy his bacchanal dance, accompanied by Pan and the Satyrs."* (In Greek Mythology Demeter is the goddess of harvest who presides over crops and the fertility of the earth; Dionysus is the god of wine.)

Antiochos goes on in the same vein, and it appears that he doesn't find anything pleasing about the place whatsoever – *"the apples are all wrinkled like they have aged in a dungeon and the pears look like wrestlers who have fought with their fists and were left with scars and blemishes on their skins, the figs, like raisins, tight as if they are preparing for a long journey, have lost their sweetness, the grapes themselves with dry seeds as if trodden upon, appear to be coming from far away and remaining just skin and bones. The fruits of Sardica, as they say, are not eaten by a blazing fire but by interchangeable cold and big frost. "* This is a bit rich; the Arab geographer Muhammad al-Idrisi (1099–1166) actually emphasised the numbers of fields and vineyards and the abundance of grain and fruit in his description of cities in the region, Sardica being one of them.

Then Gregory Antiochos is having a go at the bread, complaining that *"it is made of millet and bran, not fully baked and covered in ash; and the wine is acid, an enemy of the* stomach, that attacks it as if with a spear; the salty fish stinks and there is mud in them, while the freshwater fish from lakes and rivers are full with silt and reek of swamp". He can't understand why the cow, "the biggest of the four-legged animals is valued more than the fish" and declares that the milk is delivered at a very low price in whole buckets or cauldrons and that baskets of fresh smelly soft cheese cost very little.

He then criticizes the dwellings of the locals and funnily enough, the following extract from his letter is displayed in the Archaeological museum of Sofia, as a testament of the living conditions during the medieval period: *"To say nothing about the stuffy, thatched-roof huts, about the little cabins of reed, cattail and various other shrubs, of small size, made by thrifty and uneducated craftsmen, who don't know anything about proportions and can't be accepted seriously but rather as a child's play.*

If our friend Gregory comes across as Mr Grumpy Pants from this letter, wait and see what he comes up with in his next letter, where even as he continues to allow his wit a free reign, his views have taken a U-turn. It's not clear where the letter, still addressed to his mentor, was written from; it appears that Gregory, a civil servant, is following the Byzantine troops on some military campaign. Anyway, it starts with a proverb, stating that *"what is in the past is always better"*.

His whinging persists of course, but now he regrets for everything that he said about Sardica; about its lands, that the Bulgarians are so proud with, and although he found it so awful before, it has now become a sought after refuge for him. He admits that he had been very unfair in expressing such disdain, showing such ingratitude, biting the hand that had fed him. He explains that although they did not live in luxury, their repast was always plentiful, they always ate well. He goes as far as to say that this is *"the land of the blessed, not the land of the Bulgarians"*; having since left, they were now based in such an infertile place, that they had just the bare necessities.

Gregory's letters, albeit subjective, are still a fascinating read and give us some insight into the life of the city of Sardica/Triaditsa. Whatever the truth, Sardica had been enjoying a bit of a respite during the time of Gregory's visit. But there was trouble ahead.

THE MAGYARS AND THE HOLY RELICS OF A BULGARIAN SAINT

In 1183 the city walls were destroyed by the Magyars of King Béla III of Hungary. Béla had just awaited the demise of Manuel I Komnenos, his benefactor, to make his move. The moment was well chosen for there was a power struggle going on in Constantinople. So the invaders came and razed Sardica and even seized the remains of St. John of Rila and took them to their capital.

Why on earth would the Hungarians do such a thing? It seems that after all this time, the fame of the Bulgarian saint and his reputation as a healer, even from beyond the grave, had not faded. In fact George Scylitzes, a Byzantine author, who was the governor of the city for awhile, wrote exactly at that time about the Life of John of Rila; he firmly believed that he, himself, had been cured of chronic rheumatism thanks to the miraculous powers of the holy relics.

George Scylitzes also stated that while in Sardica/Triaditsa, the Byzantine Emperor Manuel I Komnenos also benefited from the heavenly intervention of St. John and had his arm cured from paralysis or, more likely, tendon stiffness. No doubt visits to the renowned thermal mineral baths, located nearby, would have played a role in those miracles too. At any rate, the Magyars must've believed in such stories. A contemporary chronicler claims that the Magyar Roman Catholic archbishop, who did not believe in the sanctity of John of Rila and uttered some blasphemy against the Bulgarian saint, lost his voice. He did not recover it till he asked for forgiveness. The raiders, repentant, then decided to gain the saintly pardon and returned the holy relic to the city of Serdica/Triaditsa after placing it in a new casket, incrusted with gold, silver and precious stones.

In fact the relics were not returned until 1185, that is 2 years later; some historians even go as far as to imply that Béla held the whole *thema* Niš-*Braničevo*, including Sardica, throughout this time: *"Béla was able to establish unopposed his control across the whole* Niš-*Braničevo from Belgrade as far as Sardica, whence the body of St. John of Rila was taken and returned only after 1185."* (Paul Stephenson, "Byzantium Balkan Frontier").

Hungarian history writer István Vásáry asserts (quoting Moravcsik Gyula, a Byzantiologist) that the new Byzantine Emperor Isaac II Angelus managed to pacify the Hungarians by marrying the daughter of King Béla, which is entirely plausible: *"Isaakios, a widower, married Margaret, the young daughter of the Hungarian King Béla. Margaret (later named Maria in Byzantium) was under ten years old at the time. The marriage must have taken place in the autumn of 1185. As a dowry, Isaakios was given back some of the territories and towns that had been conquered by Béla III in 1185, including Branicevo, Nis and Sredec...As a sign of reconciliation, the relics of St. John of Rila, plundered from Sredec during the campaign in 1183 and brought to the royal town Esztergom in Hungary, were returned to Sredec around that time."* Therefore, it is the marriage of Emperor Isaac II to Margaret of Hungary that was instrumental in getting back the city of Sredetz/Triaditsa plus the relics of the Bulgarian Saint!

BARBAROSSA AND HIS CRUSADERS IN STRALIZ

At any rate, the brother of Béla, prince Geza, joined the Third Crusade of Frederick Barbarossa in 1189, which passed, of course, through Triaditsa - Straliz for the Crusaders (the rest of the Crusaders, led by Richard the Lionheart and King Philip II Augustus of France took the sea route). The Third Crusade (1189–1192), also known as the Kings' Crusade, was an attempt by the European powers to re-conquer the Holy Land from Saladin. The Byzantines did not welcome Barbarossa and co with open arms. There had been enough mistrust already between Byzantines and Germans during the Second Crusade, but during the Third their relations went from bad to worse. Nevertheless they had already reached an agreement at Nüremberg at the back end of 1188, on the eve of the Crusade, allowing for safe passage of the Crusaders through the Balkans and furnishing them with food, shelter and fodder, the army of the cross had a lot of hurdles to jump on the way.

The Byzantine Emperor Isaac II Angelus feared that Barbarossa would lead an invasion of his realm. The Germans had to swear that they would not harm Byzantine lands, otherwise the Byzantines would block the passes and deny them passage through Bulgaria. Both sides, distrusting each other, took various precautions. Consequently, despite the guarantees given by the Byzantine envoys, the advance of the Crusaders was made increasingly difficult. On reaching Straliz on 13th August 1189, the Crusaders found that the inhabitants had evacuated the city, local dignitaries included, thus no provisions were awaiting them (says Choniates, the Byzantine chronicler). Moreover, Barbarossa got wind that Isaac Angelus had allied himself with Saladin and according to the clauses agreed, he was to do everything in his power to impede Barbarossa from reaching the Holy Lands. The Crusaders, enraged, continued, making their own way across the peninsula, plundering as much as they could.

The passage of the Crusaders with their display of western prowess and power, despite the inevitable pillage that went with it, must have surely encouraged certain locals, bent on casting off the "Byzantine yoke" that western rulers might be more sympathetic towards their plight and recognise their independence.

Let's not forget that at that time the Second Bulgarian Kingdom with its capital at Tarnovo had already been established a few years earlier, but Triaditsa was still part of the Byzantine territory. However Barbarossa was not willing to get involved in such conflicts and having made up with Isaac Angelus, he crossed into Asia Minor, while the Byzantines who had provided him with food and ships rubbed their hands in glee at having managed to get rid of him so easily.

The Serbs and the Bulgarians meanwhile, inspired by the Crusaders, now became bolder and attacked fortified cities; Choniates, a contemporary Greek historian, tells us that they *"advanced on Triaditsa, the ancient Sardica where they razed the greater part of the city."* However the Byzantines managed to retake the city and the surrounding area. Nevertheless Triaditsa had a very rough time for the next few years, while the Byzantines were busy dealing with the Bulgarians and the Serbs. The war continued for awhile, but Isaac Angelus was not getting anywhere. In 1193 a Bulgarian army led by King Asen I, assisted by the Serbs, managed to recapture Triaditsa and the whole plain around it. In the autumn of the same year the Byzantines took it back again! It seems that the city finally became Bulgarian in 1194.

THE TREASURES OF BOYANA CHURCH

In 1194 the city of Triaditsa/ Sredetz was once again annexed to the Second Bulgarian Kingdom and knew at last a long spell of peace and prosperity – a new golden age that lasted about 160 years or so. It was a time when a number of monasteries started to materialize in the vicinity of the city; 14 all in all, plus various churches, chapels, hermitages, spread around the foothills of Vitosha and other surrounding mountains. People even started to refer to this complex as "The Little Holy Mountain of Sofia" as opposed to the renowned Holy Mountain on Mount Athos in Byzantium.

The first in the hierarchy was St George near Bistritsa, but later The Holy Mother of God at Dragalevtsi became quite famous and retains its position to this day (both Bistritsa and Dragalevtsi are districts of Greater Sofia). About 100 religious centres altogether were functioning in Sofia plain until the end of the Second Bulgarian kingdom and with them the importance of Sredetz grew all the more. At one stage Sredetz even found itself in the middle of the Bulgarian Empire, which had in the meantime extended far to the west and to the north during the rule of King Ivan Asen II.

The city and its region were given as an appanage to the brother of the King, Sebastocrator Alexander Asen. The grant of an estate, title, office, or other thing of value to a younger male child of a sovereign who would otherwise have no inheritance (the firstborn son was entitled to the entirety of the family's inheritance), was the accepted practice in Europe in those days. Information about Sebastocrator Alexander Asen is scarce; his title indicates that he was second only to the King. It is also known that he defeated the Hungarians who attacked Sredetz in 1232 and he drove them from Belgrade (a city which at that time formed part of the Bulgarian state).

A period of political power struggles, of wars and uncertainty started soon after the demise of King Ivan Asen II (1241). At that time, Sredetz and the whole region was ruled by a certain Peter, a son-in-law of King Ivan Asen II (husband of Anna, the former King's daughter from his third marriage to Irene Comnena). Sebastocrator Peter became Regent to his brother-in-law, the young Michael II Asen, along with his mother-in-law. He enjoyed a position of influence at the Royal Court in Tarnovo until the marriage of King Michael to Anna (1256), the daughter of Prince Rostislav Mikhailovich, an ambitious Russian noble in exile, who quickly supplanted him. However, it's known that Peter's descendants eventually succeeded to the Bulgarian throne, to become the last Royal dynasty in power before the Ottoman invasion.

The intrigues and the frequent *"coups d'état"*, that marked the life at the Royal Court in Tarnovo at that stage, would've been felt in Sredetz as a distant echo, at a time when communications between the two cities would've been difficult, due to the distance and the political unrest during this period, not to mention the Tatar incursions. Besides, the city of Vidin, on the Danube, had been gradually gaining in importance, leaving Sredetz somewhat behind. It was probably for the best, giving Sredetz a bit of a respite, at least until the Ottoman conquest...

Next we hear of a Sebastocrator Kaloyan, a very wealthy and influential nobleman, who was related both to the Serbian and to the Bulgarian Royal family. Was he the son of Sebastocrator Alexander Asen? It is not clear. Whatever his pedigree, he is connected forever with the history of the city of Sredetz and the collective memory has retained his name, while others, more illustrious, and maybe more deserving, have long since been forgotten.

An area in the centre of Sofia is associated with him and it is believed that he renovated the magnificent palace of Constantine the Great and used it as his residence. His name is also linked to both the church of St. Petka (the old), which is now incorporated in the building of the Diocese of Sofia and to the church just opposite, St Nicholas. Both benefited from his patronage and both are still in use today. However, the street passing between these churches, is now erroneously named "King Kaloyan", no doubt as a result of confusing the Sebastocrator with the great Bulgarian King of the same name, who might have been his uncle; although, based in his capital Tarnovo, the King would have had very little to do with the city of Sredetz.

Little is known about the Sebastocrator and the odds are that he would've been forgotten by history altogether if it wasn't for his involvement in the renovation and extension of the church in Boyana (at the time a village in the foothills of Vitosha, now a district of Sofia) in 1259. Money was not an issue for him, from what we can gather, and Kaloyan, like any rich and powerful man, wanted to leave his mark. As the one who had commissioned the work, he wanted the best he could get for his money. Whether the reconstruction of the church gained him a place in paradise, no one can tell. But this investment got him something else which was probably beyond his wildest dreams – immortality of a different sort, a lasting legacy that he is still remembered for, despite the passage of time.

The edifice itself is modest enough. A two-storey extension – the second floor served as a family chapel – has been skilfully added to the existing church, but the whole composition is unfortunately somewhat spoilt by a later, 19th century addition. However, the real treasure is inside this unassuming building. The frescos, produced by the 13th century master artist named Basil (Vasily for the Bulgarians) and his apprentices, are not only superb, but a work of art way ahead of its time.

The portraits of the donors should've been done on a smaller scale, as was the practice in those times, but here the images of the handsome dark-eyed Kaloyan and his wife, the beautiful Desislava, are placed amongst the portraits of saints who led exemplary lives. To balance it somehow, on the opposite wall are the portraits of the Bulgarian King Constantine Tikh (1257 – 1277) and Queen Irene, sister of the Byzantine Emperor John IV Doukas Laskaris. It is interesting to note that while the Royal couple, depicted frontally and looking rather stilted, have their eyes turned slightly towards the face of Christ – *Chalkites* (based on an original from the Chalke gate in Constantinople), Kaloyan, holding a model of the church and his lady, her arms outstretched in a similar gesture and eyes demurely lowered, are both turned slightly towards another image of Christ- *Evergetes* (blessing).

Kaloyan clearly wanted to underline his relationship with the King, for they were cousins, but also to appear as his equal. The clothes the Sebastocrator and his wife are wearing, are as elaborate as the ones worn by the Royal couple. Let's not forget that the title Sebastocrator indicates that he was second to the King only, and the coronets, adorning the foreheads of Kaloyan and Desislava reinforce this idea.

Thus towards the end of the medieval period we find Sredetz a thriving city, the seat of the Sebastocrator. It continued to prosper for another 100 years or so, till the Ottoman invasion. Gradually the name Sofia must've crept into common usage, although it was still used interchangeably with Sredetz.

The first written Bulgarian document referring to the city as Sofia, but still persisting with the designation Sredetz region, dates from around 1376 and is a charter, granted to the Dragalevtsi monastery "The Holy Mother of God from Vitosha" (just outside the city) by King Ivan Shishman. In the charter, the Bulgarian King emphasises the status of the monastery and a nearby village as being autonomous, outside the jurisdiction of the Bishopric of Sofia and giving it a sort of feudal immunity, while cautioning the governor of the Sredetz region that he *"should not interfere with the monastery"*, neither with *"the people from Novachevo village when they are in the Royal city of Sofia"*. The Dragalevtsi monastery subsequently became known as the Royal monastery, emphasising the King's patronage.

The name of the King himself is now closely linked with the fall of Bulgaria under Ottoman rule. Sadly, the once mighty Bulgarian Kingdom found itself fragmented and weakened by internal struggles. Ivan Shishman's older brother had taken the region of Vidin on the Danube, while another noble had laid hands on the fertile Dobrudja, a large area to the south of the Danube, stretching all the way to its delta on the Black Sea. Ivan Shishman, although in possession of the largest chunk, then found himself like the piggy in the middle. While the Bulgarians were involved in their petty squabbling, the Ottomans were quick to act. They saw their Empire as the successor to the Byzantine Empire, keen to reintegrate its former territories, they went into expansion mode

A TRIP IN TIME BUT NOT IN SPACE

INTERLUDE

Our itinerary is:

Serdonpolis – Serdica – Sardica – Sredetz – Triaditsa – Triadizza – Stralis – Straliz – Hesternit – Starnen – Sternes – Sternys – Scernys – Ny – Sophia – Sofya – Sofia

In the Middle Ages the Western, mostly Latin speaking, travellers were rather confused while travelling through what we know today as the Balkans. No GPS, no travel maps, no road signs to help them to ascertain their whereabouts. Besides the unfamiliar language, the unusual place names added to the confusion. Thus old *Serdica – Sardica*, (or even *Sartica*) of the Roman era, had become *Sredetz* for the local population, *Triaditsa/Triaditza* for the Greeks; as to the Western visitors of these parts, the city has been referred to as ....well, you name it - whatever sounds even remotely similar to the above names would do the job, such as *Stralis, Straliz, Stralicia, Hesternit, Starnen, Sternes.*

In 1069 and 1079 the Byzantine emperors Isaac I Comnenus and Alexius I Comnenus who used the city as a military base for their campaigns against the Pechenegs, refer to it as *Sredets*. In the Anonymous Notary of King Béla, the oldest extant chronicle of the history of the Hungarians, we even find it as *Screducy*!
"Some days later, Zuard and Cadusa with their whole army, emblazoned standards aloft, crossed the water of the Danube and captured Barancs [Borons] castle, after which they went to the castle of Screducy. Hearing this, the countrymen of the Bulgarians and Macedonians feared greatly before them. Then all the inhabitants of that land sent their envoys with many gifts to surrender the land to them and hand over their sons as hostages. Zuard and Cadusa, inclining to peace and taking their gifts and hostages, left them in peace, as if they were their own people, and riding beyond the Wacil Gate [ultra portam Wacil], they took the castle of King Philip." (*Wacil Gate* here refers to the Trajan Gate, also known as Succi, the fortified pass located between modern-day Sofia and Plovdiv - the latter obviously indicated here as the *castle of King Philip* – Philippopolis!)

Muhammad Al Idrisi (1099–1165), the well-known Arab geographer and cartographer, who travelled extensively around the world, has left the following account in his "Book of Roger" (*Tabula Rogeriana*, a comprehensive geographical book with maps, compiled for King Roger II of Sicily): *"The distance between Istibuni (today Ihtiman) and Atralisa (Sofia) is covered for one day. Atralisa is a town in a valley with densely populated districts and numerous buildings, wherefrom start a series of cultivated plots and orchards..."* Al Idrisi places Atralisa in *"Ard Burdzhan"*, (the Bulgarian lands). And he adds: *"Atralisa, as we already described it, is located in the fifth climate zone, and is a marvellous town."*

Gervase of Ebstorf, who drew the Ebstorf map for the cathedral of the same name, notes the *"puszta of Bulgaria"*, which is *"the land of the Vlach"* (he means King Kaloyan of Bulgaria, 1197–1207). *"The end of the puszta comes with Stralis (Sofia), main town of Romania"* - which presumably means what we call today the Byzantine (Roman) Empire, although at the time of Kaloyan, Sredetz was a Bulgarian city and Wallachia, on the other side of the Danube was a vassal territory of Kaloyan's.

Odo, Odon, or Eudes of Deuil (1110 – 1162), a historian and participant of the Second Crusade (1147–1149) in his narrative of the Crusade, entitled *De profectione Ludovici VII in Orientem* (On Louis VII's journey to the East) explains that *"the towns of Nish, Hesternit [Sofia], Philippopolis [Plovdiv] and Adrianople [Edirne] are at a four-day distance from each other, and from the latter town to Constantinople it takes five days.*

Jehan de Mandeville or Sir John Mandeville in his *"Travels of Sir John Mandeville"* (1357 -1371) also mentions Sofia, albeit under a different name. The trouble with Mandeville's accounts is that his travel stories, which had become quite the bestseller of its time – that is at the dawn of printing - are not only taken very much as fictional today, but they are also to be found in so many different versions, that it becomes almost impossible to make head or tail of them. Take this one for example (from a publication of the University of Cork): *"Thence men go to Belgrade, and thence to Buigris, where they find a bridge of stone over the river which is called Straet Ombarrocc, and thence through the land that is called Pinnseras, and thence to the city of Sternes in Greece and thence to the city Apimpane and thence to the city of Bradinoble and thence to the city of Constantinople, which is named Balsamson."* Apart from Belgrade, Greece and Constantinople, the rest of the place names are unintelligible.

Mandeville's travels, according to the Cambridge History of English Literature, were translated into almost every European language and some 300 manuscripts are said to be still in existence. The three standard versions are the Latin, the French and the English, all of which were attributed to Mandeville himself and date from as early as 1403. The best manuscript is the oldest, in French, 1371; there are three English versions – of

Cotton, of Egerton and a "Defective" manuscript (which misses pages etc). The quote above is Egerton's from 1781, written *'probably in Brefne, not later than 1484'*, by two scribes.

The way Sofia seems to change its name in each version, is bamboozling – anyone for a game of Scrabble?! The Cambridge History of English Literature gives it as an example of the "transformation" of place names – some transformation indeed: *"...thus the town Hesternit appears in Latin as Sternes ad fines Epapie, in a French version - as N y e puis a fin Pape, in Cotton as - Ny and to the cytie of fine Pape, in Egerton - as Sternes and to Pe cite of Affynpane"*

Lost in translation? You won't be after you read the next few lines when all will be explained. Or shall I leave it to my readers to make sense of it? Anyway, in fact everything is simple enough if you know some geography and have a map of the area, which was not the case in those far away days. The above mumbo jumbo means only that they (Mandeville and his mates) went to *Sredets* (for the Bulgarians) but *Sternes, Hesternit, Sternez,* or whatever the foreigners chose to call it, and then on to *Philippopolis*, the city of Philip of Macedonia – today simply Plovdiv, located some 3 days ride from *Sredets*. Two very distinct cities: the first one is *Hesternit / Sternes / N y / Ny /* and the second *– fines Epapie / a fin Pape / cytie of fine Pape / Pe cite of Affynpane*. Yet from the quote above, and that from a reputable source - The Cambridge History of English Literature, one is left with the impression that it's a question of one place only. Thus the city of Hesternit might become Sternes in Latin, but why on earth should it appear as N y in French and then to be reproduced as Ny in the English version of Cotton? A printing mistake?

The trouble is that mistakes like this frequently get copied - without the authors or printers verifying the accuracy of their sources - and then passed on. That would explain how Sternes, spelled as Sternys in an English version happened to become the NY that puzzled us so much at first; a simple misspelling (omitting letters in this instance), causing a city to be renamed. All right, no chance of confusing it with The Big Apple which didn't exist at the time, but still, it makes it very difficult to follow the fortunes of any city when the name is constantly being changed. Thus tracking the elusive Sternes throughout the years may become the work of a lifetime!

Anyway, here is another version of this excerpt of Mandeville, a pure joy (especially if you are able to decipher it):

6 THE VOIAGE AND TRAVAYLE OF SIR JOHN MAUNDEVILLE KNIGHT
with so great might that the water is freshe xxx [1] myle within the sea and afterwards go men to Belgrave [2] and entereth the lande of Bugres [3] and there pass men a bridge of stone that is over the river Marrock [4] and so men passe through the lande of Pinseras [5] and come to Grece to the citie of Stermis [6] and to the citie of Affinpane [7] that was sometime called Bradre [8] the noble and so to the citie of Constantinople that was sometime called Bessameron [9] and there dwelleth commonly the Emperor of Grece.

[1] Pynson and others say 20 miles.
[2] Belgrade.
[3] Bulgarians.
[4] Now called the Morava, nothing to do whatsoever with Morocco.
[5] Pynson says Pynteras, others Pyncemartz, and Pyncoras (now Pirot).
[6] Pynson says Sternys, others Sternes, or Scernys (now Sofia).
[7] Written elsewhere Affynpayn, Assynpayn, and ad fines Epapie (Philippopolis, now Plovdiv)
[8] This one best illustrates the difficulty of placing the localities, for this means Adrianople, a city between Philippopilis and Constantinople (now Edirne, Turkey).
[9] Byzantium, the ancient name for Constantinople, the seat of the Roman Empire; obviously this account was written prior to its falling to the Ottomans, which happened in 1453.

For the record Pynson - Richard Pynson (born in 1448 in Normandy – died in 1530) was one of the first printers of English books. He came from France – a Frenchman – and was to become a printer to the King - first to Henry VII, then to Henry VIII. Bearing this in mind, we can trust Pynson as far as accuracy goes.

The name Sofia, according to the majority of sources, was actually first recorded in writing in *The Vitosha Charter*, awarded to the Holy Mother of God, the Vitosha Monastery in the village of Dragalevtsi, located in Mount Vitosha near Sofia, the document itself being discovered in the Zograf Monastery, where it is preserved to this day. This medieval Bulgarian Royal charter was issued between 1371 and 1385. The name Sofia must've been used interchangeably with the other names, well into the time of the Ottoman Empire. However this was the name that remained.

As you see we started from Serdonpolis, we then passed through a dozen cities, to arrive at Sofia, but in fact we did not move one bit. Different names, changing times, but one, and only one location.

OTTOMAN TIMES

"The first view of Sophia, rising up in the centre of a vast basin, with its domes and minarets picturing their fair forms on the horizon; over which we behold in picturesque grandeur the encircling chain of the Balkan, is one of surprising beauty."

Edmund Spencer

THE SHISHMAN ROYAL DYNASTY AND THE OTTOMAN INVASION

The Ottoman raids on Bulgaria started in the middle of the 14th century and numerous battles were fought before they finally managed to conquer it. The Bulgarian Empire had started its decline towards the end of the rule of King Ivan Alexander (1331-1371), who divided the country between two of his sons, thus weakening it exactly when it had to face the Ottoman threat. Ivan Alexander is known to the Anglo-Saxon world thanks to the illuminated manuscript he had commissioned in 1355/56, now referred to as the Gospels of Tsar Ivan Alexander, and described as "*the most celebrated work of art produced in Bulgaria before it fell to the Turks in 1393*". The pages of the holy book are lavishly illustrated with 367 colour miniatures and King Ivan Alexander himself, together with his family, are depicted there. This is a full length portrait of the Royal family on a double page; on one side are the Royal son-in-law with his wife and two sisters-in-law and on the other side – the King in imperial dress, joined by his second wife, Theodora, and two sons – Ivan Shishman, his co-ruler, and Ivan Asen. The Gospels are now preserved in the British Library, having miraculously found their way there, after being brought to England from Mount Athos by a British collector who received them as a gift from a monk.

But let's go back to Bulgaria and see how Sofia was doing during this time of mounting Ottoman incursions. The first was an Ottoman cavalry of some 20 000 under the leadership of Sultan Murad's brother, which got as far as Sofia, where they were met by the Bulgarian troops led by Prince Ivan Asen IV, the son and also co-ruler of the Bulgarian King Ivan Alexander. The young Prince lost his life during the battle, but the Ottoman army was driven away. One anonymous Bulgarian chronicle states that: *"The Turks killed Asen and a great number of Bulgarians perished."* According to a Turkish chronicle, a lot of janissaries (the Sultan's personal troops recruited from slaves and prisoners) lost their lives in the same battle too; however, some Bulgarian historians (Andreev) reckon that the Prince lost his life later, in 1355.

The confusion comes from the fact that not one, but two sons, both of whom were co-rulers with King Ivan Alexander of Bulgaria, fell on the battlefield at Sredets in two separate battles. *"And so Amorat, the son of Orhan, crossed over with the Turks in the year 6834 [according to the Islamic calendar/ 1326, but more likely 1349, according to the Western one] and set off against Sredets. The Bulgarians gathered an army under their leader Asen, the son of Alexander and a great battle was fought. Then Asen (Ivan Asen IV) was killed and a great multitude of Bulgarians perished. Again did the Bulgarians come together under the leadership of Michael, the son of Alexander (Michael Asen, and his co-ruler) but he too was killed and many people were captured and carried across Gallipoli." (Bulgarian archive sources).*

In fact the next bid for Sofia is six years later, in 1355, when the Ottoman army is repelled again, but both sides pay a high price. The Ottomans had gained control of the fortress at Gallipoli in 1354 and freely crossed over to the Balkans. Still, after this battle, the city gets some breathing space.

Even so, the city becomes a bone of contention between King Ivan Shishman and King Ivan Stratsimir, his half-brother, whose fiefdom is to the north (with his capital at Vidin on the Danube). It's not clear why, but it seems that at one point Ivan Stratsimir managed to take control of the city of Sofia/Sredets and to keep it for awhile, but in 1373 Sofia appears once again within the domains of Ivan Shishman. The two brothers had an uneasy relationship and were unable to show a united front. Each was trying to keep the Turks at bay, without much success. The bitter rivalry between the two brothers was of long duration. Ivan Stratsimir felt hard done by, by his half brother, because by rights he should've been the heir of the defunct King Ivan Alexander, yet Ivan Shishman was the one chosen to rule over the Kingdom of Turnovo. So when the Ottomans started to exercise pressure on Ivan Shishman, Ivan Stratsimir did not come to the rescue.

When Ivan Shishman gave his sister Maria Thamara (Kera Tamara) in marriage to the Turkish Sultan Murad I, angling after the pretty widow since 1371, he must have been convinced that this union would ensure peace between the two countries. Or else it must've been an act of desperation, for at the time he was already a vassal of the Sultan.

THE FALL OF SOFIA

At any rate, soon afterwards, in the beginning of the 1380s the Ottomans resumed their campaigns and besieged the city of Sofia/Sredets, which they deemed important, because it controlled major communication routes to Serbia and Macedonia. And yet, it was said that Maria Thamara had done a lot in order to preserve the sovereignty of the city of Sofia. *"It was under siege for a long time,"* states Hajji Khalfa (in his work 'Rumeli und

Bosna') *"by Lala Şahin Pasha and in 780 of the Hegira (1378 AD? According to other sources 1382, 1385 or even 1388) it capitulated to the beylerbey of Filibe, Bulken Pasha."*

The city of Sofia was apparently very well fortified and the Turkish leader Lala Şahin Pasha failed to capture it, despite all his efforts, and there is no doubt that he did try, for he really coveted it, otherwise would he refer to Sofia and Sofia plain as Paradise Apple Gardens? In the same report he explains that the fortress is unassailable and all direct attacks had failed. He considers it impossible to take, unless they use either deception or some clever military stratagem. Further on he states that *"Inside the fortress there is a large and elite army, its soldiers are heavily built, moustached and look war-hardened, but are used to consume wine and rakia [eau-de-vie] - in a word, jolly fellows. The fortress is well provisioned with wheat, flour and livestock."*

According to legend, the person in charge of the defence of the city was one named Ban Yanuka. Some suggest that he was in fact the Transylvanian ruler John Hunyadi later involved in the crusade of 1443, led by King Władysław. That's not very likely because at the time of the siege of Sofia he would not yet have been born. Other speculations point to Prince Ivan Asen V, brother of King Ivan Shishman. This prince, possibly named after his half-brother, also called Ivan Asen, mentioned earlier, who had perished in battle against the Ottomans, is known to have resided in Sofia/Sredets. "Yanuka" might well derive from Ivan – Ivanko, while *"Ban"* is a title given to the governor of a city and its region.

The story goes that a young Muslim man gained the confidence of Ban Yanuka and they frequently went hunting together. Once when they were out hunting, just the two of them, the Muslim managed to disarm an unsuspecting Ban Yanuka; he then proceeded to tie him up before taking him to Indjèh Balaban who was then in Filibe (Philippopolis, present day Plovdiv). The Ottoman troops then marched on Sofia, taking their captive with them. The defendants of the city of Sofia, seeing their leader in the hands of their enemy, prayed Indjèh Balaban for mercy and opened the town gates for him...

In fact Sofia was besieged numerous times by the Ottomans. It was under siege in 1382 and it must've been then when the young Prince Ivan Asen V was captured by the Turks and was forced to convert to Islam, before going back to Sofia. Later, after his apostasy, he was killed by the Turks, presumably at the time of their conquest of Sofia.

Mavro Orbin, a writer and historian from the republic of Ragusa (Dubrovnik,) affirms that Prince Ivan Asen V led the armies of his brother King Ivan Shishman.

To be sure, Bulgarian folklore is full of references to Ban Yanuka, King Yasen, Shishmanovich Yane. More to the point, from a tombstone, discovered in Turnovo, the old Bulgarian capital (possibly ordered by the Queen, Maria), it becomes clear that Ivan Asen was buried in 1388, fallen while fighting the Turks. In the inscription it is disclosed that he was exposed to the risk of *"failing the beauty of the Faith"*, presumably an allusion to his conversion. King Ivan Shishman outlived his younger brother, but only to see his country being gradually overrun by the Turks. He was forced to accept not only the position of vassal to the Sultan but, it seems, that in the end he was even stripped of his Royal title. It is believed that he was killed when Turnovo was captured by the Ottomans in 1395.

Yet, Bulgarian folklore has elevated him to the position of a great hero, a tragic figure, fighting a losing battle. This Bulgarian King Arthur has inspired the popular imagination and his ghost still haunts the environments of Sofia. According to some sources, like the history written by Paisius of Hilendar, the King managed to escape from the invaders with his entourage and to reach Sofia. He buried his treasure somewhere along the Iskar gorge and fought the Ottomans for 7 years before being killed in battle. That's what a very popular folk song says:

> *Since, my dear mother, dawn has broken,*
> *Since then, my dear mother, the army has marched,*
> *Horse by horse, my dear mother, hero by hero*
> *Their sabres, my dear mother, as bright as the sun,*
> *Fire glows, my dear mother, in the green forest,*

Their leader, my dear mother, Tsar Ivan Shishman himself,
Responds, my dear mother, Tsar Ivan Shishman himself:
God Almighty, my dear mother, Lord our Maker,
May He help us, my dear mother, with strength and courage!
We are to fight a battle, my dear mother, on Sofia plain,
We are to spill blood, my dear mother, in the name of Christ,
For the glory, my dear mother, of the Christian faith.

    The fortress of Urvich, just outside the city of Sofia, is said to be where he made his last stand. Urvich is just one of the many fortifications along the Iskar River. Built during the Second Bulgarian Kingdom, its strategic position would've been much appreciated for it is encircled on three sides by the river. It has been said that the waters of the river were diverted when need arose and people even believed that the legendary treasure had been buried in the river bed.

    According to legend, the local people had worked on the fortifications and knew a secret passage that led to the fortress. The Turks wanted to take it, for it opened the road to Sofia itself. One day the Pasha captured a shepherdess with her small child and threatened to kill them if she didn't tell him how to find the secret passage. The woman, terrified, told him everything he wanted to know, breaking the oath she had sworn.

    The defenders of the fortress got wind that she had betrayed them. The King had them bury the treasure under a rock and divert the waters over it, then ordered them to leave during the night before the enemy attack. He told them that although they might hold the fortress for awhile, without access to the river, where the secret passage led, they would not have any water and would die of thirst and starvation. So they left the fortress, which was then taken by the Turks and demolished; the King himself was killed during the foray. Meanwhile the shepherdess and her child had been turned to stone.

    In these seemingly far-fetched stories, there is at least a grain of truth. A treasure of a sort was recently discovered in the small, half-demolished church at Urvich; 18 silver coins from the time of King Ivan Alexander, the father of King Shishman. The archaeologists believed that there were probably more, but that treasure-seekers got there first. There were also some rings dating from the Middle Ages.

The struggle of the Bulgarians, and more especially in this case, the Sofianites, against the invaders did not stop with the conquest of Sofia, even if, to all intents and purposes, from that time on the city was an Ottoman possession, or so it would seem.

For things were not as clear-cut as that. For a start, certain European states, including Rome, continue to refer to Constantine II Asen (son of Ivan Stratsimir) as the King of Bulgaria till 1422 (the year of his death). In Fra Mauro's 1459 map of the world (there is an 1804 copy in the British Library), Bulgaria figures as "Bolgaria". Then there are numerous written materials, indicating that Sofia and its adjacent territories were governed by Bulgarians, presumably vassals of the Sultan, as late as the end of the 15th century, notably Radivoy, the *voevoda* (governor) of Sofia, who in 1493 restored the Kremikovtsi monastery, in the vicinity of the city, believed to be initially founded by King Ivan Alexander. The murals of the monastery church, St. George, preserved to this day, are the proof that Bulgarians still held power in the region, as we can see the portrait of the donor himself, Radivoy, presenting a model of the church to its patron St. George in the presence of the Metropolitan of Sofia, Klevit; as in Boyana church, the donor and his family seem to be elevated to the same status as the patron-saint. The two young children of the couple, standing just in front of them, have their hands crossed on their chests, indicating that at that time they were not amongst the living anymore, having succumbed to the Black Death in 1492.

Come what may, life went on. It is said that the *Sanjak* (district) of Sofia was established circa 1393 and existed till the end of the Ottoman rule (1878); that soon after the establishment of the *Sanjak*, Sofia became the seat of the Rumelia Eyalet, where the Governor–General (*beylerbey* or *beglerbeg*) of Rumelia resided; and that the *Sanjak* itself became the Principal *Sanjak* of Rumelia, also referred to as *Pasha Sanjak*.

Rumelia for the Turks meant "the land of the Romans", for the Byzantine Empire was then known as the Eastern Roman

Empire. Today the name "Rumelia" has long since dropped out of use and we refer to these lands as the Balkans. If you look at a map it becomes pretty obvious why Sofia was chosen to be the capital of Rumelia – it is situated at the very centre of the province, i.e. the Balkan Peninsula! And let's not forget – on a major crossroads too! Travellers still continued to use good old *Via Diagnalis* and Sofia remained a very important post on their itinerary.

In 1433 Bertrandon de la Brocquiere, a counsellor to Philip le Bon, the Duke of Burgundy, makes a stop in Sofia on his return journey from Jerusalem. He estimates that the city must've been considerable, judging by the town walls, now razed to the ground, but despite that he still perceives it as the best Bulgarian city. *"It has a small castle and is situated near a mountain on the southward, and at the beginning of a great plain sixty miles long by ten wide."* Afterwards Bertrandon goes on to say that its population is predominantly Bulgarian, as it is too in the surrounding villages. The Turks are a small minority, which gives the others a great desire to overthrow their yoke, if there were someone to assist them. The Turks that he spotted coming back from Hungary were not at all heavily armed: *"there were many more that had neither bow nor sword than those who were armed with both. The best equipped had a small wooden target. In truth we must confess that it is a great shame for Christendom to suffer itself to be subjugated by such a race for they are much below what is thought of them."*

THE ILL-FATED CRUSADE OF KING WŁADYSŁAW OF VARNA AND JOHN HUNYADI

Whatever the brave Bertrandon thought about the chances of success of a potential uprising, when the time came just 10 years later, the events took a different course and, sadly, even with someone to assist them, the subjugated Christians didn't manage to overthrow the foreign yoke.

And yet at the onset everything started just like in a fairy tale, when a gallant prince, a knight in shining armour came to the rescue; Władysław was his name, Władysław III, King of Poland

and King of Hungary. The Pope had helped him to keep his throne in a civil war and asked him to fight the Turks in return. So the Hungarian/Serb led Crusade of 1443 was a venture sponsored by the Pope. It is also known as the Long March.

The Hungarian army, led by King Władysław, John Hunyadi, and Serbian Despot Đurađ Branković, attacked in mid-October. They had several advantages over the Ottomans, which gave them victory in their first encounters, such as forcing Kasim Pasha of Rumelia and his co-commander Turakhan Bey to abandon camp and flee to Sofia to warn Sultan Murad II of the invasion. For the record – Murad spent a considerable amount of his time in Sofia, taking advantage of the mineral baths there. But this time the Sultan had rushed there to muster an army.

The record of the contemporary Ottoman historian Oruc Bey and another, anonymous Ottoman chronicle, *"Ghazavat-i-Sultan Murad bin Mehmed Han"* ("The Holy Wars of Sultan Murad Son of Sultan Mehmed Khan"), recording the battles of Sultan Murad II (1421 – 1451), both describe the events of 1443.

Apparently the Sultan was determined to get to Sofia before the arrival of the Crusaders. He needed reinforcements though, if he expected to halt their advancement. Therefore he issued quite a few decrees to hasten the mobilisation; one of them in particular sounded rather desperate, for he was offering the earth to whoever joined him in the jihad: *"It should be known that whoever accompanies us on this victory-crowned campaign and offers assistance out of love for the religion of Islam, my imperial assent has been granted for whatever it is they request. Whatever it is they wish – whether timar or zeamet, whether a post in the janissaries or the household cavalry or whether release from the yürük status – I have accepted."* For reference: *timar* and *ziamet* were forms of land tenure in the Ottoman Empire, consisting of a grant of lands or revenues by the Sultan to an individual in compensation for his services, especially military services; while the *yürüks* were nomadic tribes; the *yürüks* in the Balkans had the obligation to provide auxiliary military services to the Ottoman Sultan. It is unclear if the above incentives did the trick. Oruc Bey notes that the *serahor* – that is, mercenaries, that they were aimed at, simply took the money and went back to their farms.

Meanwhile in order to slow down the Hungarians, Turakhan Bey and Kasim Pasha, the two underlings of Sultan Murad, on their flight to Sofia, left a trail of fire behind them. Burning all the villages in their path, they were in fact waging the so called scorched earth campaign, which involves destroying anything that might be useful to the enemy in advancing through or withdrawing from an area. In this case there was another consideration – winter was coming and it was going to be a cold one. When they arrived in Sofia, Turakhan bey advised the Sultan to burn the city as well and retreat to the mountain passes beyond. According to *Ghazavat*, whose author (judging by his detailed and vivid description) had presumably served in the entourage of Sultan Murad II, this is what Turakhan bey had to say: *"My Padishah, there is a way out of this. We are no match for these infidels. They cannot be resisted. All we can do is to leave the city and retreat. You should give the order to burn the city and the surrounding villages. My hope is that, when the infidels, who are as low as the dust, enter the plain of Sofia, a storm will blow up and when they find no shelter, they will lose their hands and feet. After that the matter is simple. If there is no possibility of resisting them, this is the only solution."*

It appears that the Sultan trusted his advisor's judgment well enough for he *"commanded everyone to take his family and belongings and to set fire to the city and its villages. Now see what chaos and confusion there was! The people of Sofia willy-nilly took their families and possessions and with sighs and sobbing, scattered in all directions. Meanwhile Kasim Bey, on the orders of the Padishah, set fire to every part of Sofia and its surroundings, destroying even its hot water springs. In short it was such that mothers forgot their children. Not a straw was left in Sofia or its surrounds."*

This is a pretty thorough account of the events that took place in Sofia at the back end of 1443. Yet why is it that Western accounts make it that the Hungarians rather than the Ottomans set the city on fire? Western propaganda, intended to impress the enemy? Janos Thuroczy for example, just a child at the time, states that the Crusaders *"stormed the city, which they sacked, plundering and burning everything"*, while Giovanni Campisio chimes in with *"the Crusaders had not only reduced Sofia to ashes, which had long since been reported, but that it was rumoured they had taken Edirne itself."* It seems that it was heard on the grapevine! However, the account given in *"Ghazavat"* concurs with another narrative, that of Laonicus Chalcondyles, a contemporary Byzantine historian ("Proofs of Histories"), adding yet more weight to the *"Ghazavat"* account.

The Crusaders arrived in the city on a freezing December's day to find ashes and cinders. They looked for a church and not finding one, they went towards the Siyavus Pasha Mosque, for the mosques, of course, had been spared. This one in particular awoke their interest and saddened them, for this is what had become of the famed cathedral of St. Sophia; the onetime proud symbol of the city had been turned into a mosque. Once there, the Crusaders hung a big bell inside, lit candles and brought the Metropolitan Bishop. A Holy mass was solemnly held, presided by the Orthodox Bishop and attended by the Latin/Catholic Crusaders, a rather moving occasion which must've uplifted the hearts of all present and must've been seen as a step towards a reconciliation between the Eastern and the Western Christian Churches.

From *Ghazavat*, we learn that Władysław had informed the local populace that their goods wouldn't be touched if they voluntarily provided help to the Crusaders. According to it, the Bulgarians welcomed and helped the invading army and elected a *"Vladica"* (Bishop) as their representative in Sofia. It goes on to say: *"Most of the people in fact submitted to these accursed men. Some began to bring provisions to sell. Some mounted their horses and acted as guides. In short that year they paid their tax to the infidels, who are as low as the dust, and many of the subject infidels mounted their horses and joined Yanko's [Hunyadi's] army."* According to *Ghazavat*, Hunyadi was very pleased with this development and was planning to send these local reinforcements as a vanguard, reasoning that *"if the Turks attack us, they will make an excellent shield."* Meanwhile the Crusaders had to press on, pleased with their progress so far and with their new friend, the Orthodox Bishop, whom they left in charge.

The Sultan in the meantime was grieving for the "fair city" that he had ordered to be set on fire: *"The Padishah was extremely low-spirited and regretted what he had done. But for what purpose? What had happened had happened, and it grieved him night and day. 'Alas!' he worried, 'What a fate we have visited on fair Sofia! The man who told us to do this is not our friend. Alas! We acted without thinking when we followed the word of a man who is a calamity.' He suffered bitter pangs of conscience, but seeing that there was nothing to be done, he issued orders with the thought 'It was God's decree'."* Nevertheless, the Sultan's grief quickly turned to anger, when he was told of the "treason" of the local citizens.

Meanwhile, the Pasha of Sofia who had fled to the town of Radomir, some 44 km to the southwest of Sofia, on hearing that the Crusaders had left, emboldened, he gathered his troops and rode back to Sofia where he took the Cathedral and beheaded the Bishop. Problem solved!

In the wake of the "humiliating peace" of Szegedin, signed in 1444, after the defeat of the Crusaders at Varna, where King Władysław lost his life, *"the citizens of Sofia,* says the British historian Bury, *which ten years earlier had been the most flourishing town in the whole country, lamented among the ashes of their ruined houses the vain attempt of the Christians to set them free. Their city famous for its baths became the residence of the 'Beglerbeg of Rumelia' – the viceroy of the Sultan in the Balkans."*

OTTOMAN MILITARY CAMPAIGNS IN THE WEST AND THE BLACK DEATH

In the aftermath of the 1443 Crusade, for their participation in which many citizens of Sofia were persecuted, particularly those from the elite classes, Sofia's urban layout and appearance started to change. The population increased in the still predominantly Bulgarian town during that time, as Sofia rose to become in 1444 the capital of Rumelian beylerbeylik, spanning most of the Ottoman possessions in Europe, remaining the centre of the region until the 18th century.

In 1448 Hunyadi, who had survived the 1443/44 Crusade, led another campaign against the Ottoman Empire and suffered another crushing defeat at Kosovo. The Ottomans had mustered their troops in Sofia; according to Ottoman reports some 50 to 60 000 armed men, although Western sources put it up to 150 000. At that time Sofia, understandably, was used as the base of the Sultan during his Serbian campaigns.

Hunyadi finally managed to settle scores with the Ottomans at Belgrade in 1456; although his old rival Murad II had long since died, Hunyadi was victorious against his son and successor, Mehmed II, known as the Conqueror. Venting his anger on his generals, Mehmed retreated to Sofia to nurse his wounds and for awhile nothing was heard of him, so rumours started to circulate that he had succumbed to his injuries. However he was alive and kicking; instead it was Hunyadi who did not live for long to enjoy his success; plague broke out in his camp only 3 weeks later and he was struck down at the age of 70.

The Black Death, it seems, was on the side of young Mehmed; it had spared him, not just during that outbreak, but also during the previous and subsequent epidemics; or rather he kept out of harm's way. The Byzantine historian Dukas describes how in 1455 during one of the outbreaks, he went on a merry-go-round before he was able to find the Sultan, moving from one place to another to escape the pestilence. He finally caught up with him, the Sultan, near Sofia.

Meanwhile the Ottoman conquest of Serbia was finally brought about in 1459 when the Serbian despot Tomasevic gave up without a fight. The Serbs arrived in Sofia to hand over the keys of their fortified capital Smederevo.

In 1466, while Istanbul was in the throes of another especially devastating outbreak of plague, Mehmed headed for the mountains of Bulgaria with his troops. In October 1466, the Milanese Ambassador to the Segnoria reports from Venice that because of the plague, the Sultan intends to spend the winter in Sofia and not to return to Edirne or Istanbul until the danger had passed. The Venetians were at war with the Ottomans at the time, that's why the whereabouts of the Sultan was of paramount importance. Apparently he had set up camp on a mountain top (maybe in Mount Vitosha) and no visitor was allowed within a day's journey to him. However other maladies troubled Mehmed, notably gout, the hereditary ailment of the Ottoman rulers. In June 1464 recovering from a painful attack of gout, he had to set off on yet another campaign against the Hungarians. In Venice it became known that he had mustered an army in Edirne and sent it ahead to Sofia. The campaign turned into a fiasco (the aim was to take Jajce, an important strategic outpost in Bosnia), the Sultan returned to Sofia to levy more troops, but Jajce remained elusive for many more years to come.

PATRON SAINTS MAKE THEIR APPEARANCE IN SOFIA

Meanwhile, in the year 1460 the citizens of Sofia had seen the arrival of the relics of King Stefan Uroš II Milutin, St. Kral (the Saintly King), which have been kept in Sofia ever since (in St. Nedelia Church). The initiative belongs to the widow of the Turkish Sultan Murad, Maria, a descendant of the Bulgarian Royal dynasty who used her influence with Mehmed II, to obtain various dispensations from him. In the year 1469 Maria also arranged for the relics of St. John of Rila to be moved from the old capital Turnovo to the Rila monastery. On the way to the monastery the procession halted in Sofia (then Sredets) and the relics of St. John were laid alongside of the relics of the Saintly King in St. George Rotunda for the benefit of the Christian population of the city.

This event has been described by the medieval Bulgarian chronicler, Vladislav Gramatic. He states that the aroma emanating from the relics of the Saints amazed everyone and soon the entire populace gathered there with candles and float lights. The remains of St. John stayed in Sofia for 6 days. A rich woman - a benefactress - had a new coffin made for the Saint, manufactured out of good quality wood and her husband donated money for an expensive shroud to cover it. On the day of departure a big crowd of people accompanied the relics out of the city, bidding a tearful farewell to the Saint. It appears that at that time the Christian population of Sofia was predominant and had churches, monasteries and the liberty to worship there.

In 1476 Radoslav Maver, a Bulgarian *boyar*/noble from Sofia, restored the church of the Dragalevtsi Monastery "The Holy Mother of God from Vitosha" (just outside the city) and its frescos. That's the same monastery mentioned earlier in connection with the 1376 charter, granted by King Ivan Shishman. Radoslav Maver, his wife Vida and his sons Nicola and Strahil are depicted alongside the other personages on the murals, all impressive portraits, all surviving miraculously the vagaries of time.

A later record from 1493 concerns the restoration of the Kremikovtsi Monastery "St. George the Victorious" (also outside the city of Sofia) and its frescos by Radivoi, the Bulgarian *voevoda* (governor) of Sofia, and the bishop, Kalevit. Fortunately the frescos, of great artistic value, are still preserved.

THE RETURN OF THE BLACK DEATH AND VARIOUS OTHER EVENTS

In May 1475, the Black Death showed its face in Istanbul again. And true to form Mehmed and his entourage left his capital and headed west. He spent the whole month of October in Sofia. If the Black Death didn't get the assiduous Mehmed, other forces, aiming at his life, were in motion. In 1481 his time was up. He was not yet 50. Rumours of poisoning started to circulate, but it was never discovered who was behind it. Was it his son Bayezid II who succeeded him, as some implied? It will never be known.

At the time of his succession, the Ottoman Empire was at war with Hungary, amongst others. Bayezid immediately issued an order for his troops to gather at Sofia. Sofia remained the main base for the Ottoman troops throughout the campaign, which went on and on at the frontier during 1482/83. In 1497 there was yet another outbreak of plague, which affected Sofia as well. In those times, it seems that the plague would spread to Ottoman lands from European ports such as Venice or Ragusa (today Dubrovnik) and from there go through the overland routes of the Balkans and/or the sea route eastwards. Not a welcome traveller on *Via Diagonalis*!

In the 16th century the city of Sofia had a population of around 7,000. It was at this time that many mosques, fountains and hammams (bathhouses) materialised on the urban landscape. Here is the place to say that the Ottomans were obsessed with water. Sofia, with its abundance of thermal waters, must've appeared to them as a paradise on earth; sitting near a fountain or a stream and having a cup of coffee – the ultimate pleasure. Water and cleanliness were closely connected with the Muslim religion. Turks were known for their strict observance of hygiene, especially where the ritual ablution before prayer was concerned. Therefore a washing fountain would be found near each mosque and in some cases public baths would be built in the vicinity (Banya Bashi for example or the Knyajevo complex).

Springs were seen as a gift of God for both Muslims and Christians. Therefore if a stream ran or a spring surged, the Turks, keen to build a fountain, would often erect a marble slab and embellish it with an inscription from the Koran. The Bulgarians followed a similar tradition; to build a water fountain or a well was seen to be praiseworthy, a valuable gift to offer and a way to achieve immortality - that is the donor will be remembered by all those whom it's intended for, for the time it remains in place.

However, if the richer households often had a well in their courtyards, the poor had to rely on the nearest public water fountain in their neighbourhood. Such fountains were often found on crossroads and had taken the role of social centres where people met and exchanged news and/or gossip. In fact the different districts were usually organised around a fountain and often took on its name. So during Ottoman times in Sofia there were the districts of "Mala cheshma", "Bash cheshma", "Kuru cheshma", "Nova cheshma"; *"çeşme"* signifying water fountain (or tap) in Turkish, bulgarized into *"cheshma"*. Hot water, carried on a cart in a keg, was also offered to the citizens, but most people preferred to go to the public baths and soak there, meeting their friends and associates; not unlike the ancient Romans in earlier times.

There was no shortage of public baths in Sofia during the Ottoman rule. True, segregation existed; different ethnic groups went to different baths and women had a particular time schedule that they had to follow, but nevertheless all citizens of Sofia were able to indulge themselves in the public baths on a regular basis.

Of the many Ottoman buildings from that period, only a few are still in existence today, including a single mosque, Banya Bashi (the name comes from the phrase "numerous baths"), built by the renowned Ottoman architect Mimar Sinan.

SOFIA, A FAVOURED STOPOVER FOR TRAVELLERS

Most travellers in this region had to pass through Sofia, especially on their way to or from Constantinople. It goes without saying that their descriptions are one-sided and not always reliable. But nevertheless their impressions of the city are interesting and well worth reading, offering rare insights into a period long since forgotten. And although they are far from objective, let's see what they have written and decide for ourselves.

Ogier Ghiselin de Busbecq, an ambassador on behalf of Ferdinand of Austria, passed through Sofia in 1555 on his way to Constantinople. He didn't stay long and his account is very general and sketchy. This is what he has to say: *"Sophia is a good-sized town, with a considerable population both residents and visitors. Formerly it was a royal city of the Bulgarians* [in fact Sofia, known then as Sredets, was only briefly a Bulgarian capital around the time of Boris II, who had been captured by the Byzantines!]; *afterwards unless I am mistaken* [which he is!] – *it was the seat of the Despots of Servia whilst the dynasty still existed, and had not succumbed to the power of the Turk."* [the city in question is in fact Smederevo on the Danube, 40 km downstream from Belgrade].

Austrian diplomat Hans Dernschwam, who took over Ogier's mission and visited Sofia on his way to Istanbul at about the same time (1553/1555), was looking at different features – the Turkish baths. He describes the baths situated on a square near a mosque (*"a big quadrangular building in front by the entrance, with a round* Greek-*style dome on top, like the Pantheon in Rome"*). It's impossible to identify the baths in question because at the time there were several baths situated near mosques in the city. And despite the temptation to go for the central mineral baths next to Bania Bashi Mosque, those baths are precisely the ones we could most certainly discount, because the mosque in question was not yet built, not for another 10 years or so. Besides, the baths Dernschwam is talking about, were not hot water mineral baths like the ones in the centre. Dernshwam gives full details about the different parts of the building; starting from the changing rooms with their decorative water fountain, with a base in the shape of an octagon, placed in the centre; he then goes on to a big communal bathroom, then 5 smaller bathrooms and finally the room where the water was heated. The rooms were rectangular in shape with floors, covered with polished white marble; topped by semi-spherical domes with lead coverings on the outside.

Further he explains that natural lighting was provided by round openings *"as big as plates"*, situated in the cupola, the light coming through *"unusual glass"*, secured to the openings by way of plaster. He also describes the heating system – hot air, conducted through under-floor canals; the hot and cold water running through lead conduits, while the water for the bath itself – through clay pipes: *"The big water conduits that lead the water into the baths are made of potter's clay. Each tube is approximately one Viennese cubit long and the separate tubes go through each other. They are plastered up like I have seen in Siebenbürgen* [Transylvania] *too, in old buildings in Thorenburg*

[Turda]."

In 1616 (1617) the Austrian diplomat Count Czernin who stopped in Sofia while going on his first diplomatic mission to Constantinople, has left a favourable and more detailed account of his stay in a travel diary, written by his secretary Adam Werner von Crailsheim. *"Sofia,"* he writes, *"owes its name to a church which has been converted into a mosque by the Turks. A capital of Bulgaria in the past, it is now an open city, agreeable and well populated. Its importance is equal to that of the Imperial city of Worms and it is well situated in a pleasant and fertile plain. One can see nice churches, an imaret* [an Ottoman soup kitchen of this period], *a caravanserai* [an inn], *a bezestein* [bazaar] *and hot water baths. Sofia was taken in 1362 by Murad I and today it is inhabited by Bulgarians, Ragusans, Greeks, Turks and a great number of Jews, who are trades people and have an important commerce here*[1].*"*

The comparison with the city of Worms is interesting – Worms was at that time basking in the light of a Golden age and enjoying various privileges. But the other thing that strikes us when we read these lines is that the appearance of the city has already changed – it has become a typical Oriental city! But the mineral baths are still in use! Count Czernin also seems to think that Sofia has been a capital of Bulgaria in the past.

The impressions found in a travelogue about the mission of Louis Deshayes, Baron de Courmemin (1621) are a bit mixed; not very positive as far as the climate is concerned: *"the high mountains in the region make the winter here longer than the summer and bring greater precipitation."* Then the term "open city", used by Count Czernin, is clarified: *"It is not closed within walls and the houses are separated one from the other and most of them avail big gardens. The latter make the city look bigger. The main mosque, which is very beautifill, in the old days would've*

---

[1] For example, from the accounts of a Venetian merchant, Giacomo Badoer, based in Constantinople, we gather that he was dealing with a certain Jew from Sofia, Jachob; in November 1439 Badoer bought from him wax (from Zagore) and sold him cloth (from Palma de Majorca)

been a Christian Church under the name of St.Sofia." But then he goes on to say that *"there is nothing remarkable there, as the city is far more poorly urbanized than some other towns in Turkey and its location is so unhealthy because of the marshes, which spread on one of its sides. If it wasn't the Rumelian Beylerbey to make his seat there, it [the city] should not remain in such condition…* Still, in the end it is admitted that *"Sofia is one of the biggest crossroads in Turkey, as one has to pass from there on his way to Constantinople, Venice, Dubrovnik and Hungary…"*

These observations correspond with those of Louis Gédoyn, the French Consul in Aleppo, who passed through Sofia on his way to Syria in February of 1624 and wasn't very happy with his stay. What probably didn't help in his case was that it happened to be a particularly cold winter: *"…there isn't a living man in this country who remembers to have seen anything like it and it is 67 days since I haven't seen an inch of land because the snow covers it to at least 10 feet height…"* He says that Sofia is a big and densely populated city, but not very pleasant; that a high mountain is to the south of it and the city gets its *"good water"* from there by way of aqueducts. He also mentions a *"little chapel that remained a Mecca for the place, having been the venue for the Sardican Council at the time when the city was known as Sardica"*. He then goes on to describe his encounter with a certain religious Jacobin, an astrologist and clairvoyant, who had been banned from Ragusa (present day Dubrovnik) because of his predictions (the demise of Sultan Osman, Philip II, King of Spain and Pope Gregoire XIV amongst others). Gédoyn doesn't indicate the name of this fortune-teller, although he is taken aback by his revelations and discouraged on hearing that his mission is not going to be successful.

Sir Henri Blount, a seasoned traveller from England, who stayed about 20 days in Sofia in 1634, seems to have had altogether a good time there and was left with a much better impression of the *"Chiefe Citie (after the Turkish division) of Bulgary …nor hath it yet lost the old Grecian civility"*. After a few words about the geographical position of the city, Blount makes an interesting observation concerning the houses of the local people: *"The Iewes and the Christians have here the doors of their houses little about three foot high, which they told me was, that, the Turkes might not bring in their Horses, who else would use them for stables in their travel, which I noted for a sign of greater slavery than in other places."* The buildings that mostly catch the eye of Blount are: the Seat of the Beylerbey - Viceroy of all Greece (Rumelia for the Turks); the mosques – the most impressive one in the city centre, another one with a College - to the south; *an exquisite Baths, the principal with a hot fountain;* many stately *hanes* (inns) or *kirevanserahes*.

Caravans (groups of carriages, pack mules etc travelling together) were, it seems, the favoured means of transport in the Ottoman Empire, rather than waterways. They were extensively used by the Ottoman merchants throughout the 17th century and were under state control. The caravanserais (*kirevanserahes* for Blount), the Ottoman equivalent of the coaching inns, where the travellers were able to stay for the night and to have a break, were an important part of the infrastructure, as much as the hotels/motels of today; they marked the various stages of a journey, situated at key points along the way. Istanbul was linked to Belgrade and Buda by the same road that had existed in Roman times and before; *via Diagonalis*. It was by and large used by Europeans entering the Ottoman Empire and for that reason it is the best known of them all.

Dubrovnik, this little Adriatic city, had become a major trading partner with most European powers and Dubrovnik merchants were all the time back and forth on via Diagonalis. In Sofia they were buying wool. Records show great variations in the price of wool, depending on the political situation in the Empire, and they would rocket in times of war.

It seems that the long-distance traffic in this period was taken predominantly by non-Muslim merchants. On the whole, little is known about the relations between the Muslim and non Muslim craftsmen in Sofia, although tanners, furriers and cap-makers would've worked in much the same conditions and their concerns, judging by the records of court cases and such, were predominantly related to the increasing prices of raw materials or the competition of newly fledged artisans.

Vincenzo Maria Coronelli (1650–1718), a well-known Venetian geographer and cartographer, in his map, *"The Flow of the Danube from Vienna to Nicopol and the Adjacent Lands"*, made notes about Sofia in 1692: *"Sofia is said to have been built by Emperor Justinian I from the ruins of ancient Sardica and to be the seat of a Beylerbey, as well as the birthplace of St Helen, the mother of the Byzantine Emperor Constantine I the Great (306–337)."* On the map Sofia appears with its name in Italian (Sofia), in French (Sofie), in Greek (Triadizza) and in Latin (Sophia). The location of ancient Sardica or Serdica is marked separately. It is not clear why Sofia is indicated as the birth place of St. Helen; most present day historians now maintain that she was born in Asia Minor. Why the change? Rewriting history to suit some interests? Yet in Bulgaria St. Helen is particularly venerated along with her illustrious son. Their joint Saints day is on 21st May. This Christian feast is connected with some ancient pagan practices involving fire-walking - dancing on hot coals while in a trance. The Christian element is the icon of St. Constantine and St. Helen held by the dancers which, they believe, protects them. Constantine, as we know, loved Serdica. But what about his mother? It's plausible that she was born here; or did she have some other connection with the Balkan city?

THE CATHOLIC PRESENCE IN SOFIA

In 1610 the Vatican established the See of Sofia for Catholics of Rumelia, which existed until 1715 when most Catholics had emigrated. Peter Bogdan Bakshev, a Bulgarian Catholic Bishop, came to Sofia in May 1640. He has left a detailed account of his impressions, a very important source of information for later historians. He confirms that Sofia didn't have city walls (it seems that by that time they were mostly demolished), then he goes on to describe its geographical position – *"between two mountains, Haemus to the north, The Rhodopes to the south; Haemus, or as the Italians call it, "the Chain of the world"* (Bogdan has done his studies in Ancona, Italy and the Vatican) *divides Misia and Thrace, now all this called Bulgaria..."* Peter Bogdan is impressed with just how fertile the Sofia plain is – there is plenty of wheat, wine, farm animals and fruit; horse breeding is well established, the horses are *"good and swift"*. *"Fresh fish is not always available, he pursues, for the Danube is not so near, but one can always find salted fish* (no freezers at the time!); *also Mediterranean fruits like olives, figs, raisins etc. There is a lot of meat like everywhere in the Turkish Kingdom."*

Being such a major commercial centre, Sofia attracted merchants from all over the place, even from countries like Hungary and Poland, and any stuff, any commodity could be found there *"even Italian"*! *"Sofia is also the seat of the Pasha or Vizier and the Great Kadi – like the Archbishop and another one, the mufti, that is the interpreter of the law; when the other judges can't decide on a case, he is consulted and according to their law and rules, he gives a letter, a fatwā and the judge can't do otherwise but to follow the law. But otherwise the mufti doesn't interfere in anything else apart from the affairs of the jurisprudence."*

Peter Bogdan of course dwells on the state of the Roman Catholic Church in Sofia at the time – the one and only building they had was really small – *"10 feet long and 6 feet wide"*, it was dedicated to Our Lady of Purification, but was not consecrated. It had been built a long time previously by tradesmen from Dubrovnik. The priest was lodging under the same roof...The congregation at the time was tiny – 50 adults and 8 children, mainly originating from Dubrovnik. This number apparently fluctuated with the passing of merchants on their way to and from Istanbul. On the other hand, Bakshev states that there were about 6000 houses belonging to the Schismatics (that's how the Roman Catholics were referring to the Eastern Orthodox Christians at the time!), which would amount, according to his rough estimate, to 25 000 people. There were only 5 churches for all those people, but two of them were demolished by the Turks in the previous couple of years before his arrival. That leaves 25 000 with only 3 churches! Moreover *"the Orthodox Archbishop, who resided in the city,* Petar Bogdan explains*, was always of Greek origin, while the congregation was Bulgarian"* (this did not change until the 19th century).

Other information about Sofia that we owe to Bakshev is that at the time, the basilica St. Sofia, already turned into a mosque, had been rebuilt and was so high that it could be seen from afar, from *"half a day distance from the city"*. There were about 30 000 Turks living in the city, according to Peter Bogdan's estimates (he admitted that he didn't dare ask the Turkish authorities about the exact number) and about 150 very well built mosques. The Jewish population amounted to 4000 families, according to Peter Bogdan, or about 15 000; they had their synagogues and schools for the rich and were mostly involved in commerce and money lending; it seems they enjoyed certain privileges and despite being heavily taxed by the Sultan, they would mutually help each other to pay all their taxes on time. There were also some Greek and Armenian residents in the city, who worshiped in separate churches, *"each of them seeing the others as the heretics"*(despite the fact that Greeks and Armenians both belong to the Orthodox Christian Church, as do the Bulgarians themselves).

Peter Bogdan also comments on the secular buildings in Sofia, such as inns and other accommodations for travellers, and emphasizes the numerous water sources in town, *"brought from the mountains"*, in addition to the natural hot waters, which are used in the *"many magnificent public baths and in quite a few places to do the laundry"*. In the end Peter Bogdan mentions a church, just outside the city, *"in a nice, high spot, there, they say, the Sardican Council took place, in Bulgarian this place is named Triaditsa."* The so called Sardican Council, he is referring to, is, of course, the Council of 342/343 when the Western and the Eastern bishops could not reach an agreement and held separate sessions in Sardica and in Philippopolis respectively.

In 1642 Pope Urban II declared Sofia to be the seat of the Bulgarian Catholic Archbishopric and appointed Peter Bogdan

Bakshev as the Archbishop. Peter Bogdan left quite a few historical works, *History of Sofia* being just one of them.

EVLIYA CHELEBI'S SOJOURN IN SOFIA

Next we meet Evliya Chelebi, the nephew of Melek Ahmed Pasha, the Sofia based Rumelian Governor, who wrote in his travel chronicle about all sorts of things that impressed him in the city of Sofia during his stay. The year is 1652. This is what this seasoned traveller had to say about the fortified city of Sofia: *"According to Latin sources this fortress is as big as the one in Constantinople and measures 47 000 paces circumvention. I, myself personally walked around and examined its buildings and foundations ...According to the story of Yanuan, the fortress of Sofia had 27 gates, 1700 towers and 70 000 merlons. Sofia of today is just one district of the old city and is situated in the corner of the fortress."* Evliya Chelebi was particularly impressed with a *"famous area"* in the vicinity of the city, between Vitosha and Sofia, known at the time as Korubaglar (now Lozenets, a district of Sofia), that in the whole of the Ottoman Empire, according to him, with its beautiful parks, there is nothing to compare with this *Garden of Paradise*. To be sure, Korubaglar of old would've been nothing like its present day appearance. Contemporaries describe vineyards amongst forests, meadows, cherry trees and see it as a holy site and a favourite destination for the Turks. Presumably, the Christians, having left their own holy edifices to rack and ruin, had little to do with this area, favoured by the Muslims. Evliya Chelebi mentions the ancient vestiges on the west slope of Lozenets, (that Peter Bogdan rightly supposes to have been the ruins of a monastery, dating from the time of the Serdican ecclesiastical Council) and declares that the locals continue to demolish them in order to use the material for their buildings.

How much we can rely on the accuracy of the account of Evliya Chelebi, is another matter. His extensive use of superlatives makes one think of some elaborate advertising campaign, he's been paid to conduct. Some of his stories are so far-fetched that they are more like fairy tales or fables such as the one about the storks. According to this story, a pair of storks built a nest on the lead-covered roof of the Celebi Camii mosque (The Gentlemen's Friday mosque,) just opposite the Pasha's palace in the city of Sofia. A practical joker named Debbag-oglu (meaning the tanner's son), decided to play a trick on the unsuspecting birds and exchanged their eggs for crow's eggs. Soon afterwards a couple of crow chicks hatched, to the dismay of the storks. The father stork, greatly distressed, called upon all his mates who came in their thousands, making such a racket, that the whole city was startled. The birds spent the entire day there without eating or drinking, disturbing all the city; everybody interrupted their activities to watch their carry-on. Eventually, the storks killed the crow chicks, followed by the mother stork, whom they blamed for infidelity. The father stork went off with another female and his mates flew back to their nests...Everyone present was astonished. The Pasha was going to punish Debbag-oglu, but then he decided to let him be, believing God would punish him anyway. Which is what happened soon after. Debbag-oglu was seen running away, pursued by a jealous husband, who had just caught him in flagrante with his wife. Reaching Banya Bashi square (the place where the Mineral baths stand today), Debbag-oglu saw that some janissaries were squabbling over his "whore", or rather his "servant-girl". Rushing to her rescue, the rogue fell under the swords of the janissaries along with the girl. Some tannery apprentices found him there and asked the Pasha for justice for their master. As he was unwilling to do anything about it, they left the corpse under the eaves of the mosque, facing the Pasha's house. There was the Divine Justice! The corpse of Debbag-oglu ended-up in the same place that the storks had left the remains of the crow chicks and the mother stork. The Pasha said that the fellow got what he deserved and ordered the corpse to be removed from the mosque, shrouded in a mat and buried. The tannery apprentices removed the hide of the tanner's son and brought it to Banya Bashi where it was tanned, which made quite a show. After the Debbag-oglu affair, the Pasha banned all the prostitutes from the town, to the relief of the honest folk. But the men, who were upset about it, started a rumour that there would be a famine and death, even a plague. And indeed the plague started to spread in the city and lots of people died; others fled. Tens of high officials lost their lives as well and even the Pasha was struck down by the horrible disease and almost died. Happily for him he eventually recovered.

More informative though is Evliya Chelebi's account of the public baths in Sofia (there were a lot of private ones too). *"In this country hot springs are called 'bana',* he explains. According to him there were five of them and they were hot water mineral baths. There was one known as *"the women's"*, another – as *"the Christian's"*, a third was *"the Greco-Latin"*, a fourth –*"the Jewish"* and the fifth – was in the centre of town. He then takes pains to explain that *"other nationalities don't go to the Jewish bath, because they have an aversion to it"* and that men don't go to the women's bath lest *"they'll lose the hair from their heads and beards";* such remarks today would be seen as racist or sexist, but let's not forget that the values of the 17th century were not the same as today. Evliya Chelebi elaborates further on the baths in the centre of the city. It's a building with a big dome and has room for up to 1000 people. He mentions a water fountain, a big pool and two *"halvetas"* (separate rooms for bathing). One was known as "the white", because it was light and covered with *"pure white marble"*, while the other was "the black", for it was quite *"dark"*. He also notes some decorative features, like the metal zoomorphic figurines on the water-taps; one of them, in the shape of a frog was, according to Evliya Chelebi, to remind the bathers not to waste the water, for they were not frogs. The tap for the main pool was in the shape of a lion's head, water gushing out of his jaws. Evliya Chelebi also describes 3 mineral baths in the surrounding area of Sofia. One of them, supposedly at present day Pancharevo, *"were to be found near the manor of Kinan Pasha, which is a palace similar to a lodge, in the foothills of Vitosha, near Iskar River, in a place covered in greenery. The water is healing, but the building is not so nice. In olden times Gazi Hudavendigar* [The Godlike one, nickname of Sultan Murad I, the same who married the sister of the Bulgarian King Ivan Shishman] *built for this bath a small, but beautiful dome. This mineral water is reputed to cure 7 diseases and all the sick from all over the place, who suffer from problems with the joints and various other ailments, come to take the waters or to have mud baths. With God's help they are healed and get fit. Especially the city ayans* [notables] *come here in July with their families and bathe the whole Sunday, they feel re-energized."* Evliya Chelebi added that after the fall of Sofia, Murad I *"remained in this city for 3 years to organize the administration of the newly acquired territories."* To the west of Sofia, there was another bath with very hot water and proven curative properties, helping in cases of pleurisy and chest infections. The third mineral bath Evliya Chelebi talks about, is situated in Knyazhevo, now a district of Sofia. The building described had a *"low dome"*; the water – lukewarm with the smell of sulphur, was beneficial for syphilis and leprosy. That particular bath – or the building at any rate, still exists (albeit having since undergone internal reconstruction), but those who suffer from the above mentioned diseases, now have the choice of more up to date treatments.

THE HABSBURG WARS

At the time of Sultan Suleiman II (1687 – 1691), the headquarters of the Ottoman army was to be found once again in Sofia, while they were waging war with the Habsburg Empire. In 1689 the Sultan had accompanied his army from Adrianople (Edirne) to Sofia, where the governor Arab Receb Pasha was appointed as supreme commander, succeeding Yegen Osman Pasha (the previous governor of Rumelia who had lost Belgrade and turned traitor). Apparently it was unusual for an Arab to rise so far up the ranks in the Ottoman Empire, but Receb was well known for his courage. Unfortunately neither his popularity, nor his courage, helped him to deal with his troops during this disastrous campaign. They fled the enemy at Belgrade, refused point-blank to regroup at Nis and marched back to Sofia to complain to the Grand Vizier. The Sultan was there, and when he received the news that his advance guard was defeated at Nis, he hastened to retreat to Philippopolis (Plovdiv). However he appointed a capable Grand Vizier, Kiuprili Zade Mustapha, who was able to somewhat remedy the situation. Unfortunately he was killed near Belgrade a couple of years later and, with his death, the same old discipline issues re-surfaced, with some of the troops again on the run all the way back to Sofia, their numbers increasing as bandits joined them as they went.

In 1695 Mustapha II acceded to power. The young Sultan insisted on leading his army in military campaigns despite the reticence of the Divan (the Imperial Council led by the Grand Vizier). In the summer he started his first campaign against the Habsburg Empire. At first he was doing well and was rather pleased with himself. But when Prince Eugene took the command of the Imperial Armies in Hungary, Mustapha mustered his troops in Sofia for what later proved to be another disastrous campaign. The year is 1697.

In Sofia the Grand Vizier had a dream. Elmas Mehmed Pasha had been appointed as Grand Vizier in 1695. His nickname Elmas (diamond) signifies that he must've been a very handsome man. At any rate he is remembered for his abilities and his courage. After a succession of incompetent Viziers, the Sultan had finally found a man after his own heart. In his dream Elmas saw Kiuprili Zade Mustapha Pasha (one of his predecessors) entering his tent with a cup of sherbet and offering it to him after taking a sip of it. *"God knows, exclaimed the Grand Vizier, this is the cup of the martyr that I am to taste at this campaign!"* The army left Sofia on the 10th August 1697 and marched towards Belgrade. On 11th of September Elmas fell at the battle of Zenta. According to some, he was killed by his own soldiers while trying to organize an orderly retreat.

In 1698, in the midst of peace negotiations with the Western powers, Mustapha was still preparing to resume the war if things did not go his way. His Grand Vizier, Amcazade Huseyin, leading an army to the frontier at Belgrade, was met by the Habsburg

Imperial envoys with peace proposals at Sofia. But the peace process was taking time.

AN ENGLISH LADY GOES TO SOFIA'S HAMMAM

Lady Mary Wortley Montagu, the wife of the British Ambassador to Istanbul, who stayed in Sofia on her way there, wrote that it was *"hardly possible to see a more agreeable landscape"*. She states that she had a tedious journey, but *"must not omit what I saw remarkable at Sophia, one of the most beautiful towns in the Turkish empire"*. Lady Montagu hired a coach and went – incognito, she announces excitedly, to the hot mineral baths the city was famous for, as they were *"resorted to both for diversion and health"* and describes an edifice, built of stone *"in the shape of a dome"*, or rather five domes *"joined together"* with skylights to provide sufficient daylight inside. She then gives the details of her visit; the relaxed atmosphere, the sulphur vapours, the marble surfaces, the women, come to pamper themselves and to socialise with their friends (as they would do today in any spa centre), her reluctance to join them (due to the heavy riding habit she was wearing and the difficulty of taking it off), all of this vivid detail brings to life this long gone hammam.

The description of the baths in Sofia, a real eye-opener, can be found in her letter (XXVI) to a lady-friend, dated 1st April 1717. Lady Montagu's so called Turkish letters were later published in England and in France. Her quite erotic portrayal of the hammam in Sofia, full of charming details, impressed the French artist Ingres so much so, that he copied the following lines from it: *"I believe, upon the whole, there were two hundred women ... so many fine women naked, in different postures, some in conversation, some working, others drinking coffee or sherbet and many negligently lying on their cushions, while their slaves (generally pretty girls of seventeen or eighteen) were employed in braiding their hair in several pretty fancies."* Ingres went on to create a masterpiece, just based on this description – "The Turkish

Baths" *("Le Bain Turc")* in 1862, an oil painting, which is now in the Louvre.

This must have been the golden age of the public baths in the Empire. The majority of hammams in the Ottoman Empire were built in the 16th-17th century. But it seems with time they were becoming less and less profitable and besides, the wood, used for heating them, was less and less available (no wonder that with the deforestation going on unchecked, towards the end of the 18th century, according to contemporaries, Mount Vitosha was all but bare!). In 1768, due to the lack of wood, Sultan Mustafa III decided to suspend the building of new public baths.

THE ARCHIVES SPEAK OUT

Now it's time to look at another source of information. The Turkish authorities had a heavy duty administrative machine set up and, it has to be said, that the Ottoman Empire was quite advanced, as far as accountancy and bookkeeping were concerned. According to a Venetian representative named Garzoni, stationed in Istanbul in the year 1572, the revenue office kept systematic records and, at the end of the fiscal year, prepared annual balance sheets showing revenues and expenses. Estate accounting in the Ottoman Empire was performed by clerks under the supervision of officials. An official had to go personally to the place of the estate, to perform the necessary investigations, to decide the dispute and also, to decree the distribution of real-estate assets among the inheritors, in cases of estate disputes.

Happily some of the archives, notably the so called *tereke* or *muhallefat defters* (estate or inheritance registers) for Sofia for much of the 16th and 17th centuries, have been preserved to this day. The difficulty is that they contain so much data, on so many different issues that it's a challenge to find anything tangible on any one topic. Several historians have already tried to prove various theories, researching these documents. But even today, using the wonders of modern technology, a study based solely on administrative sources would appear inadequate and fragmented.

However they can prove quite useful to check and confirm what is already known or believed.

These registers are deemed reasonably accurate[2]. From them we can get a glimpse into the lives (and deaths) of the well to do residents of Sofia, the landed gentry, so to speak. The majority of the estates recorded, involved the "socially vulnerable" that the *kadi* (the judge) had to protect whatever their religious background; notably under-age children, widows etc. The agent of the Treasury, of course, was quick to collect his due and, in the case of unknown heirs – the whole estate.

The majority of the rich landowners were Muslim, as we can imagine, however, the records show that there were quite a few Christians as well, both local citizens and temporary residents, among the wealthy inhabitants of Sofia. Actually, one of the latter, an Armenian merchant, left one of the biggest estates and, due to the fact that he had no close relative with him, his estate would've probably been more easily accessible to the agent of the Treasury (it would've just been seized). As we can gather, the local elite was not very homogenous at the time – the city of Sofia was more than ever a melting pot of various cultures. Despite the differences, some status quo was maintained and everybody got on with their lives. As in other parts of the Ottoman Empire during

---

[2] The tax registers of the 16th century witness a significant rise in the Muslim population at the expense of Bulgarians, with 915 Muslim and 317 Christian households in 1524–1525, 1325 Muslim, 173 Christian and 88 Jewish in 1544–1545, 892 Muslim, 386 Christian, 126 Jewish and 49 Roma in 1570–1571, as well as 1017 Muslim, 257 Christian, 127 Jewish and 38 Roma households in 1573. The Ottoman rule saw a major demographic growth, as the city grew from a total population of 6,000 (1620s) through 55,000 (middle 17th century) to 70-80,000 (18th century data from foreign travellers, albeit possibly exaggerated). During the 16th century, Sofia was a thriving trade centre inhabited by Turks, Bulgarians, Romaniote, Ashkenazi, and Sephardic Jews (in the 16th century there were 126 Jewish households, and there has been a synagogue in Sofia since 967 AD). There were also Armenian, Greek and Ragusan merchants. In the 17th century, the city's population included even Albanians and Persians.

the seventeenth century, many of the neighbourhoods in Sofia had a mixed population, though some must have been entirely Muslim, and others presumably entirely Christian.

Statistically speaking, it comes as no surprise that the rich tended to live in the centre of the city, although not exclusively. They usually married within their class. The majority of the local rich Muslims had a military background. Another group of wealthy citizens included trades and craftsmen – there is a dyer, a cloth merchant, a shop owner, a gun merchant, an ironmonger/blacksmith, a tanner and a barber...The learned classes (the so called *ulema*), it seems, were not so wealthy; however there were women amongst them and many did leave their collections of books to posterity.

Concerning the Judicial Procedure, Sofia, like the rest of the Ottoman provinces, was subdivided into judicial districts headed by special judges (*kadis*) appointed from Istanbul; their task was to apply both the civil and religious law. Each of these courts kept records of their procedures, day by day and year by year, and many of these record books, called *Sicil*, have been preserved in the archives. One of the most interesting facts that might come as a surprise for some, is the widespread existence of slavery in the Ottoman Empire. There were taxes levied on the slave market and it appears that the state profited greatly from this unsavoury business.

SOFIA FROM THE MEMOIRS OF A FRENCH ARISTOCRAT

In 1782 another traveller stays in Sofia and mentions it in his memoirs, Louis François de Ferrière count de Sauveboeuf, a French aristocrat. He refers to the city as the main town of Bulgaria, governed by a Pasha who resides there. Bearing in mind that he comes from France, rich with Renaissance buildings, it comes as no surprise that he is not at all impressed with the state of the city – he finds its city walls in bad shape (either they've been rebuilt in meantime, or he refers to what was left of them, because earlier visitors mention Sofia as being "an open city"). And then *"the houses would've been comfortable enough if the*

Turks were able to repair them". Everything seems to have been left to rack and ruin and *"the stay of the Grand Vizier who camped last year for 3 months at the city gates contributed a lot to devastate it."* (Presumably that was Mehmed Pasha).

Other than that, something else was causing a stir at the time; something that brings to mind Jane Austin and her vivid descriptions of the Bennet girls obsessing about the what's-its-name Militia stationed nearby, in her best known novel Pride and Prejudice, written some 15 years later. Sauveboeuf's description of the betrothals of the janissaries to the local young beauties, *"who seemingly thought that the whole army shouldn't leave anymore their territory"*, comes across as a typical Austin scenario. These girls, almost all of them married, were having a rather good time, until being left behind or even widowed soon afterwards, as the Vizier took his troops away to Nicaea; keeping them away from their men did not prove to be an easy task! The girls in question were not Bulgarian; in fact most of the Bulgarian populace had abandoned their houses to avoid the *"unrestrained soldiery"* and had retired to the mountains. The young Bulgarian girls, explains the Frenchman, *"whose only coquetry is to pleat their long hair that reaches almost to the heel, demurely help their mothers to prepare a rustic meal for their visitor."* What a contrast! But we shouldn't doubt the accuracy of this narrative – the Bulgarians, subjugated at the time, had to keep a low profile; it was vital to keep the girls at home, out of harm's way and to give them a strict upbringing; this Patriarchal model survived well into the times after the Liberation.

Back to Sauveboeuf, the Count has another amusing story to tell, well, probably not so amusing if you happen to be a cat lover, because you would certainly find it shocking! But here goes: Sauveboeuf reports that a collection of contraband items had been seized and the culprits were threatened, in case of a repeat offense, with a particular punishment which was popular in Turkey at the time; that was to put a cat in one's pants (usually very baggy) *"and the poor animal, which is flogged mercilessly, can't be prevented from using his claws"*. Sorry, we can't put the "no animals were harmed" disclaimer at the end of this story – but it happened so long time ago, before the French Revolution, that we can't possibly sue anybody for it!

ANOTHER FRENCHMAN IN SOFIA

Ami Boué, a physician, scientist, and linguist, who journeyed extensively in European Turkey (1836 - 38) and recorded his observations in a travel log, published in France, stayed in Sofia and gave a fascinating account about his time there. *"Sofia is admirably placed, he states, to become a populous and beautiful city, because it's situated in the middle of Turkey at the crossroads of at least 7-8 arteries."* However from a strategic point of view, his estimation is that the city, although advantageously positioned to become a stronghold, is almost entirely open, with the exception of a few temporary redoubts. He suggests moats, which would be easy to dig in the alluvial soil and also, there is plenty of water to fill them with. Further Ami Boué goes on to describe the *"green lawn"* surrounding the city and the numerous tumuli there. *"Vast burial grounds precede its entrance, he declares, its mosques and its 22 minarets announce a considerable population, however this city doesn't amount to more than 5000 houses or 20 – 25 000 people, mostly Bulgarians."*

Then he explains that once inside it becomes obvious that the city has suffered a lot - the old town walls *"have all but disappeared, the streets are irregular and badly paved with lots of holes and mud and the pavement so worn out, that one has to be particularly careful while walking..."* (it seems that more than 150 years on things haven't changed at all in this respect!) Worst – *"many grand squares have been covered with huge dunghills that date probably more than a century. The bazaar consists of narrow streets, covered and stinking. The ancient Palace of the Pasha hasn't been rebuilt since the fire and part of this considerable plot of land is covered with rubble and garbage, another is used for drying of wool. Next to it, to top it all by way of contrast, rises a grand mosque with nine domes, sombre interior without ornaments and supported by square and very massive pillars."*

Ami Boué also mentions that the cathedral St. Sofia was at that time to the eastern end of town, a sign that the city used to be bigger. He found that the altar was either left unfinished or had been demolished later on; the edifice had been turned into a mosque by the Turks and they had altered it. Next to it were the ruins of another building which, according to the Turks he spoke to, used to be a grand caravanserai, a large hostelry, where the travellers would stop for the night. But only some *"miserable blacksmith's workshops"* remained in front. At any rate he wonders if it was not, in actual fact, the ruins of the ancient Bishop's palace. The Pasha himself had an extensive *konak,* residence that is, but Ami Boué didn't think much of it. It was built at the side of a small square with a brook running through the middle and a few trees around. To the side there was a small garden with a kiosk (pavilion) and a big wooden wheel used for watering. Not very impressive for the mid 19th century! The Pasha however had some bright ideas or let's say an entrepreneurial spirit, for he showed the Frenchman a little wooden model of a foundry in the English style, that he was having built in Samokov (a town to the south of Sofia, a major iron producing centre in the Middle Ages). The Pasha was very hospitable and our French traveller was favourably impressed. The Pasha's fiefdom was not very big and apart from its main city, Sofia, there were no other big towns. What towns there were, such as Etropole, Ihtiman or Samokov, Boué refers to as *"bourgs",* that is market towns. Otherwise there were a lot of villages with a predominantly Bulgarian, Christian population. The Turks, he says, considered the Bulgarians as *"good labourers and easy to govern, if one knows how to be just and humane."*

Afterwards Ami Boué talks about Mount Vitosha and how easy it is to climb to the top of it, for its foothills are two steps from the city and are *"watered by thousand streams, which turn on about fifty or so mills."* It took the intrepid traveller 3 hours to climb the mountain, following paths that went through oak, beach and conifer woods. He doesn't specify the peak he reached, stating only that *"the view from its rocky summit compensated* amply the trouble when you find yourself as in the centre of a panorama and surrounded on all sides by diverse mountain chains..."

It is interesting to compare Ami Boué's impressions with those of Neofit Bozveli, an eminent Bulgarian born cleric, who fought for an independent Bulgarian church and who visited Sofia at about the same time (1835). He writes about the glorious past of the city, its geographical location and explains that Mount Vitosha was *"famous for its mineral wealth (ore, precious stones)"*. Then he enumerates the *"ancient remains: there are 8 churches, Diocese (metropoleis), the temple of Sv. Kral [St King] where rest the relics of St. Stephan of Serbia. In the city there are located 2 thermal water springs, one of them named Elitsa, the other – communal, used by the tanners. Two more baths are located at less than one hour journey away: Gorna Bania and Bali Effendi (Knyajevo) next to a Turkish mosque."* Bali Effendi was a Turkish saintly figure, buried there in the 17th century and his grave was famed for its healing properties.

Neofit Bozveli then cites the monasteries in the environs of the city, 12 in total and goes on to say that *"this famous city has 46 000 inhabitants, mostly Turks, Bulgarians and some Jews."* Note that Ami Boué estimates the number to be about 20 - 25 000 inhabitants (5000 houses) and mostly Bulgarians! Also, he only mentions the mosques with the 22 minarets, but not the churches that Bozveli talks about, although the latter mentions *"Turkicised churches, one of them – exquisite and magnificent St. Sophia that could be seen from a distance of 6 hours trek"*.

THE IMPRESSIONS OF A BRITISH TRAVEL WRITER

Captain Edmund Spencer was a prolific British travel writer of the mid-nineteenth century. In 1850, Spencer undertook an extensive voyage through the southern Balkans, which he describes in his two-volume "Travels in European Turkey, in 1850, through Bosnia, Servia, Bulgaria, Macedonia, Thrace, Albania, and Epirus, with a visit to Greece and the Ionian Isles" (London 1851). He spoke some Bulgarian and his description of the Bulgarian lands offers much rare insight and is well worth reading. His impressions of Sofia, which he visited at the same period as Ami Boué, confirm more or less what the Frenchman thought, but also add some additional information concerning different facets related to the city.

Sofia, as seen from a distance, appears lovely but on approaching the city, Spencer is disgusted at the view of the *"dreary waste, which encircles the town and to increase the tristesse pass through a funeral forest of turbaned pillars"* – the vast burial grounds that Ami Boué mentions. Spencer is further disenchanted seeing the *"miserable wooden bridge thrown over the Isker and the still more miserable wooden gate with the dilapidated fortifications that a child might leap over…"* The beautiful, populous city, that was so prosperous at the time of Lady Montagu's visit in 1717, 140 years later had dwindled into a *"miserably poor"* Turkish village, as another British visitor, a statesman, Mr Shaw-Lefevre attests. *"The Turkish landowners,"* he wrote, *"had driven the Bulgar inhabitants into less fertile localities."* But then Spencer, who aims to present an objective account, goes on to say that *"Sophia, however decayed an appearance it may present to the eyes of the traveller from the west, has by no means lost its local importance and the associations connected with it must ever be interesting when we remember the degree of commercial prosperity it had attained long before London, the mighty emporium of modern commerce, was even heard of."*

There follows a rather romantic legend, forgotten today, about the origins of the city. Sofia, like so many other cities, is believed to have been founded by a celestial being who fell in love with a mortal girl, Serdicé, and left heaven for her sake. The city they founded was named after Serdicé (which sounds very much like the Slav word for "heart"), now Sofia.

Spencer finds the basilica of St. Sofia (then a mosque) impressive as indeed the few other churches around the city and *"one or two other public buildings, memorials of the wealth, industry and civilisation of the Bulgarians."* Then Spencer comes to the caravanserai (han), also described in the account of Ami Boué, although the Frenchman had thought that it might have been the ancient Bishops palace: *"It's partly in ruins,* Spencer informs us, and it was the *"most magnificent building ever erected in these provinces for the reception of the traveller and his merchandise. It was constructed entirely of cut stone arched throughout, and fire proof. In wandering through its vast stables, warehouses, galleries, and endless private rooms, we have abundant proof of the great commerce of Sophia, in the Middle Ages, when this han alone, the only one that escaped utter destruction, was sufficiently large to accommodate a thousand travellers. At the same time, the torn and shattered state in which it had been left by the cannon balls of the Turks, shows the protracted resistance made by the inhabitants against their Mahometan invaders."*

Spencer then talks about a *"Grecian temple"* that, according to him, dates from the time of the Macedonian Empire. He also mentions the ruins of a Roman amphitheatre that must be the same that were recently re-discovered and integrated into the basement of the Hotel Arena di Serdica in the vicinity of the basilica St. Sofia.

Spencer also makes the almost prophetic statement that *"the only remnant of the Turkish rule that is likely to go down to posterity, is the fragile minaret! invariably added to the churches of the Christians when they were converted to mosques."* Apart from these architectural features, Spencer is similarly unimpressed like Ami Boué, by the *"ill-paved narrow streets, badly ventilated bazaars, wooden huts with their booth-like shops, coffee-rooms"* etc. Spencer connects the *"abominable accumulation of filth in towns and cities"* with various diseases such as typhus, cholera and even the plague. *"From the statement of Dr. Roberti, in the service of the Ottoman Porte, it appears that the town of Sophia, in 1836, when the plague broke out, was reduced from a population of 45 000 to 35 000, since then from repeated attacks of cholera and other maladies, we find it now numbers less than 20 000."*

Spencer shares his opinions about the political situation in the country, the unsuccessful uprising in Vidin in 1850 and the scepticism of the Bulgarians who were cajoled into submission by both threats of excommunication, coming from their Archbishop and also by the promises of the Sultan. However Spencer thought that some good at least had come out of the failed uprising - indirect taxation had been abolished, the Christians were allowed to build churches, repair monasteries and found educational establishments without having to pay for permission from the Divan (the Imperial Council).

EDUCATION

In 1859, Dr. Elias Riggs, an American missionary, while touring Bulgaria, was in fact extremely surprised to note how many Bulgarian schools had appeared despite the fierce opposition of the influential Greek Orthodox Church and the displeasure of the Turkish government. He visited a school in Sofia, attended by 400 boys and another one, for girls, attended by 120. *"When we remember that we are in Turkey,"* he writes, *"it is interesting fact to notice that the Bulgarians do not limit their laudable endeavours for education to boys alone. This is striking indication that they are training themselves to give the right place to women even at the very beginning of their educational system."* In fact Sofia had been lagging behind other towns as far as education was concerned. Data about the first Bulgarian schools in Sofia is scarce - in 1825 and 1827 the church authorities of St. Nedelia and St. Petka Church respectively, had money allocated for teaching, but in the second case the "teachers" had also the task to paint the murals in the altar of St. Petka!

Then in 1828 a certain Stoimen Rilchanin opened a private school in his house. The curriculum followed by the children included Reading, the Scriptures, Catechism, Geography, Greek language and Bulgarian Orthodox Church chant. These were the core subjects, taught in the schools in those days, but with time they corresponded less and less to the needs of a new and dynamic class of merchants, craftsmen and entrepreneurs. They needed a more up to date education, that would not only help them to create and maintain international commercial links, but would also give them access to knowledge in various other spheres, like philosophy, history, literature.

Those who chose teaching as their vocation had to be idealistic, enthusiastic and prepared for anything. Such was the case of Zachary Krusha who had a very challenging time throughout his career. He started teaching in 1839 and pursued it on and off until 1852. For a start, let's make it clear that Bulgarian schools in those times owed their existence either to the initiative of the local churches or to the generosity of rich philanthropists, so the conditions left much to be desired, the pay was not going to make anybody rich and the expectations were high. Zachary Krusha relates some of the difficulties he had to face, such as how a humble structure was converted to the needs of the school *"furnishing it with seats and writing tables and fitting it with windows"*. Besides being the teacher, it was expected from him to also fulfil the roles of cantor, scribe and translator of texts from Greek into Bulgarian language. The school attracted about 150 children who were taught Bulgarian language and grammar, arithmetic, geography, history, religious studies and Greek language. Interestingly, a large number of his pupils grew up to become in their turn teachers, but there were also those who became merchants, craftsmen, consuls or priests, as he later states in his report to Marin Drinov, head of the State Department of Education in 1878.

However, Zachary Krusha also managed to attract the wrath of the Greek Orthodox Bishop, who saw him as one of the causes for the waning of Greek influence and, as a result of the bishop's efforts, in 1845 Zachary Krusha was replaced by a Greek teacher. Discontent with the supremacy of the Greek clergy had been building up in several Bulgarian dioceses as early as the 1820s. But it was not until 1850 that the Bulgarians initiated a resolute struggle against the Greek clerics in a number of bishoprics, demanding their replacement with Bulgarian ones. However, until the end of the Crimean war (1853-1856) secular education in Sofia remained firmly under Greek authority.

Despite the removal of Zachary Krusha, the local Bulgarians were determined to have their own schools. Luckily for them in this period, today referred to as the period of National Revival, there were rich benefactors who were prepared to spend their money on education. One example being a certain Ivan Denchev, known as Denkoglu, who came from a poor background but amassed a fortune during his commercial activities in Russia. On his return to Bulgaria he became a philanthropist; it was he who opened a public school in Sofia in 1858, a two-storey building in the courtyard of St. Kral (today St. Nedelia) church and a lot of dignitaries were present at the opening ceremony, including the governor of Sofia, the military commanders Osman Pasha and Suleiman Pasha and the Austrian consul Zamero. Denkoglu appointed his friend Sava Filaretov, who had studied philosophy in Moscow, as the head teacher. Sava Filaretov was a brilliant teacher and the school was a great success. But it was a boys' school only. And girls also wanted to attend school. There were, of course, plenty of conservative Bulgarians, who were opposed to the idea of education for girls, arguing that it was sufficient for the girls to be taught how to sew and how to spin. Probably for this reason, the woman recommended for the post to teach girls, was a certain Nedelia Petkova, a poor widow with a large family, who had a very basic education herself, but had managed to impress Naiden Gerov, the Russian consul in Plovdiv, with a beautifully hand-embroidered icon of St. Mina, commissioned by a provincial cleric.

Nedelia Petkova embraced her new vocation with fervour. The city municipality did not have the means to provide a building, so the classes were conducted in a private house. The newly-fledged teacher was at a bit of a loss in the beginning, but thanks to Sava Filaretov himself, who helped her, and the two senior students he sent to her, she quickly got her bearings. A year later the school numbered 200 pupils and the premises were not sufficient to house them, so the need for a purpose-built school became apparent. Another city notable, Dimitar

Traykovich, was approached this time and it was he, who built the school for the girls.

According to a memoir of Nedelia Petkova, written by her daughter, Stanislava Karaivanova, also a teacher in her own right *"the Turkish women were envious of the Bulgarians, saying that since the gyaur girls went to school, the harvest increased;"* and also that a notable Turk *"wanted to close one of the school windows, because from there it was possible to see into his harem."* The girls were also discouraged by their own grandparents: *"Once an old woman met three senior girls from the school and said: "It's a shame for grown up girls like you to go to school, why don't you stay at home to do the house work? Didn't I get old without studying books – look at my white hairs!" – "Oh, but we don't want to die like you," replied the girls.* And here the author, this unassuming 19th century woman makes the following, quite profound remark: *"Even now there are people who misunderstand the purpose of science. They study either because education is in fashion, either for some speculative reasons. In fact science has the task to save humankind from its own misconceptions, to teach them the real reasons of natural phenomena and to ease their toil. So what is needed, is diligence, hard work, observation and experience."*

EARTHQUAKES

INTERLUDE

Sofia is situated in an earthquake zone and has had some very destructive quakes throughout its history. Not a lot is known about the earlier ones – the first one recorded was in 1450 with a magnitude of 6 on the Richter scale. Better documented are the earthquakes of 1818 and 1858, both known to have caused a lot of damage and to have frightened the population.

The worst earthquake in Sofia was that of 18th September (30th in the Gregorian calendar) 1858; it was also better documented than the previous ones and from all that was written about it, it becomes clear that it was really devastating and was felt even in more distant places like the Rila Monastery. About 70-80% of the buildings in the city suffered badly; the poor had to rely on charity to repair their houses before the winter set in. Ivan Denchev, a Bulgarian entrepreneur and philanthropist, better known as Denkoglu, was one of those who sent donations for them. Public buildings were also badly damaged and some of them completely destroyed. 19 out of the 24 mosques lost their minarets and only 2 out of 7 churches were still functional afterwards. The Syuvush mosque (former St. Sofia Church) suffered serious damage – the minaret fell and subsequently a rumour spread amongst the Muslims that they must've displeased the Christian God, so as a result the building was then abandoned. In the west a new hot geyser erupted but afterwards gradually receded. The flow of the mineral water in the city diminished for a few days, but afterwards reached its previous level.

A newspaper article of the time (issue 399 "Tsariogradski Vestnik"/4th October 1858) states that Sofia suffered a lot and the quake was felt for days in a row; that up to 40 stone buildings were brought down, plus 20 minarets, a mosque and the Telegraph office were all demolished; there were lots of casualties. Sava Filaretov, the prominent Bulgarian educator and well known public figure, was an eyewitness and describes it vividly in letters and articles: *"On 18th September 1858, Thursday at lunchtime, the sun was shining in a peculiar way over Sofia plain and was so scorching that one didn't know where to go to in this unusual heat and oppressive atmosphere. At that time, all of a sudden, in a moment, a blast was heard, but such a blast, loud and deafening, as if thousands and thousands of cannons went off. At the same minute the earth shook and trembled so much and so terribly, that everyone was in distress and thought that the world was coming to an end...They say, that Mount Vitosha, 1 hour south-east of Sofia, had got cracked in one place half a yard wide and half an hour walking distance between the villages of Boyana and Dragalevtsi..."*

A certain Spas Vatsov who has documented the 19th century earthquakes, wrote that *"at that moment the earth shook so* terribly that everybody thought that the end of the world was coming. After 2-3 minutes it was seen that out of 24 mosques only 5 kept their minarets...but cracks had appeared on the domes of the former as much as of the latter. In half an hour in the fields to the west, where there was never any water, hot water appeared...the earth core wasn't shaking, it was jumping; either it was rising, say a yard upwards, either it was falling with ineffable speed and a horrible echo...at the Bash Cheshme Mosque* (a mosque that used to stand at the crossroads of Vitosha Boulevard and Solun Street) *the metal, conical minaret roof which had been ejected upwards by the quake, had afterwards nosedived, piercing the gallery for the muezzin of the said minaret..."* Things didn't calm down for a long while. Spas Vatsov quotes a peasant naively complaining that he thought that *"once it gets frosty and the earth freezes, it won't be able to move and shake, but I can see that it still jumps and bounces for the fun of it."*

DECLINE – THE ROAD TO INDEPENDENCE

SOFIA LOSES ITS STATUS IN AN ADMINISTRATIVE SHUFFLE

The earthquake of 1858 only exacerbated the conditions in the city, which had been left to rack and ruin for a long time. No improvements had been made since the stay of Ami Boué 20 years or so earlier. In a travel guide to the East, published in France in 1861 (*Itinéraire descriptif, historique et archéologique de l'Orient,* oeuvre d'Adolphe Joanne et d'Emile Isambert) only a few lines are given to Sofia and this description is far from flattering: *"This historic Bulgarian metropolis is just a little town today with about 20 000 inhabitants and doesn't offer anything more than rubble and a cluster of narrow streets unhealthy and stinking."*

The only sites worth mentioning are the ruins of the ancient Palace of the Pasha, that Ami Boué mentions, still not restored since the fire and *"the mosque that used to be the metropolitan church at the time of the Bulgarian kings"*- that is the basilica St. Sofia. The authors actually quote Ami Boué and concur with him in that, judging by the situation of the church, the city must've been a lot bigger and that the actual Palace of the Pasha *"is vast and comfortable, but lacks character as is the case of such buildings in Turkey"*.

The city of Sofia had been the centre of *Rumeli Eyalet* (Rumelia province) for a very long time. But in 1864 as part of administrative reforms, it became part of the so called *Tuna Vilayet* (that is the Danube region where the main town was Ruscuk, present day Rousse, which had grown into one of the most important Ottoman towns on the Danube and an administrative centre of *Tuna Vilayet,* which extended from Varna and Tulcea to Sofia and Niš). It appears that the Sofia citizens of Bulgarian stock were not that concerned about this reform, which downgraded their city. One might say they were even somewhat pleased, because the name Rumelia (*Rumeli* in Turkish), making an allusion to the Christian, but more specifically Greek population (the Greeks were known as *Romaioi* - Romans from Byzantine times), was not much appreciated. Anyway, it's doubtful that any reforms would've diverted the Bulgarians from striving for their independence.

From the onset, under the first Governor Midhat Pasha (1864 – 1868) the reformed province did really well as far as *"modernization" in the fields of legal and institutional reform, infrastructure, communications, economic development, medical care, hygiene, and urban development"* was concerned. Only a decade later, it was to become the nucleus of the new autonomous Bulgarian state.

The centre of Sofia in this final period of the Ottoman rule, according to architect T. Goranov (1938), appeared to have been the square at the Central Mineral Baths and the mosque Banya Bashi. Five main avenues, leading to the five exit points of the city, formed a star-like junction at this square: the cross mountain road, traversing the Balkan range, leading to Lom and Vidin on the Danube; the main road to Niš (Nish) and Belgrade; the road to Kyustendil (and Macedonia), the main military road to Constantinople (*via Militaris*) and another cross mountain road to Pleven and Ruscuk (Rousse). The construction of these streets was owed to unpaid labour in the period of 1860-1870, and, unlike the customary haphazard approach commonly seen from the Turkish authorities in those times, they were very well thought out – traced straight from the centre to the respective roads, something that at times involved pulling down entire rows of houses. These avenues were lined with trees – cherries, plums and willows to give them a more European aspect."*The five main streets constructed in Sofia before the Liberation,* writes Goranov, *form the skeleton of the city.* The city itself was encircled by a big moat enclosing an area within of about 284 ha (2.84 sq km).

There were about 20 neighbourhoods in the town at the time consisting of 3106 houses (according to Ottoman sources). There were about 100 public buildings, which included: churches, mosques, baths, schools, inns. There were also a number of separate graveyards (Bulgarian, Turkish, Jewish) and a few specialised markets (Wheat Market, Horse Market, Cattle Market).

Another initiative of Midhat Pasha was the founding of a vocational handicraft school at Knyazhevo and also a large textile factory, for which he brought machines and a skilled workforce all the way from Austria and Belgium.

While all this was going on, the Bulgarians, still dreaming of independence, were preparing an uprising. And it was a man of the cloth, who *"finding the monastery too constrained for his soul"*, as the poet Ivan Vazov put it *very* succinctly, and forsaking his vocation, went amongst the people to preach liberty and to organise a revolutionary network throughout the country. This took him 9 years and, by the end of this term, the entire Ottoman police force was pursuing him, but that did not deter this remarkable man, it was as if he knew his days were numbered. In the words of Vazov:

"He was invisible, a phantom or a shadow,
He'll show up in a church, come to an assembly,
Appear, disappear without sign or trace
Everywhere hounded, everywhere received."

His nickname was Levski, from lion (*lev* in old Bulgarian), given to him for his courage and strength and referring, according to legend, to a lion-like leap over a precipice, a feat dating from the time of his youth, when he had joined the Bulgarian Legion in Belgrade, mustered to fight the Ottoman Empire.

THE HANGING OF LEVSKI, BULGARIAN NATIONAL HERO AND A REVOLUTIONARY

"One man's terrorist is another man's freedom fighter."

This tragic event happened on the 18th February 1873 at, what was then, the outskirts of Sofia. 140 years on, the city having grown at quite a pace, the place of Levski's execution is to be found in the centre and a monument is erected to mark it.

Hristo Botev, a fellow revolutionary, deeply affected by the loss of his friend, expressed his sadness in a heartbreaking poem,

"The Hanging of Levski"

O my Mother, my dear Motherland
Why are you crying so pitifully, so sadly?
And you, raven, you hateful bird -
At whose grave your ill-betiding croak?

Oh, I know, Mother, I know, you lament,
Because you are a wretched slave,
Because your holy voice, Mother
Is a feeble voice – a voice in the desert.

Weep! There, at the bounds of Sofia
Towers – I saw it – a bleak gibbet
And your one and only son, Bulgaria
Hangs from it with frightful weight.

Ghastly, ominously croaks the raven
Dogs and wolves howl out in the fields,
Old people pray to the Lord with fervour
The women weep, the children scream.

The winter chants its dreadful song,
Gales sweep thistle across the field
And chill and frost and hopeless lament
fill your heart with such great sorrow.

In his last letter Levski expresses his sadness at falling into the hands of the enemy before the struggle is over but implores his mates to keep going because his demise is not going to prevent the liberation from happening and it shouldn't paralyze their hearts and their souls. He believes that a lot more sacrifices will have to be made at the altar of freedom, but a lot more will be needed afterwards, in the struggles after the liberation.

"If you let the present day Turkish lackeys and all those usurers and masters, that exploit you today, to rule you tomorrow, when you are free, it will be better to remain in the shadow of the Sultan."

"Don't let yourselves be manipulated, for those who hold the money, hold your future, because they've taken the money from you, while you are bowing before them and praise them as if they are the sun in your eyes."

"For those who incite hatred amongst the people who live in our dear Fatherland, either on ethnic or religious grounds, aiming at making money while you are killing each other, the punishment is death, death and again death. For those who promise a lot, just for the sake of being elected to rule you, and then afterwards go back on their words with the excuse that times have proved to be difficult and, you see, they didn't expect this, the punishment is confiscation of their property and exile abroad."

"And don't forget – I've told you more than once: "Whoever liberates us, will also enslave us."

"Time is in us and we are in time, it turns us and we turn it."

Today, some 140 years on, these words sound prophetic. The suggested death penalty may be viewed too harsh to the 21st century reader, but desperate times give rise to desperate measures! Otherwise these ideas may seem very left-wing, but were more likely inspired by the French Revolution; the suffering that the ruling class has been inflicting on the rest of the population before and since, if justice is to prevail, should have to be offset in some way or another.

APRIL UPRISING – THE AFTERMATH AND THE BATTLE FOR SOFIA

The uprising finally went off 3 years later, in April 1876 – premature and badly organised – no surprise that the Ottoman authorities were able to put it down without much difficulty. The repressions that followed were terrible and the rest of the world was shocked when they learned of these atrocities. Sofia, initially planned to be the centre of the 5th revolutionary district, was dropped by the organisers, due, it was said, to the deplorable situation of the local revolutionary committees. However, in the wake of the uprising, the Bulgarians from Sofia suffered along with the rest.

The city at the time was nothing more than a big village, *"a fortuitous concourse of mean, red-tiled little houses and cabins of wood and plaster. Its crooked, narrow lanes, leading nowhere in particular, were unpaved. In rainy weather they were no better than open sewers"*, declares John Macdonald in his book about Bulgaria *("Czar Ferdinand and his people")*. He adds that *"in Turkish Sofia no Christian woman dared venture out of her house after dark or far from it in the daytime. There were no street lamps. No man went out of doors in the night time without a lantern. Arrest, perhaps a beating, was the punishment for breach of the regulation."*

We might well wonder about the law-enforcement at the time, but, as Macdonald explains, the *zaptieh* – the Turkish gendarme, *"as often as not an ex-bashi-bazouk was an irresponsible tyrant."* He goes on to explain that *"highway robbery by Turkish gendarmes and soldiers – whose pay was usually months, or even years, in arrears – was of frequent occurrence in the Bulgaria of 1877."* (*bashi-bazouk*, literally "damaged head", was an irregular soldier).

The French consul, Léandre François René Le Gay, in his detailed reports to the French Embassy in Constantinople, describes those troubled times in detail. He feels for the

Bulgarians, amongst whom he lives, and their plight. In the aftermath of the April uprising their properties were plundered, set on fire, the booty, taken by their oppressors, was then sold at the markets. In a report from 24th May 1876 Le Gay testifies that Turkish soldiers, recently back in town, were selling objects snatched from the Bulgarians at the market. *"20 000 head of livestock were seized from those wretches, 6 500 of which were sent here to be sold in town or in the surrounding area."* The newly arrived soldiers were having a good laugh as they sold their booty, while the local Muslim kids, armed with sticks, were amusing themselves by knocking off the hats of the Bulgarian peasants at the market.

In another instalment from 31st May 1876 Le Gay recounts: *"Yesterday at 10 am 3 wooden cannons were brought and 60 Bulgarian prisoners. This event made a sensation. Word went round that they were going to take pictures of the cannons."* The cannons in question were secretly made by the Bulgarians who participated in the uprising and were seized by the Ottomans when it was put down. From the same report of Le Gay we learn that *"at 10:30 am the local authorities received an official telegram announcing the succession of Sultan Murad (V) to the throne. This news made the personnel at the konak to lose their senses. At 11:00 o'clock the troops gathered. The first two-gun salute was fired* [the guns were produced by the renowned German steel manufacturer Krupp]. *Despite the public announcement made beforehand, when the cannons were heard, widespread panic took place amongst the local population who thought that another massacre was going to occur and rushed about with their carriages; screaming women darted and scurried after their husbands; the cattle, also scared, ran all over the place. This commotion lasted about 10 minutes and when the Bulgarians realised what was going on, they calmed down."*

Things simmered down as the days went by. In a report from 14th June Le Gay informs us that: *"The prisons were full with Bulgarians. Last week 11 heads of rebels were brought in dribs and drabs. Mazhar Pasha made sure that they were buried in the*

Bulgarian cemetery to soften the impression of their exhibition to the public." Lots of prisoners were passing through the city; amongst them were the troops of the great Bulgarian poet and revolutionary, Hristo Botev, who were captured after his heroic death.

There was a bridge in Sofia, the so called Colourful Bridge (*Sharen Most*), built over a river that the Turks used to call "The Bloody River" (*"Kanla Dere"*), for according to legend, the name came from the blood of the Bulgarian defenders of the city during the Turkish invasion. Whatever the truth, during the time of the Ottoman Empire, in spite of its vibrant red and yellow colours, the bridge or rather the place by it, was connected with some rather gruesome happenings. It was here that local criminals were executed. Non-residents on the other hand, were hanged near the respective city gates, where they had entered the city (Levski for example, was hanged by the Eastern gate). Thus, in the aftermath of the April uprising, a few Bulgarian bookshop keepers, who had been involved in it, all local men, were hanged at the place by the Colourful Bridge.

The American reporter, J. A. MacGahan, in his book "Turkish Atrocities in Bulgaria" (1876) also recounts some horrific stories. Other than the large scale slaughter, a more profitable business was quickly organised. There was a certain Ali Bey, a notable from Tatar Bazardjik (present day Pazardjik), for example, who *"arrests men of the well-to-do class upon a charge of having belonged to the Insurrectionary Committee, puts them in prison and maltreats them in various ways until they are glad to ransom themselves at the rate of from 15 to 50 pounds apiece."* He goes on to add that *"the same thing occurs in Sofia on a much larger scale. There the business is taken in hand by the Kaimakam (the Governor of the province), who often exacts as much as £500 ransom."*

This assertion is corroborated by Le Gay who states in a report from 19th October 1876 that he intended to procure some proof of the racketeering going on, i.e. lists with the amounts of money that the Bulgarians were giving to their oppressors to buy themselves out of being arrested and convicted *"with the* agreement of the Turkish authorities, who naturally receive their share; however the cases are so many, that I renounced to continue with this investigation and will just tell Your Excellency that the Turks used the alleged Bulgarian uprising to enrich themselves at the expense of the Bulgarians."

It appears that it was a time of lawlessness, for MacGahan says that there were some *"Turkish notables who virtually govern the place and in whose presence the Kaimakam doesn't pretend to any authority. In our presence they gave orders which it was the business of the Kaimakam to give without even consulting him and he stood by, silent and obsequious, without offering an observation."*

The events of April 1876 acted as a trigger for the Russian-Turkish war that followed. In Sofia the authorities were building new fortifications around the city. It was mainly the soldiers who were involved in this task, but according to Le Gay, the local civilians were also supposed to give them a hand and work there for a number of days, although people were hoping to buy themselves out of it, for the authorities were amenable to the idea – it was going to bring money in and the solders would finish the job as they had done elsewhere. Despite all these preparations the Austro-Hungarian Consul Josef Waldhart stated that the Russians were going to raze Sofia before too long.

Indeed, by late 1877, the Ottoman Empire was losing the war and the Turkish civilians were fleeing the Bulgarian lands. The city of Sofia, as a major supplier of food and munitions for the Turks, was of great strategic importance for the further advance of the Russian troops in Thrace, so the Russian Generals Gurko and Rauch headed for Sofia Plain with 20,000 men, crossing the Balkan range in the throes of winter, to face 15,000 enemy troops around Sofia under the command of Osman Nuri Pasha.

The mood in Sofia amongst the Muslim population was grim. Captain Fife, a British military attaché, observed on 20th December *"the feeling of alarm amongst the inhabitants and the daily departure of a large number of them from the town"* despite the bitter winter weather. On December 28th a relief worker reports that *"women and children were begging government officials for carts for the journey south."*

The battle for Sofia started on New Year's Eve, 31 December 1877, at the village of Dolni Bogrov, situated nearby. After setting fire to the villages of Dolni Bogrov and Botunets, the Turkish units attacked the column of Gen. Velyaminov. However his troops resisted and then counter-attacked on New Year's Day, 1st January 1878. The cannon fire could be heard in the city centre and when the defeated troops of Osman Nuri Pasha returned with their wounded, it became clear that the Russians would soon invade the town.

Meanwhile the troops of Gen. Rauch endeavoured to cross the Iskar River at the village of Vrazhdebna, where the Turkish troops set the bridge on fire with the intention to slow them down, but the fire was put out and the Russian advance continued. Three more villages to the south-east were taken on 3rd January. During the ice-cold night of 3rd-4th January, it was a Bulgarian man, who led the troops of Gen. Velyaminov in the direction of Kumarica (today Novi Iskar, a district of Sofia).

Faced with a real risk of being surrounded, Osman Nuri Pasha issued the order that very night for an immediate retreat towards the town of Pernik, situated to the southwest of Sofia, abandoning some 6,000 sick and wounded soldiers in the city. Osman ordered Sofia to be set on fire and the arsenal to be blown up. He then warned the ambassadors of the various foreign embassies and consuls of his decision. He proposed to put 30 carts at their disposal to ensure the evacuation of their families and their luggage. Chaos and confusion reigned everywhere. Sofia plain was swarming with terrified Muslim civilians trying to flee. The city itself was rife with disease.

Sofia escaped the fate of Stara Zagora - one of the largest towns in the Bulgarian lands, which, just a few months earlier (31 July 1877) had been burnt to the ground by the Ottomans after the massacre of some 14 500 Bulgarian civilians. Sofia owes its lucky escape thanks to the Italian Consul Vito Positano, the French Vice Consul Léandre François René le Gay and the Austro–

Hungarian Vice Consul Josef Waldhart who all refused to leave the city.

Positano not only refused to do so but did everything possible to save Sofia and its people. With the help of the French and the Austro-Hungarian consuls he called upon the diplomatic corps to defend Sofia. *"In sign of protest against your inhuman intentions to set Sofia on fire, we declare that we will remain in the city together with our families, our entire staff and also with the Health missions who have been tending your wounded to this day."* He also threatened Osman Nouri Pasha with grave diplomatic consequences should he continue with his plan. By doing this, Positano risked his own, and his family's, lives. Using his experience (he had the rank of captain in the local fire-brigade in his native Bari, Italy), Positano directed fire-fighting efforts to save houses, engulfed by flames. He organized rescue operations and led patrols of Bulgarian volunteers on the streets of Sofia. After the Ottoman retreat, Positano even organized armed detachments to protect the population from looters (regular Ottoman Army deserters, bashi-bazouks and Circassians).

Gen. Gurko entered the city, enthusiastically applauded by its citizens on 4th January, and a solemn church service was performed at the St Nedelya/St Kral (Sveta Nedelya/Sveti Kral) Church in the centre of Sofia. You may well ask why this service was not held at the basilica St. Sofia. Sadly, this church, once a symbol of the city, had become a virtual ruin at the time of the Liberation. However, on that fateful day, to honour this momentous event, it is said that in front of the basilica, a bell was hung from a tree and rung - for there was no bell tower - a practice preserved to this day. After the arrival of the Russian Forces, the population of Sofia gathered under Positano's balcony to express their gratitude for his efforts.

The first Sofia city council declared Positano an honorary citizen on 20th December 1878. The citation read: *"Were it not for his direct involvement, there would have been no trace left of Sofia and thousands of Sofia residents would have died that winter."* Léandre le Gay was also declared an honorary citizen of

Sofia on 26th May 1878. Three streets in Sofia were named respectively Positano, Lege (le Gay, misspelt in Cyrillic) and Josef Waldhart in honour of the three ambassadors for their timely and courageous intervention that saved the city.

AFTER THE LIBERATION (1878)
THE REBIRTH OF THE CITY

"The capital of Bulgaria occupies the same site as the squalid, poverty-stricken town once governed by the Porte. No mushroom city in Western America ever sprang so quickly into a prosperous being from the ashes of filth and a corrupt administration. Twenty years ago (1887) the mean looking buildings and foul dark streets of Sofia rendered the place a nest of filth and disease and its rapid conversion into a modern city of fine buildings, broad, well-paved streets and pleasant parks and gardens, is one of which Bulgarians may well feel proud."

Harry de Windt, Through Savage Europe; Being the Narrative of a Journey (undertaken as Special Correspondent of the Westminster Gazette), throughout the Balkan States and European Russia, 1907

Sofia woke liberated on 4th January 1878 and its citizens went out on the streets to celebrate this liberation that cost so many lives. On 3rd March 1878 - the Treaty of San Stefano is signed by the plenipotentiaries of the Russian and Ottoman Empires. A temporary Russian government is formed and on 21st May 1878 Prince Alexander Dondukov-Korsakov takes office as Imperial Russian Commissioner in Bulgaria.

In the wake of the Russian-Turkish war, however, the Great Powers in their collective wisdom decide to split Bulgaria in two distinct parts – the Principality of Bulgaria; an independent state, and Eastern Roumelia, a semi-autonomous Turkish province (13th July 1878, Treaty of Berlin).

Sofia, having been left to rack and ruin in the last years of Turkish rule, on 4th April 1879, suddenly found itself the capital of the new Principality of Bulgaria. At the time it was neither the biggest, neither the best suited for this role – Turnovo, the old capital or Plovdiv, the ancient Philippopolis were deemed, by some, as more suitable candidates. Yet, for various political reasons and strategic considerations, Sofia was the one chosen. Needless to say, it took some time to reconstruct it and make it fit for its new role.[3] The prominent Bulgarian writer and poet-laureate Ivan Vazov describes Sofia in his memoir in the aftermath of the Ottoman era as *"a capital young, muddy, raggedy, poverty-stricken"* and is appalled by the condition of the city centre, revealing that the square of St Nedelya Church (then known as St. Kral) was *"a maze of Jewish and Bulgarian houses, crammed above winding stinking streets and blind alleys; a horrible ghetto that only 10 years later was going to be cleared away by the axe of Dimitar Petkov, the Mayor at the time."*

Dimitar Petkov was indeed about to start on a grandiose building campaign. If he could, he would've torn down the entire dirty old town and started from scratch. On his list of condemned buildings along with the basilica St Sofia, were the rotunda St George, St Petka's church, the Synagogue, the Banya Bashi Mosque etc. But about his endeavours we'll talk later on.

At the inaugural meeting of the National Assembly, 13th April 1879, a proposal was made and unanimously accepted for the building of a monument, a temple in memory of the Russian troops who had lost their lives during the Russo-Turkish war. Alexander of Battenberg, the newly-elected head of state, suggested Sofia as the site of this edifice and also launched a fundraising campaign. The temple was to be named St. Alexander Nevski - the patron saint of the Russian Orthodox Church and of the Russian Emperor, the latter known in Bulgaria as the King-Liberator – *Tsar Osvoboditel*. The construction of this temple almost brought about the complete demolition of the basilica St. Sofia a few years later. Building materials were scarce and it was

---

[3] According to data from the archives of the Municipality of Sofia, the city had "11 694 inhabitants, 2 schools, 7 churches, 30 mosques and dervish lodges, 10 inns, 120 shops, 62 taverns, 19 bakeries and 3306 houses."

thought a good idea to knock down the ruins of St. Sofia and use the materials for the new cathedral. A certain Architect Bogomilov firmly opposed this notion and declared that if the Bulgarian government wasn't prepared to restore this historical monument, he would appeal to the Russian Archaeological Society. This fortuitous intervention saves the symbol of Sofia city, for the time being at least.

Meanwhile, on 1st July 1879 the first electric light in Bulgaria – the so called "electric sun" illuminates the City Garden and the clock tower in honour of Prince Alexander of Battenberg, who is expected to arrive at his capital. The initiative comes from a certain Dr D. Mollov, an eminent doctor of medicine, who had the equipment imported all the way from Vienna, especially for the occasion. However the city will have to wait till 1900 for the first street lighting to be installed.

Konstantin Jireček, the Czech historian and diplomat arrived for the first time in Sofia on the evening of 9th November 1879. Coming from the "Golden Prague", then an important and flourishing city of the Austro-Hungarian Empire, his first impressions of the new Bulgarian capital, described in his Bulgarian diary, are far from flattering: *"very unfavourable impressions"* (*"impressions le plus défavorables"*). *"Tired, disappointed and angry"* he slept with his travel clothing on, in a dreadful hotel in Sofia, where he had expected to find *"an Eldorado for tired travellers"*. The morning didn't bring any agreeable surprises – the city didn't improve on a closer look: *"Crooked street with trees, opened oriental shops on the side, horrible uneven pavement and awful mud. A big village! Finally I found a plaza. On the left - one-storey building with 16 windows on the facade and guards at the entrance. This must be the palace."* In front of the palace he saw *"the beginnings of a garden with a bandstand and a cafeteria"* – the City Garden. The huge puddles in the streets provoked the sarcastic analogy of a *"Bulgarian Venice"*. Then he arrived at a huge wooden building of the sort that *"at home they build for cattle fairs, entirely decked out with little flags. This must be the Parliament"*.

Another visitor, James Samuelson, a British barrister, remarked on *"the baths fed by natural hot springs, the execrable pavement which makes progress in a carriage very difficult; the wooden skeletons of triumphal arches which are permanently retained throughout the country, so that the people may n ot be put to any unnecessary trouble in preparing joyeus reception in turn for Russian general, German prince, or a national hero!"*

This is what had become of the splendid city Constantine the Great loved so much - buried under centuries-worth of rubble with a shanty town on top. The territory covered by the city was little more than 2,8 km^2 (1,1 sq.mile), surrounded by a defensive moat. The moat was then transformed into a peripheral boulevard - the first ring road of Sofia (traced today by the boulevards of Slivnitsa, Hristo Botev, Patriarch Evtimii, Vasil Levski and Rakovski Street). It encloses 2,84 km^2, but at that time only 75 % of this area was built on. Outside the built-up area lay orchards and fields. However, that was about to change very quickly as the city started to expand.

The first census of the Principality of Bulgaria, from 31/12/1880, indicates that the population had risen to 20 501; only 11 395 were born in Sofia, while 9 106 (nearly half) came from elsewhere. The next census, from 31/12/1887 (after the unification with Eastern Roumelia), shows that the population continues to grow, reaching about 31 000. At that time the city becomes a major waypoint on the railway line connecting Western Europe and Turkey (where the Orient Express was to run) and so, five years later, from the census of 31/12/1892, it becomes clear that with its increased population of 46 593, Sofia had finally become the biggest city of Bulgaria.

Sofia's railway station together with the Bulgarian State Railways was inaugurated on 12th August 1888, at midday, to coincide with the arrival of the first international train, coming from London – Paris. It departed the next morning heading for Plovdiv – Edirne – Istanbul. The Bulgarians were justly proud of this station, the most important of its time, not only in Bulgaria, but also on the whole of the Balkan Peninsula.

But there was still a lot to be done. Sofia's makeover was not accomplished overnight.

Konstantin Jireček, who had meanwhile become the Bulgarian Minister of Culture, informs us in his "Travels in Bulgaria" (1888), that in the first winter after the arrival of Prince Alexander of Battenberg, the newly-elected head of state, the Bulgarian capital looked worse than during the time of Ami Boué (1836-38).

And yet life went on amongst the ruins; the shopping area, extremely poor, but lively, was busy from the early hours of the day till late at night with the clamour coming from the yelling coachmen and the din from the passing carriages mixed with the shouts of the street-vendors, trying to sell their wares. Thousands of crows circled above the city, looking for any leftovers, competing with hundreds of stray dogs, who mostly favoured the taverns and the butcher shops. More than hundred years on, the stray dogs are once again a serious problem, despite all the changes that have meanwhile occurred in the city that doesn't age...

"Neither gas nor candles, even tallow ones, Jireček pursues, *are used at night for lighting, but torches, just like in the villages."*

Prince Alexander Battenberg, used to the opulence of the family Schloss Heiligenberg, would've found his new lodgings, let's say, wanting. *"The Prince's Palace,* says Jireček, *is the konak of the Turkish Pasha, built in 1873, just before the war. The initial building was one-storey with 23 windows, with a balcony above the entrance. When the Prince arrived, it was in a poor state. On the upper level, only two rooms were suitable for habitation while in the others barrels were placed here and there, indicating a leaking roof, whereas downstairs, in the secretary's office, that doubled as a waiting room, there were frogs, joyfully jumping around."*

Felix Kanitz, the Austro-Hungarian geographer, ethnographer and naturalist in his travel notes *"Danubian Bulgaria and the Balkans"* (1882) explains that the konak had to be quickly reconstructed into a palace, albeit a very uncomfortable one, and the furniture of a bankrupt Viennese singer was bought for the salon of the Prince. He also makes it plain that at the time no social life as such, existed in the Bulgarian capital; and seems to think that only one grater was to be found in the whole town and the entire neighbourhood would've had the use of it.

A grater is certainly a useful kitchen appliance, but one may well wonder why such great importance is bestowed on it and what role it was supposed to play in the social life of the Bulgarian capital at the end of the 19th century. *"Only Burmov's family,* pursues Kanitz, referring to the mayor of Sofia at the time, *who had spent time in Istanbul, had managed to arrange their home in the European way, and that was the only house which the Prince would visit with pleasure. For a young man, who had been the favourite of the high aristocracy of Berlin, life in Sofia must have been a great ordeal indeed. "* Prince Alexander couldn't remain long in his dismal palace in urgent need of repairs; in 1880 he bought a stately home near the Black mosque (now Sveti Sedmochislenitsi Church) and moved there. It was initially built for the Russian General Parensov, the Minister of War in 1879/1880. This building became known as the Little Palace and was his home for the duration of the official Palace's reconstruction, that is, for about 2 years or so.

On 3rd March 1882 (the 4th anniversary of the San Stefano Peace Treaty) Prince Alexander placed the cornerstone of the St. Alexander Nevski Cathedral. The place chosen for the edifice was to the east of the basilica St. Sofia, and, when it was discovered that underneath lay an extensive necropolis (which shouldn't have come as a surprise), it was too late to stop the project. So the Prince arrived at 11:30 a.m. on a cold winter's day and saluted the troops waiting there along with a big crowd of people. A metal casket containing golden coins was placed along the cornerstone of the Cathedral, according to a Slav tradition. Later that evening a big banquet was held at the Slavic Discourse Club.

The building of St. Alexander Nevski was on its way, but various other civic buildings were needed in the new capital. The Parliament at that time had to hold meetings in the Russian Army

Club, a wooden structure, large enough to accommodate the 300 odd Russian officers stationed in Sofia. When in 1882 it burned down, the Third National Assembly had to start its sitting Parliamentary sessions at the newly built 1st High School for Boys. Interestingly, Konstantin Jovanović, the young architect who designed this edifice, was later commissioned to do the Parliament building as well. According to Kanitz, three Government ministries had to share the same roof, that of an old ramshackle two-storey Jewish house (located on Lege Street); i.e. the Ministry of Foreign Affairs, the Ministry of Justice and the Ministry of Finance.

All that said, technological progress was not slow to start its march in the new capital.

On 26 November 1884, the very day when the new Parliament building was inaugurated, the first telephone call was made in Sofia to the bemusement of Stefan Stambolov, the eminent politician, chairmen of the Parliament, and Petko Karavelov, another well-known figure, who were invited to witness this historic moment. Three Bulgarian officers – Gruev, Nikiforov and Blaskov, had organised the demonstration.

The three young people had brought a telephone set on their return from Russia. The telephone, although well known at the time, was seen as an amusing gadget and even as a toy and hardly anybody could foresee its future as a powerful means of communication; doctors then, as they do now, were expressing their concerns about the harmful effects it could have on the health. All the same, the three officers were very excited with their new toy. One unit was to be installed in their house (18, Ivan Vazov Street), while the other was intended for Colonel Reshetin, just a few houses away, at Number 13. The proximity of the two houses was important for the project, but no doubt the young and attractive daughter of the colonel, also influenced their choice. Captain Gruev was the one who installed and connected the two telephone units and organised the demonstration. When the guests of honour arrived, he turned the handle of the gadget and lifted the receiver. Colonel Reshetin at the other end, answered immediately. Stambolov and Karavelov were clearly impressed. Even more so, when Miss Reshetin joined in with a song – Stambolov in turn replied with a folk song.

Two years later, in 1886, the first telephone exchange connecting five subscriber lines, was established in the workshop of the Post Office in Sofia. Those subscribers, who were able to talk to each other on the phone, were the Palace, the Prime Minister, the Head Office of the Posts and the 4th Police Station. The 5th subscriber was a private individual – a prominent trade representative. On 15th January 1892 the first long distance call was made between Sofia and Plovdiv – everything considered, not bad going to accomplish this in such a short time!

The first pushbikes had also appeared in the city by 1886 – 1888. In those times the bike in question was not the same as the one we use today, but its predecessor – the high wheel bicycle, the penny-farthing. A contemporary wrote in his memoires how one of the first cyclists in Sofia, Mr. Mitovich, *"pinned as a grasshopper on the high seat was galloping on his iron horse in the streets of Sofia, followed by a crowd of spectators of different ages."* It appears that this new mode of transport won great popularity in a short time and in 1889 the first velodrome appeared just outside the city (now in the very centre, near the national stadium, Vasil Levski). The Cycling Club had obtained from the local authorities, not only the site for the velodrome, but also a horse-drawn carriage with a barrel full of water and a man for the initial preparation of the tracks.

While the bicycle was gaining popularity, its fellow companion, the motorbike, was a great disappointment for the citizens of Sofia. The first motorcyclist, architect Stavrev, shattered the peace and quiet of the city with his noisy machine and, riding at the "high" speed of 20km/h, represented a danger to the hapless pedestrians, still not used to keeping themselves to the pavement.

The automobile, which appeared a bit later, about 1896, had more success. The first one was delivered on Easter Day 1896 to the Central Station of Sofia, to a certain August Schedevi, a Czech, working in the Bulgarian capital – he ran an iron workshop in Sofia, which along with its main activity - production of iron fences and other products, also produced springs for carriages. It is not recorded exactly what type his automobile was and so there is some speculation about whether it was powered by a steam engine, an internal combustion engine or was an electromobile. However, until the turn of the century the French manufacturer "De Dion Bouton", whose make the car supposedly was, only produced steam engines. Eyewitnesses recall seeing Mr Schedevi, proudly sitting behind the wheel of his new automobile on a leather-covered red seat, pressing a bulb horn on his way home from the station. He triumphantly crossed The Lions Bridge, to the applause of the crowds emerging from shops, inns and eateries to see him as he pursued his way towards the centre. Somewhere at the beginning of Vitosha Street, the engine suddenly stopped, to everybody's disappointment. It had to undergo repairs, but even after these it appears to have been a great failure. Nevertheless, following this first appearance, the automobile gradually arrived on the scene and stayed there.

By the way, Lions Bridge wasn't built till 1889-1891. Presumably the eyewitnesses in question meant the so called "Colourful Bridge" ("*Sharen Most*") which stood there before. This bridge, according to the legend, was built by Halil Sali Efendi, an eccentric Turkish merchant. One year, when the harvest was good, he bought lots of hay from the local peasants; the following year the harvest was bad and the peasants had to buy hay from him; so he made a good profit. The money he gained, was used to build the bridge and he put a sign on one side of it, saying *"I sold at the right moment, created a bridge"* and another sign on the other side, which read: *"If there is no bridge – build one, if there is no water fountain, build one"*. Turks used to call that river – "The Bloody River" ("*Kanla Dere*"), for according to the legend, the name came from the blood of the Bulgarian defenders of the city during the Turkish invasion. As we've already said, during the time of the Ottoman Empire, this was the place where local criminals were executed. In the aftermath of the April uprising, a few

Bulgarian bookshop keepers, who were implicated in it, were hanged at the place by the Colourful Bridge.

Therefore after the Liberation there was a proposal for a new bridge to be built in memory of the revolutionaries. Accordingly a project was made for a very lavish memorial complex with the bridge itself at the heart of it. The Bulgarian based Czech firm of the Prošek family erected the bridge. The cost was enormous – 260 000 BGN, Bulgarian golden Levs, (the Lev at the time was equivalent to the French Franc) and presumably that's why the rest of the memorial was never completed. The bridge itself has just gone through a very major modernisation with the tram crossing the otherwise pedestrianized bridge, in the middle of a busy roundabout and with the metro passing beneath!

The bridge is 26 m long and 18 m wide. It is positioned on an important road leading to the north, to the port of Lom on the Danube River. The newly built railway station, inaugurated in 1881, was situated just 1 km to the north of the bridge. So at the time it was one of the entrance points into the city. The four bronze lions on each end represent the four bookshop keepers, hanged by the Turks. They were manufactured by the Viennese engineering company *Waagner Biro AG*. The Sofianites quickly realised that the lions lacked tongues and wondered why. Some wit suggested that the reason was that this way they would be unable to tell how much money was embezzled from the building funds. Others were joking about preventing revealing the secrets of the "priestesses of love", for the area was then notorious for its brothels.

The Prošeks erected another bridge at the same time – the so called Eagles Bridge which was also situated on a very important artery – the old Roman *Via Militaris*, (now known as "Tzarigradsko Shose"), leading to Istanbul. However the first major project of the Prošeks was the largest Beer Brewery (1881-1884), for which they are remembered to this day!

This is how step by step Sofia was turning its back on its Oriental past and was embracing the new technological wonders, coming from Europe and the New World.

History hasn't recorded how the "grater crisis" was solved that Felix Kanitz was so concerned about. The foreign visitors, coming from Western Europe, used to higher levels of comfort and luxury in their countries of origin, obviously had trouble adjusting to life in the newly liberated, poor Bulgaria. Their criticisms may not be objective or fair, but remain interesting as they show the outsider's point of view.

Emile De Laveleye, the eminent Belgian economist, who came and stayed in Sofia for some time in the 1880s, wasn't that impressed with life in the Bulgarian capital. The city at the time has 20 000 inhabitants and 2968 houses. The old town has an unmistakably Turkish atmosphere about it – narrow twisting streets with shops open on both sides and poor wooden houses. The only buildings that date from the past are the 7 or 8 mosques, the public baths – where hot water runs abundantly into a large marble-lined pool, and there is one other old building, transformed into a library/printing house. More than 5 000 Turks having emigrated, their houses, in the eastern part of town, have been demolished and a new district is being built in their place, with large streets laid out in a grid pattern.

The newly renovated palace of the Prince is also to be found there, an imposing building, which, Laveleye has been told, has a price tag of 4 000 000 francs (the Bulgarian currency, the Lev, is based at the time on the French Franc). It must've been worth the expense for James Samuelson, another visitor (who wrote a book on Bulgaria well worth reading – Bulgaria, Past and Present, 1888) refers to it as a *"fine structure of modern French Renaissance, resembling portions of the Louvre and Tuileries."*

A magnificent hotel stood opposite the palace, in *"imitation of those at the Viennese ring (Ringstrasse), with a restaurant, café with much gilding about it and boutiques with grand window displays"*, according to Laveleye. More splendid buildings followed a bit further, housing the respective consulates of England, Russia, Austria, Italy and Germany. On from there are located some large white buildings accommodating various Ministries, a Military School, created by the Russians, a casino for the officers and, in the gardens, a number of sumptuous villas consisting just of a ground floor – in the ancient Roman fashion, which although convenient, takes a lot of space.

Laveleye then, by way of example, describes the floor plan of the house of Mr. Queillé[4], where he lodges: on the right, from a central vestibule opens the dining room and the salon; opposite – the office and the master bedroom; to the left – three more bedrooms; in the back – a little outbuilding for the kitchen and its adjacent parts; lots of cellars but no loft; flat roof, covered with painted metal sheet. Laveleye estimates the value of the house at 30 000 francs and adds that the land goes for between 40-50 francs/m² in the vicinity of the big market, elsewhere – 14-15 francs/m². Let's not forget that this is an economist speaking here! The constructions, he pursues, are made of rubble-stone, brought in from somewhere in the vicinity and are then decorated laboriously with stucco. The wood for construction is very expensive, because it's brought in from a distance of 4-5 days on ox-drawn carts. *"I don't know, he testifies, a more unfavourably situated town than Sofia. In every direction as far as you can see, stretches a vast deserted plain and only to the south is towering the severe granite massive of Vitosh, the highest peak of which at an altitude of 2330 m is covered with snow for part of the year. But this rather imposing mountain is completely bare. The trees had been cut and the goats leave to grow nothing but bushes."*

Now here is the place to explain that throughout the Turkish rule, deforestation went ahead at an alarming pace and as Will Monroe clearly explains (*"Bulgaria and her people"*): *"When Turkey conquered Bulgaria more than five hundred years ago, the country was covered with virgin forests; but during the five centuries of Ottoman rule no control was exercised over the destruction of the forests, and no measures were taken for their preservation. Entire liberty was granted to the people to pasture their flocks and herds in the forests, and the right to cut wood upon the payment of a tax hastened the deforestation of the*

[4] Eumène Queillé, a French financial controller, a personal finacial adviser of Alexander Battenberg (1881-1884)

country. When Bulgaria won her freedom in 1878 the forests had largely disappeared."

Macdonald in "Czar Ferdinand and his people" concurs with Monroe: *"For the Turks, in nearly five centuries' occupation, had shown no interest in preserving any of its cultivable beauties, except at their official residences. Mount Vitosh, for example, which rises high over Sofia plain, and from whose peaks some of the finest prospects in Europe are obtainable, was in its lower parts almost stripped of its forests. To reproduce a few words from the present writer's past account of the matter: 'The Turk has no notion whatever of the art of forest conservancy. When he wants wood he simply butchers a tree and takes of it what he needs. He would say that preservation was "God's business," and that trees were made by God for man's use...in saying it he would consider he was doing something religiously meritorious.'"*

According to Laveleye, it was the Turks, purposefully got rid of the trees, as was also done in Bosnia, to *"avoid surprises"*. He describes Sofia plain as *"ten times the size of the Roman plain, but more desolate and melancholic..."* which brings to mind Peter Mundy's impression when he arrived in Sofia about 200 years or so earlier: on his approach to the city, the sweeping view of the plateau enclosed by the mountains in which Sofia is situated, greatly impressed him, but on entering it, he thought it quite dreary. At the end of the 19th century Laveleye corroborates his view and furthermore, he doesn't like the climate at all – he finds it harsh – *"in winter the northern wind freezes you and in summer the sun scorches you"*. The deviation of the thermometer is frightening – in January it goes down to minus 20^{0}C, in August it goes up to 39^{0}C; that is – a difference of 59^{0}C and the daily temperature variations are at times 15-16^{0}C! Nobody spoke about climate change in those times – people took it the way it came. However such dramatic temperature differences probably hadn't been recorded in Sofia since then, until very recently, with the so called global warming!

The Belgian then mentions the risk of earthquakes; *"the one from 1858, he explains, knocked down quite a few houses and provoked the eruption of thermal springs"*. Then he suggests planting trees and creating parks around the city to make it more pleasant. Laveleye really felt strongly about this issue, emphasising that *"it is more urgent to plant trees here, rather than build palaces!"*

To be fair, trees were being planted at the time to shape what was to become Boris' Garden. This was the idea of Ivan Hadjienov, the mayor of Sofia who wanted a garden to rival those in Vienna; therefore on 22nd March 1882 a decision of the local council was taken and the creation of a nursery garden was set in motion. The decision however was not unanimous. Lots of people thought that a garden was hardly a priority for a capital with muddy streets and gas street lighting. But by 1889 the park was taking shape and even the lake, known today as Ariana, was already created. Still, it seems that these developments were not good enough for Laveleye, who remained unimpressed with the Bulgarian capital. Yet, at the end of the 14th century Lala Şahin Pasha who coveted Sofia so much, thought the city and its plain wonderful, a paradise on earth; is this the same place that Mundy and Laveleye are so uncomplimentary about? One can't help but wonder about that. Is it a question of "call a place paradise, kiss it goodbye" or just the normal way things go – with their ups and downs, rise and fall...

In Laveleye's report there is a lively description of a dinner given by the British Ambassador, Mr Frank Lascelles, attended by the majority of the foreign ambassadors to the country. It seems though that it was difficult to break the ice and the only lively topic – to decide the best way to deliver fresh fish from the Danube! After the coffee, the Belgian has a chat with the high-spirited Mme Lascelles, who tells him about the hardships she experienced at the beginning of her stay in Sofia; she complains that in the city's new streets you can't circulate in whatever way – *"walking, one loses one's shoes, in a carriage one gets stuck as in the time of Mme Sévigné."* (Marquise de Sévigné was a French aristocrat who lived in the 17th century and is remembered for her letters). Expensive new paving stones were laid with great care;

the following spring after the thaw, it seemed that they had disappeared, but in fact they had sunk into the liquefied clay. But it appears that despite such mishaps, things had improved, the society in Sofia is very pleasant not least because it has become intimate - people meet often, almost every day. Also the hunters and the skaters are very happy here. Bear-hunting in Mount Vitosh or the Balkan is apparently unrivalled. But dining is still an issue; nothing can match the dinners at the French Ambassador's. Unfortunately his chef, a Belgian, is away, taking the waters at Carlsbad, to the annoyance of all the gourmets. Then Mme Lascelles sings the praises of the Bulgarians; they are sober, honest, industrious, disciplined, a nation with the highest of qualities.

Danish traveller André Lutken passing through while travelling "From Adria to the Bosporus" in 1892, concurs: *"One must admire the élan vital of this nation..."* and further on he adds: *"The very same day the pressure was gone and the yoke lifted off their necks, the Bulgarians gave themselves a quiet shrug and started working where they left off 500 years before. They got down to it with a sobriety and a practical sense that is characteristic of them."* Lutken waxes lyrical about Dimitar Petkov, the Mayor of Sofia at the time, for the major improvements and building fervour in the city: *"Everywhere along the roads you see evidence of the feverish haste of the work to make old Sofia disappear and make space for the great new city rising under the leadership of the fresh and vigorous mayor of the capital..."*

Dimitar Petkov became the Mayor of Sofia in 1888 at the age of 31. He deserves to receive credit for the transformation of Sofia from an Ottoman backwater into a modern European city. This veteran from the Russian-Turkish war, who had lost his hand during the battles at Stara Zagora and Shipka, showed incredible energy and zeal while demolishing this shantytown that had become Sofia. He is seen as the Bulgarian Haussmann and his actions were every bit as controversial as those of the illustrious French Prefect.

In 1889 he persuaded the Council to take on a huge loan, for that time, of 10 million Bulgarian Levs (=10 million French Francs) from the Central Bank of London, for town planning. But the brave Mayor was far from altruistic; neither was the Prime Minister, Stefan Stambolov. In the process of metamorphosing the city, they also managed to line their own pockets. Dobri Ganchev, a contemporary chronicler, describes the cunning scheme: *"When the old Sofia has been demolished, in accordance with the new regulation plan, new parcels were formed. They were created as a result of the narrow streets being closed, by the tiny plots of the demolished houses. These plots could not be given to the previous owners, who had very small yards. The city council was giving them to 'their people' who supposedly have had land here previously. This is how it was done: the city agent Nicola Filipov finds the Jew, owner of the house to be demolished, and advises him to sell it to so and so, telling him that otherwise he would get very little money from the municipality. He promises him also a good place in the new neighbourhoods. The place is then sold to Stambolov or Petkov, while the owners of the old houses receive new plots of land. "* Nevertheless, these two great men are not to be envied. Both of them had tragic fates – both of them died violent deaths: Stambolov – in 1895, Petkov – in 1907. Their widows became known afterwards as the "Golden widows".

But let's go back to the life in the new capital at the end of the 19th century. As time went on, the picture was changing. The Balkans attracted more and more travellers in search of romance and adventure.

William Miller, a prominent English historian and journalist, went around the Peninsula in 1894, 1896, 1897 and 1898 and published his impressions in a travel book – "Travel and politics in the Near East in 1898". At the time Near East meant the Balkans. The chapter on Bulgaria is called "An experiment in emancipation: Bulgaria" and, not surprisingly, is full of fascinating insights, for Miller was a keen observer and, having thoroughly studied the Eastern Question, selected features which were of interest. Sofia, once an Ottoman backwater, has changed dramatically since the departure of the Turks. It was now donning a European garb, and yet for the European traveller, it remained still *"in the shadow of the Orient"*. There was promise and hope in the air though, a newly found confidence and an enthusiasm to move forward. *"Sofia has, indeed, very few traces of its Turkish past nowadays,* says Miller, *although only twenty years have elapsed since the "collective wisdom" of Europe created free and autonomous Bulgaria, and Sofia became the capital of the new state, the town has completely shaken the slough of its previous existence."* He goes on to describe the significant changes that took place in such a short period of time, underlying that few cities, even in the west of America, have grown at such a pace. From the *"squalid Turkish town of 11 000 inhabitants"* it has become quite a place with *"fine streets and 'European' buildings, a delightfully cool public garden, a large palace, and a population of nearly 60 000 souls."*

Miller believes that this progress is due *"to its geographical position and the construction of the railroad from Belgrade to Constantinople"*. He then explains why, strange as it might seem, precisely Sofia, being somewhat to one side, was chosen for the capital of new Bulgaria and not say, Turnovo – the old capital, or Ruschuk (now Russe) – the big city on the Danube, which had been lately the centre of a Turkish province. But the geographical location of Sofia was in fact of high importance – amongst other, more political considerations, placed as it is, almost in the centre of the peninsula.

As for the Western innovations, according to Miller, the most striking of all was the new Parliament building, *"erected at a cost of £80 000, which is easily the most imposing edifice of the kind in the Balkan Peninsula. Compared with the mean little building in which the Servian Skupstina meets, or even the more imposing Boulé at Athens, the Bulgarian House of Parliament looks very well indeed..."* The architect, who presented the winning project for this edifice, was a certain Konstantin Jovanović, graduate of the Zürich Polytechnic in Switzerland and whose father, a Bulgarian, was the Chief of Prince Mihailo's Cabinet in Serbia.

According to an anecdote, when the design work was

completed, the young man went to see the Prime Minister himself with the accounts to claim for his expenses during this time. Just for the record: the overall budget for the Government and the Council of Ministers at the time was apparently 1 460 934 BGN (the Bulgarian Lev at the time was equal to the French Franc). The Prime Minister, looked at the accounts and the contract for 6 000 BGN due to be paid to the young architect, gave him a long hard look and said: *"Listen, my lad, have you any idea what 6 000 Levs are? That's a hell of a lot of money! Who can earn this much nowadays? Even if you take the stars out of the sky, that's too high a price to pay! Look, lad, take these 3 000 BGN and go away with my blessing. Even this sum is a bit much, but still, you've put in the effort. Mind you, when you leave, don't you start telling people what you've earned. They would kill me if they knew how I've spent their money!"* The young architect took the money and left the country. It was another architect, the Austro-Hungarian Friedrich Grünanger who was charged to oversee the work.

On June 4th, 1884 Prince Alexander Battenberg placed the building's cornerstone. By 1886 the work was completed by Friederich Wilhelm Gustav Liebe, a young builder from Saxony. The building is the focal point of "Narodno Sabranie" Square. The motto, taken from the Bulgarian coat of arms "Unification Makes Us Strong" (or *"Unity makes strength"*; paraphrase of *"United we stand"*), dominates the fronton of the edifice. Let's not forget that this magnificent Neo-Renaissance building, now proclaimed a monument of culture for its historical significance, was really very badly needed at the time. Prior to its construction, the National Assembly sessions were being held in various localities - such as the Russian Army Club, an extensive wooden construction, on Alabin Street, erected at the place where the garden of the hotel Rila is now situated (built over the remains of Constantine the Great's palace!). Constructed in 1879, it burned down in 1882 and the sessions were then held in the newly built First Secondary School (Moskovska Street).

Prince Alexander though, had other fish to fry at the time when the Parliament was finally inaugurated in 1886. The

Unification of Bulgaria had taken place in September 1885 with the Prince's blessing, something which had attracted the wrath of both the East and the West. As Lord Lytton, the British diplomat put it: *"This beastly Bulgarian Question seems likely to resemble the proverbial turd of which the Scottish proverb says that the more you tread on it, the broader it gets."* Lytton then suggests that *"the most convenient means to shake this encumbrance off Britain's diplomatic boot, would be to induce the Sultan at Constantinople, technically the suzerain overlord of the two Bulgarias, to accept their unification with the object of turning the new state into a bulwark against Russia."* So the Great Powers once again had the better of the situation. Despite a victorious war with a belligerent Serbia, Bulgaria had to sign a not very advantageous peace treaty. There was widespread discontent and a Russophile group of army officers decided to depose their Prince, so on 21 August 1886 they abducted him, took him to the Danube, put him on a yacht and sent him to Russia to be dealt with by his Russian cousin and namesake, the Russian Emperor. The latter wouldn't even meet him, but sent instructions for him to retire to Western Europe. However this move was not at all popular with the rest of his subjects. A contra coup-d'état, organised by the politician Stambolov ensued and eventually Prince Alexander returned to Sofia on 3rd September the same year. In spite of this, his Imperial Russian cousin was very cross with him and forced him to abdicate, so only a few days later, on 7th September, he had to leave Bulgaria for good, to the regret of many.

Now, according to the Berlin treaty, the Bulgarian ruler had to be someone approved by all parties: by the Great Powers and by the Sublime Porte; a difficult and quite daunting task to find such a prince, to whom no one could object. When Miller visited Bulgaria, Prince Alexander Battenberg had long since abdicated, and a new ruler had been chosen, another prince of Teutonic origin (albeit with predominantly French blood – from the House of Orleans), Prince Ferdinand of Saxe-Coburg Gotha. Prince Ferdinand compared unfavourably with the dashing, impulsive

Prince Alexander. He was as unpopular in Bulgaria, as he was on the European stage.

His election was met with disbelief. Queen Victoria herself, his father's first cousin, declared to her Prime Minister, *"He is totally unfit ... delicate, eccentric and effeminate ... Should be stopped at once."* He was seen as having ideas above his station, his *"court,* says Miller, *is one of the most formal in the world"*. *"It is generally believed that he desires the title of King so that he may be on social equality with the rulers of Servia and Roumania and may be allowed to dispense with the odious necessity of wearing a fez when he visits his sovereign at Yildiz Kiosk"*. That sovereign is, of course, the Sultan, for Bulgaria is still not entirely autonomous at that time. His interior policies were no more popular than his foreign ones. *"The Bulgarians prize economy above all other virtues, yet every municipality which the Prince has visited has been obliged to run into debt, owing to the cost of receiving him in what he considers befitting pomp and his marriage alone cost £120 000. These peasant farmers ask – not without reason – why he should keep up such unnecessary state, and compare his stiff manners with the free and easy style of the late Prince Alexander."*

Nonetheless, other foreign commentators don't see Ferdinand in such a negative light. The authors of "The Balkans: a history of Bulgaria, Serbia, Greece, Rumania, Turkey (1915)" see his reign more of a *"regeneration"*, believing that *"the young man combined great ambition and tenacity of purpose with extreme prudence, astuteness and patience"* and see him as the *"consummate diplomat"*. His *"clever and wealthy mother"*, Princess Clémentine of Bourbon Orleans, daughter of the French King Louis Philippe, *"cast a beneficent and civilizing glow around him, smoothing away many difficulties by her womanly tact and philanthropic activity..."*

Another foreign visitor, a Mr M. A. John Macdonald, in his book "Czar Ferdinand and his people" (1913), notwithstanding his acerbic humour, appears to be almost impressed when talking about the Bulgarian ruler or about his mother, *"one of the cleverest and the most accomplished women in Europe"*, who had set her mind on seeing her beloved son with a crown on his head. The author also cited a rumour, doing the rounds at the time, about his mother meeting a gypsy woman, who predicted a glorious future for her offspring – that he would assume the purple, so he was educated with this idea in mind. John Macdonald concurs that Princess Clémentine *"cherished dreams of an illustrious career for her favourite son",* but argues that even if that wasn't the case, his training would not have been different, because *"love of literature, science and the arts was hereditary in the House of Orleans."* The Prince travelled extensively all over the world and spoke quite a few languages, English included. And despite his abhorrence of violence, the Prince had displayed during the Turkish campaigns *"his twofold gift of German tenacity and French élan".*

A certain Count de Grenaud wrote a letter to a friend after being invited by the Prince to accompany him to Bulgaria in the Capacity of Chief of the Household. *"I have accepted,"* the Count writes, *"the great honour of accompanying this Prince Charming to the conquest of his new kingdom. His mother and himself have enchanted me. My new Master is twenty-six years old. He has the finest blue eyes you ever saw. He has Francis the First's big nose. He has wit, good nature, and acuteness in abundance. If he reigns, he will do it, if I am not greatly mistaken, in Henri IV fashion. Meanwhile, in our future dominions, people are locking up each other, assassinating each other. I wonder if we shall reach Bulgaria safe and sound."* They did reach Bulgaria and Prince Ferdinand did indeed reign with panache. The Count became the first marshal of the Palace and when he died, his room was preserved by his Royal Master as a memorial chapel and a service was held there on each anniversary of his demise with the King in attendance.

Everything considered, Ferdinand actually did make a success of his reign to start with, especially when he had Stefan Stambolov as his Prime Minister (known also as "The Bulgarian Bismark" for his controversial politics). In the first 20 or so years of his reign, things went swimmingly for Ferdinand and for Bulgaria.

Soon after his succession to the Bulgarian throne, his mother, Princess Clementine, found him an eligible bride, the 23-year old Princess Marie-Louise of Bourbon-Parma. Rather pleased with the prospect of such a union between the grandson of King Louis Philippe of France and the great granddaughter of King Charles X of France, Princess Clementine wrote a letter to Queen Victoria with the news, describing her future daughter-in-law as *"unhappily not very pretty, it is the only thing which is lacking, since she is charming, good, very witty, intelligent and very likable"*. While displaying a certain enthusiasm, it is not perhaps the most flattering portrait of Marie-Louise of Bourbon-Parma and certainly understates the talents of the young princess, who was exceptionally gifted and well educated – she spoke five languages, painted well, played piano and guitar and read Italian poetry.

Ferdinand was fortunate to marry into such a family and to start with was quite affectionate with Marie-Louise. He was even pleased that they both shared the typical Bourbon nose and hopefully their offspring - if there were to be an offspring, would carry the same hereditary feature down the generations. Most importantly the Bulgarians would have a prince with French royal blood in his veins at a time when the French themselves had disposed of the monarchy altogether! The trouble was that the Bulgarian Constitution stipulated that the heir to the throne should be a member of the Christian Orthodox Church while the Roman Catholic bride-to-be, whose godfather was the Pope himself, was obviously adamantly opposed to such an idea. Prime Minister Stambolov, who approved the match, managed to accomplish the unthinkable – he coerced the Bulgarian Parliament into amending the Constitution! On the whole, the Bulgarians were thrilled with the prospect of this marriage to the point that when a non-compliant Metropolitan Kliment condemned Ferdinand in a sermon, his congregation, very angry, even drove him out of his own cathedral!

The couple were married in the spring of 1893 in Parma, Italy and having had the blessing of Pope Pius, went forth to multiply. They didn't waste much time, despite the fact that theirs turned out not to be love's greatest match, producing four children in five years; the poor Queen died at the age of 29, after giving birth to the last one.

The heir to the throne arrived just 9 months 10 days after the wedding! Royal births in those days were not only painful and lengthy affairs, they were far from being private as well. In her Sofia palace, the young princess waited patiently for her pregnancy to come to its term; a worthy descendant of a Royal line, she, just like her predecessors, had to undergo labour in the presence of witnesses – besides doctors, midwives, ladies-in-waiting, there were Prime Minister Stambolov, the Minister of Justice and the Court Chamberlain – all present, to vouch for the legitimacy of the heir apparent and to make sure that there was no foul play. The whole country was rejoicing.

Named Boris after one of the greatest Bulgarian monarchs; the very one to have adopted Christianity as the official religion of Bulgaria in the 9th century, this boy, born with a silver-spoon in his mouth, was soon to become the subject of a bitter dispute between his parents. It was rumoured that Marie-Louise was so infuriated that she threw her shoe at a portrait of her husband. Ironically, the root of this discord was religion. Despite their prior agreement that Marie-Louise, a devout Catholic, was to bring their son up in the same faith, her Royal spouse meanwhile had decided otherwise. The interests of his realm had to come first and under increasing pressure from the Russian Emperor, he had his first-born boy converted to the Bulgarian Eastern Orthodox Christianity in 1896. His son was consequently recognised by Russia. Marie-Louise was devastated, while Pope Leo XIII had Ferdinand excommunicated. According to Princess Louise of Belgium, a second cousin of Ferdinand and married to his eldest brother Philipp, *"Marie Louise of Parma, mother of the souls of her children, betrayed, repulsed and broken in her belief in her husband, immediately fled from the Konak of Sofia, and came to*

Vienna to hide her sorrow and her fear in the sympathetic arms of her mother-in-law, who was equally tortured by the blasphemy of her son".

Princess Louise, also staying there at the time, perceives Ferdinand as a Devil worshipper, condemns him for giving his sons to the *"Russian schism"*, empathizes with this *"pious mother"*, whose *"innocent children had lost their hope of salvation"* and understands *"her indignation and her desire to annul her marriage at the Court of Rome"*. Unfortunately Louise of Belgium's memoir is full of inconsistencies, so we should take it with a pinch of salt. Ferdinand, also a Catholic, had found himself between the Devil and the deep blue sea. He hadn't been happy to break his promise and he had gone to the Pope personally to plead for dispensation, but found Pope Leo XIII inflexible, was told that he couldn't possibly consider such a "spiritual murder" and that abdication was preferable to the conversion of the infant. Back in Sofia, Ferdinand did consider abdication, but finally decided to carry on with the conversion, asking the Russian Emperor Nicholas II to be the godfather of Boris.

However neither Prince Kyril, the second baby boy, nor her two other children, were ever converted to the Eastern Orthodoxy and there wasn't any question of it either. Marie-Louise did run away in despair, but to start with she went to Beaulieu on the French Riviera, taking baby Kyril with her. Princess Radziwill, a friend, wrote that *"the health of Marie-Louise was greatly shaken by all her recent emotions. Her parting from little Boris was horrible. They had to tear the child from her arms and the poor woman was in a faint for two hours."*

The Orthodox Chrismation of Boris was celebrated in the Cathedral of Sofia. In the presence of Bulgaria's leading politicians and the representatives of a few non-Catholic nations, the young Prince, wearing white, girded with the red sash of the order of Saint Alexander, embraced the Orthodox faith. His mother was not present; recuperating in Western Europe, she didn't *"heroically"* (as Louise of Belgium phrased it) return to Sofia and *"to her conjugal duties"* until May 1896.

Louise of Belgium is not very kind with poor Ferdinand in her memoirs, although she admits to being fascinated with him. But that's understandable, knowing that she was a flirt and had built a rather scandalous reputation for herself, rumoured even to have had an affair with him. She doesn't admit any such thing though, but hints at passes he made to her. She recalls a visit to Sofia with her husband in 1898 when she was welcomed very warmly. However it is very unlikely that such a visit took place at that time – Princess Louise had eloped with Count Geza Mattachich, a Croatian officer, who she fell in love with, in January 1897. Her husband, Prince Philipp, fought a duel with the Count precisely in 1898. Following that, Louise, together with her lover, were involved in a scandal, linked to forgery. Finally she was granted a divorce some years later.

Come what may, this is what she has to say about her stay in Sofia: *"The life of the Sovereign was wonderfully well organized in this country which was still primitive. Nothing was wanting at the palace. There East and West were happily united."* Princess Louise had an enjoyable time, especially because Ferdinand had elected her *"the queen of these days of festivity"*. She appreciated the cuisine at the palace and the entertainment organised in her honour: *"Every night after supper there was a dance at the palace. The Bulgarian officers were most enterprising dancers. Educated at Vienna or Paris, they understood the art of conversation. They were distinguished by an instinctive air of nobility, as are all the sons of a virile and essentially agricultural race with a wholesome and wide outlook."*

Louise claims that one evening Ferdinand had offered her his whole realm, himself included. Later he took her away from the ballroom, led her to another room with a French window, open to the park and inquired if she had understood what he had said earlier. *"His tone was harsh and his look stern. There was something imperious and fascinating about him. I was much disturbed. He insisted brusquely: "It is the last time that I shall offer what I have offered. Do you understand?" My eyes wandered to the salon. I saw beside me the Prince of Bulgaria so different from his brother, still young, handsome and full of power. But the image of Princess Marie Louise passed before my eyes, and also the vision of the Queen.... I shook my head, and murmured a frightened "No."* Whether this account is true, is anybody's guess. But we will leave Louise to it and see what Ferdinand has been up to in Sofia.

Sofia benefited a lot from the endeavours of the new ruler. He was determined to transform his capital into a modern European city. Macdonald explains (in "Tzar Ferdinand and his people"): *"The only way to improve a Turkish town such as Sofia, was to begin by knocking it down. And Czar Ferdinand's predecessors did their work of demolition so rapidly and effectually that, when he first arrived at his capital, there was scarcely a vestige of the old town left. The ancient baths were there, and a mosque or two, and a rambling, picturesque, old khan, or caravanserai, the only apology for a hotel which the town possessed before the Liberation."* This notorious caravanserai was apparently quite a building, although it's not clear when exactly it was constructed, very likely towards the end of the 16th century when Hagia Sofia was transformed into a mosque. The caravanserai and various other buildings would've been constructed next to it. It is said that the vast stables of that caravanserai were intended for up to 9000 horses and it was very popular with merchants and travellers.

The Austrian diplomat Count Czernin, while on his way to Constantinople, mentions a caravanserai in his travel log, but whether it was the same one, it is difficult to assert, because there were quite a few in Sofia during the Ottoman era, although Macdonald doesn't mention any others in his book. There was certainly one near the Black mosque (St. Sedmochislenitsi Church) with a hammam to go with it. Ami Boué in the middle of the 19th century also talks about that particular caravanserai, then in ruins, with only some blacksmith shops in front and even wonders if the ruins were not those of the ancient Bishop's palace. However, Macdonald in his early 20th century account goes on to add that *"with its numberless little rooms or cubicles, all unfurnished, it was* merely a shelter, where visitors had to provide their own bedding and provide their own food. During the late Macedonian insurrection it was a favourite place of meeting for members of insurrectionary bands."

Macdonald also mentions a Turkish mosque, originally a Byzantine church, which *"Prince Ferdinand restored to its original use."* Was he talking about Hagia Sofia? He then hastens to add that *"this reconversion must not be supposed to have in any way done violence to the feelings of the Mohammedan residents."* It appears that most of them had emigrated to Turkey by this time, an emigration that had even started from the moment when the Russians were approaching the city during the Russo-Turkish war. So he estimates that *"a single mosque suffices at present day for the needs of the Muslim population in the Bulgarian capital."*

At that time Ferdinand was busy settling down after his marriage. According to a Monsieur Hepp, a French writer and for many years a close acquaintance of Ferdinand, the elaborate court life in Sofia began with Ferdinand's marriage in 1893. The ordinary, one-storeyed palace, to which the new ruler was introduced, might've been sufficient for the needs of a bachelor, but it seems was not deemed satisfactory once he started a family. *"Partly an adaptation of the Turk building*, states Macdonald, *and to a larger extent a new construction, the existing palace of Sofia was built and decorated to its minutest detail after the Prince's own plans. In its 'fastidious elegance,' it has been said, the palace is an expression of its royal tenant. Of course, the most impeccably elegant person in it is the King himself. The unsophisticated labourers and shepherds of the interior, among whom their Czar, dressed in rustic Bulgar garb, has often sauntered, and whom he had gossiped with in their own patois – about their pigs and poultry, and their crops, and the village school – would be dumbfounded by his Olympian air and magnificent apparel in Sofia palace on occasions of state ceremony. Czar Ferdinand is master of the art of* <u>mise en scène</u>. *All the elaborate ceremonial with which he has surrounded himself is an expression of his lofty conception of his role as a king – an* assertion of his prestige."

Macdonald describes Sofia during *"the first hurried years of reconstruction."* Once again it would've then been a huge building site. *"Even until a time comparatively recent, Sofia presented the appearance of a Western American town in process of being 'run up'. It reminded some visitors of the growth of Johannesburg or of Coolgardie."* (Coolgardie, in Australia was at the time the third biggest town in the country, due to the gold discovered in the area). *"The resemblance was no less applicable to the spirit of the Sofiots than the work they were accomplishing. They manifested all the go-ahead ardour, all the optimism, of pioneers. They were, in their way, the pioneers of a new state."*

This was also the time of the emergence and rise of the Bulgarian intelligentsia.

THE INTELLIGENTSIA

To start with there was the doyen Ivan Vazov, poet-laureate, novelist and playwright, often referred to as the "patriarch of Bulgarian literature". His masterwork "Under the Yoke", the Bulgarian equivalent of *"Les Miserables"*, was translated into over 30 languages. We already mentioned his poem about Levski, the first of 12 poems, part of a cycle (*"The Epic of the Forgotten"*), dedicated to the Bulgarian revolutionary process, which finishes with "Shipka" – recounting the defence of this legendary Balkan mountain pass during the Russian-Turkish war in 1877.

Vazov was born in Sopot, a little town in the foothills of the Balkan, but after the Liberation, he moved to Sofia and lived there for the rest of his life, becoming part of the cultural and social life of the Bulgarian capital. Vazov was a lady's man. However he got married relatively late and his marriage – to a woman called Athena (after the Greek goddess) was a disaster. But at any rate he didn't remain faithful to his wife for long. The greatest love of his life was also a writer, 27 years his junior whose nom de plume was funnily enough Evgenia Mars (presumably after the Roman god of war, not after the planet), and married to the well respected dentist Dr Elmazov. It was the dentist himself, who presented his wife to Vazov. To start with their relationship was platonic; the young woman was in awe of the great man, but it appears that he was smitten with her from the very beginning. He praised her work, encouraged her to pursue her own writing career and wrote the reviews for her first two books. Their closeness lasted for the rest of his life. On the occasion of his 45th birthday in 1895, Vazov, already widely acclaimed, was given a unique award – a silver lyre on a silver wreath tied together with a gold-plated ribbon. On each of the silver petals of this jeweller's masterpiece, is engraved the title of each one of his works. Later, he would offer this costly trophy to his beloved Evgenia: *"But I have no other joy than you... and hope to see you again and to cherish you"* – as the poet-laureate confesses his feelings. *"You have been so far my guardian angel, my goddess, my idol - the woman I have adored and adore... I've got no other in this world"* - wrote Vazov to his muse at the end of his life . He realises the foolishness of their liaison, which he conveys in another of the 101 letters, still preserved, that he wrote to her: *"I feel quite ridiculous to be carried away by such an adolescent infatuation at my age. But what can I do, it is stronger than me. I'm troubled by you, I live only with the thought of you, you're my sun, you are my whole world ..."* Vazov died of heart failure in 1921 and nasty rumours started to go around – the gossips were saying that he died while making love to his mistress. Evgenia Mars kept going in spite of it all. Some of her best work in fact dates from this period. But worst was yet to come. Her husband fell ill and Evgenia had to look after him and after their son. In desperation, she decided to sell Vazov's trophy to the National library; this unleashed a campaign of hatred and abuse; Ana Karima, another writer, accused her of appropriating and cashing-in on Vazov's prize and even insinuated in a newspaper article that Evgenia's stories were written by Vazov himself and that it was he who had launched her plays in the National Theatre. The litigations that followed took their heavy toll on Evgenia's health. She died of myocarditis in 1945.

    Now let's move on to another Bulgarian literary giant, Aleko

Konstantinov, and his Bai Ganyo. Aleko – a lawyer, a writer, a public figure, is best known for his "Bai Ganyo" stories, for his travelogue – "To Chicago and back" and for initiating organised tourism in Bulgaria. Mountain chalets in Vitosha are named after him Aleko and Shtastlivetsa – The Lucky One – his nickname. Not so lucky is the end he meets in 1897 at the age of 34 – shot by an unknown miscreant, it never became clear if the bullet was meant for him or for his politician-friend, with whom he had exchanged places in the carriage where he was assassinated.

His masterpiece, *Bai Ganyo* - Incredible Tales of a Modern Bulgarian, "*A rollicking, Rabelaisian masterpiece*", has been translated into most European languages, including English - "*skilfully translated. Victor Friedman's meticulous editing provides linguistic, cultural, and political context,*" (according to Harold B. Segel, Columbia University). "*A comic classic of world literature, Aleko Konstantinov's 1895 novel Bai Ganyo follows the misadventures of rose-oil salesman Ganyo Balkanski ("Bai" is a Bulgarian title of intimate respect) as he travels in Europe. Unkempt but endearing, Bai Ganyo blusters his way through refined society in Vienna, Dresden, and St. Petersburg with an eye peeled for pickpockets and a free lunch. Konstantinov's satire turns darker when Bai Ganyo returns home—bullying, bribing, and rigging elections in Bulgaria, a new country that had recently emerged piecemeal from the Ottoman Empire with the help of Czarist Russia.*" (Harold B. Segel, Columbia University)

In 1895 Aleko associated himself with another leading light on the Bulgarian literary scene – Pencho Slaveykov. Both translate and publish the work of Russian poets in the magazine "The Library of St. Clement". Slaveykov – a poet and a public figure, director of the National Library and, for awhile, of the National Theatre; Slaveykov and his father, the poet Petko R. Slaveykov – "*the earliest and greatest poet of modern Bulgaria*" (according to J. Macdonald), still live on in the centre of the capital, immortalised in bronze on a bench in the city square, which bears their name. Fittingly, the book-market today occupies this very square. Here is one of Slaveykov's poems, *While we are Young*, from "Dream of Happiness", a cycle of 93 lyrical miniatures, published in 1906:

While we are young the sun so brightly shines

The heart is basking in golden dreams

While we are young we tread with lighter step

And world's woes are not so hard to bear.

While we are young the whole thing is a joke

And sadness doesn't cast on us a shadow

Sadness may even be a fountain of joy

While we are young, ah while we are young!

In the following extract from Monroe's book (Bulgaria and Her People: With an Account of the Balkan Wars Macedonia and the Macedonian Bulgars by Will Seymour Monroe, 1914, Boston), an English literary critic, who knew Slaveykov personally, gives this account of him: "*He is the caged lion of Sofia. Great massive shoulders, a massive head, swarthy, with beard of black and silver, a brow that sets one thinking, and eyes — eyes weary with the world's troubles, eyes of the twilit woods, then of a woodland faun, eyes that lure you and dance away from you, eyes that laugh at you and their owner, unbearable eyes. Slaveikoff is the figure of revolt. As he walks painfully through the town — for his feet are unwilling travellers — he longs with a fierce desire to be where no man knows him. The passion of revolt is in his blood; it burns in the poems he wrote in Germany, whither the spirit of Nietzsche summoned him. In that series of remarkable poems he celebrates Beethoven, Lenau, Shelley, Nietzsche, Michael Angelo— men who wrote great things out of anguish.*" Slaveykov was a member of a literary circle and was involved in the publishing of a magazine, "Misal" ("Thought"), with a number of other noted writers, such as Krastyo Krastev, Petko Todorov and Peyo Yavorov.

Yavorov is one of the finest poets of turn of the century Bulgaria, whose whole life and death are determined by the two women in his life – Mina and Laura; one man, two women and a tragic fate to connect them. His first great love is Mina.

Two Beautiful Eyes

To Mina

Two beautiful Eyes. The soul of a child
in those beautiful eyes. Music, sparkle.
They want nothing and promise nothing...
My soul is praying,
Child,
My soul is praying!
Tomorrow passions and misfortunes
Will throw upon them
The veil of shame and sin
But no, passions and misfortunes
Will not throw upon them
The veil of shame and sin
My soul is praying,
Child,
My soul is praying...
They want nothing and promise nothing...
Two beautiful eyes. Music, sparkle.
In those beautiful eyes. The soul of a child.

    The girl with the soul of a child went on to do her studies in Paris in the summer of 1909. She was struck by tuberculosis soon afterwards and was sent to Berck Plage (Pas-de-Calais, France), which at the time was the place for the treatment of tuberculosis. But all was in vain. Mina died in the summer of 1910 and was buried in the Boulogne-Billancourt cemetery in Paris. The poet went regularly to her grave while he was in the French capital. And then Laura comes into his life.

Lament   *To Laura*

My soul is a lament. My soul is a cry.
Because I'm a bird they've shot:
my soul is wounded to death
wounded to death - by love ...
My soul is a lament. My soul is a cry.
Tell me about meeting and separation -
No, I'll tell you: there is hell and torment -
and in the torment - love!

The visions are close - the road is far.
Surprisingly laughing exuberance
of ignorant and greedy youth
a sultry flesh and buoyant ghost...
The visions are close - the road is far:
because she stands radiant before me,
she stands, but does not hear who calls and moans -
she - flesh and buoyant ghost!

    Later on not just his soul, but he, himself will perish by a bullet, to end his torment, the same way Laura ended hers in this drama of Shakespearian proportions. This was such a tragedy – the two were the most glamorous couple of the high society in Sofia. Laura, a socialite, beautiful, sensitive, was only 27 when she died in 1913. Cultured, she had done her studies in France. Back in 1906 she had won the first beauty contest held in Bulgaria (5th October in the Military club in Sofia). The two get married. Their happiness is of short duration. Laura shoots herself dead in a jealous row; he also shoots himself, but survives, rendering himself blind. After being tried and acquitted of murder, a year or so later, he finally succeeds with his second suicide attempt, this time taking the precaution to poison himself as well. He is only 36.
    That very year another young Bulgarian poet, Dimcho Debelianov, publishes his first poems in a magazine "Modernity" (*"Suvremenost"*). His role models are Pencho Slaveykov and Yavorov. He studied in the University of Sofia, spoke several languages (French, Russian, English) and translated works by

Verlaine, Baudelaire and even Shakespeare. He was killed in WW I (October 2nd 1916) while fighting the English in Macedonia. The following poem, *The Fallen Soldier*, was inspired by the letters of an unknown dead French soldier, found by Debelianov at the battle field.

He's a foe of ours no more
All the enemy survivors
Were swept by a mighty wave
Someplace on the other shore.

There, in the sunken verge
He lies calmly, very pale
Staring all resigned and sad
At the heavens deep and clear

All around, on the greyish ground,
Warmed by caresses from the south
Flutter shy, and now redundant
Letters sprayed with blood.

Who's he and where's he been?
Whose summons brought him hither
On a day of whirlwind triumphs
With no triumph here to die?

Poor mother's hand
T'was you in his sorry plight
With words of everlasting love
Of comfort and support.

Ridiculous pity, ludicrous pity
In such tumultuous, cruel times
As if he didn't lose his life
While taking someone else's.

As if under a command hostile
He was to show us mercy?
No, he got his just deserts;

Now gone he's not our foe.

But all this was yet to come. Back at the end of the 19th century, the Bulgarian intelligentsia was thriving. Besides the Bulgarian intellectuals living and working in the new capital city, there arrived numerous foreigners who settled in Sofia and became participants on the Bulgarian cultural scene. It was Marin Drinov's doing. A prominent Bulgarian historian and philologist, Marin Drinov was also instrumental in choosing Sofia as the capital of Bulgaria in the first instance. Assuming his role of Minister for "Education and Spiritual Affairs" (1878-1879), he summoned educated Bulgarians, living abroad, to return and participate in the establishment of the Bulgarian educational institutions. He also invited European scholars he knew, to assist in this difficult endeavour. The response was prompt and soon a number of European academics, artists and musicians, predominantly of Slav origin (Czech, Russian, Slovakian, Slovenian), settled in Sofia and set to work. The Czechs, especially, held a prominent place on the Bulgarian cultural scene.

We already spoke about Konstantin Jireček, who had become the Minister of Culture in Bulgaria. He wrote a History of the Bulgarians (Czech and German, 1876), The Principality of Bulgaria (1891), Travels in Bulgaria (Czech, 1888) etc. Czech architects, working in Sofia after the Liberation, contributed to transforming it into a European city. Antonin Kolar was one of them. He was the first chief architect of the newly proclaimed capital city of Sofia (from May 1878). And his main task was to *"clear the town, to demolish numerous houses in August and September of the same year and to repair the muddy and almost impassable streets."* He was involved in the first urban plan of the city, known as the Battenberg plan, he designed, amongst others, Levski's monument, the building of the Military academy and the Military Club.

We spoke earlier too about the Prošek family and their various projects. One of them, Bogdan, along with Antonin Kolar and the Bulgarian architect Marinov, designed Sofia's first railway station, inaugurated in 1888 that served the city for 86 years.

Czech musicians were involved in the establishment of the Bulgarian Philharmonic Orchestra. The foundations of the modern Bulgarian Art School were laid by artists who came from the west or were educated there. Jan-Ivan Mrkvička, the Czech-born artist, was one of them.

Ivan Mrkvička took an active part in the cultural life of the newly-liberated Bulgaria and is seen as one of the originators of the Bulgarian fine art tradition. Mrkvička settled in Sofia in 1889 and was one of the founders of the National Academy of Arts in 1896.

Jaroslav Věšín was another Czech artist who is closely associated with the development of the Bulgarian Fine Arts after the Liberation. He studied Fine Arts in Prague and Munich. Arriving in Bulgaria in 1897, he remained there till the end of his life. At first he was a professor at the National Academy of Fine Arts in Sofia, later on he became associated with the Ministry of War where he came to fame, producing quite a few masterpieces of military art (Bayonet Charge, The Samara Flag and many more).

We should add to this list Joseph Sebastian Oberbauer, originally from Austria, who settled in Sofia in 1889. With a background in both engineering and Fine Arts, he took an active part in producing Sofia's first cadastral map. After the completion of this job, he worked for awhile for the State Directorate for the Construction of railways and ports, but after being made redundant, he went back to the Municipality of Sofia and worked for them for the rest of his life. While working on the cadastral plan he was inspired to produce a watercolour ("Reconstruction of Ulpia Serdica"), showing the city wall of ancient Serdica, part of which was still preserved at the time, and from there used his imagination to present the city the way it looked in its heyday. As time went by he produced numerous paintings depicting churches, monasteries, mosques, inns, markets and streets of late-19th-century Bulgaria and of Sofia in particular. 70 of Oberbauer's works representing the urban landscape of Sofia are part of the future Museum of Sofia's collection, to be exhibited in the Sofia Public Mineral Baths building. A street in Sofia near the Theological Seminary, bears his name.

The task of all these people was arduous and their living conditions were far from what they were accustomed to. But they kept going nevertheless. In those times the coffee houses in Sofia, as elsewhere in Europe, were not just social hubs, but also places for conducting political and commercial activity and centres of the intellectual and artistic life. The intelligencia would gravitate to one or another coffee house, which would become their meeting place. There they will gather, usually in the evening, to socialise, to discuss things and exchange ideas. It was 11th May 1880, the day of St Cyril and Methodius, the creators of the Cyrillic alphabet, when a group of Czechs, Slovakians and Slovenians met at the coffee house "Radak". One of them, Anton Toma Bezenšek, a Slovenian linguist, working as a stenographer at the Bulgarian Parliament, came up with the idea of founding their own social club. This idea was accepted enthusiastically by everyone present and realized soon afterwards. This is how the cultural club Slavic Discourse *("Slaviyanska Beseda")* was established. It soon became the favourite haunt not just for the Czechs, but for a cluster of brilliant intellectuals of Sofia; Bulgarians and foreigners alike. The club rapidly expanded and had to have a clubhouse built for its needs. It boasted a library, a reading room, a theatre hall and even, at one stage, a cinema projection room. The club was organising various events; hosting concerts, theatre plays, literary meetings, but was also involved in charity work.

All this was very well and good, but dark clouds were gathering on the horizon. The new century about to come did not turn into an age of peace and prosperity as most people hoped.

SOFIA ENTERS THE 20TH CENTURY

"Sofia has been called a "little Brussels", and it certainly resembles the latter, although on a bright day its busy streets, alive with Eastern colour, grey, time-worn mosques, and the snowy peak of Mount Vitosch, backed by a sky of sapphire, render it infinitely

more novel and picturesque."
De Windt, Harry, *Through Savage Europe, being the Narrative of a Journey, throughout the Balkan States and European Russia*, 1907

A TIME OF RENEWAL

HOW THE CITY ACQUIRED ITS COAT OF ARMS

Sofia got its coat of arms thanks to the International Exposition (*Exposition Universelle*) in 1900. The *Exposition Universelle* of 1900 was a world's fair held in Paris, France, from April 15 to November 12, 1900, to celebrate the achievements of the past century and to accelerate development into the next. Bulgaria had been preparing for the exposition since 1897. It was important for the country, very recently liberated, to create a good impression worldwide. Each capital had to present its coat of arms at the exposition, but Sofia did not have one. The government formed a commission to get on with the task of creating a suitable coat of arms. Out of 12 projects proposed, the one designed by the young artist Haralampi Tachev won with unanimous approval to become the coat of arms of Sofia. Various small modifications have been made since then but, a century later it remains more or less the same as it was.

The shield is divided into four fields. In the upper left (seen from behind as dictated by heraldic rules) is depicted the church of St. Sophia, from where the city had gotten its name; in the upper right we see a representation of the Goddess of Fortune, Tyche, (a tutelary deity, who governed the prosperity of the city and its destiny); an image that is taken from an antique coin minted in Serdica at the time of the Roman Emperor Septimius Severus and featuring his wife Julia Domna, wearing a mural crown (a crown in the shape of the city walls). In the lower left field is pictured Asclepius/Apollo Medicus under a golden baldachin (also from an antique coin), epitomizing the mineral springs of the city, while in the lower right – Mount Vitosha, representing permanence and stability, a symbol that has endured over time. In the middle of the shield is placed another, smaller one with a lion rampant, again taken from an antique coin, found in the ancient Bulgarian capital, Turnovo, thus enforcing the bond and showing continuity. The motto underneath was added in 1911 and was inspired by the motto of Paris - *Fluctuat nec mergitur*, a Latin phrase, translated as "Tossed by the waves and does not submerge". Haralampi Tachev came up with "Grows but does not age" ("Ever growing, never aging").

THE MOST ICONIC BUILDINGS OF THE CAPITAL

"The capital of Bulgaria is young, well grown for its age, and mighty proud of itself. A trifle gawky yet and having outgrown its clothes a little where its long limbs of electric tramlines rumble out past scattered, half-built houses to the open country, and suddenly break off wondering why they have come so far. The town is working all the time, and the main street is positively busy. It has a South of France look; white house fronts, persienne-shuttered windows, and acacia trees shading the buzzing café tables along the footway."
JLC Booth, Trouble in the Balkans (Experiences of a Special Correspondent in Macedonia in 1904), 1905

"Trouble in the Balkans" is dedicated to Booth's colleague and *"travel mate"*, Frederick Moore, who also produced a book, based on the same events. His impressions of Sofia appear as variations on the theme of the "gawky" girl trying too hard to impress: *"When Bulgaria became independent, Sofia was a very dirty town without a street paved with anything but cobblestones and with but one house of any pretensions the Turkish "konak". Today, besides a palace and a parliamentary building, there are a national bank, a post office, a military academy, several vast barracks and many other Government buildings. There are parks and public gardens where bands play on summer evenings; new streets and avenues have been laid out and some of the narrow ones of Turkish times have been widened; substantial shops and hotels mark the business quarter, and modern houses the*

avenues. Still, Sofia reminds one of a lanky girl whose spindle shanks and lean arms have outgrown her pinafore. The dwellings, by setting far apart, try to reach out the long new avenues and cover the gawky child, but in places she is absolutely bare."
Frederick Moore, The Balkan Trail, 1906

This was a time of renewal. Mr M. A. John Macdonald, in his book "Czar Ferdinand and his people" (1913), recounts that in 1903, *"a large portion of the capital was little more than a desert of sand, stone, lime heaps and house walls, barely risen on their foundations."*

This was a time of changes, this was a time of contrasts, when old and new were co-habiting side by side: *"The barbaric and the civilised, jostle each other in the streets and market-places of new Sofia. The electric car just misses the long, horizontal horns and the shiny black muzzle of the buffalo, as he drags his creaking wooden cart, the fashion of which has remained unchanged these two thousand years and more."*

Macdonald is amused by the appearance of the peasant girls from the district of Sofia ("Shopi"), *"tribal remnant"*, as he calls them, *"conspicuous by their barbaric ornamentation."*

"Even with the poorest, coins – apart from the red flower stuck over the right or left ear – were the favourite ornaments. The well to-do wore them in profusion. I counted more than eighty coins, gold and silver, on the person of a peasant girl. She wore them in the form of a long rope twisted among the coils of her black hair. Another peasant woman's bust was wholly covered with silver coins as with a breastplate." He then adds that Princess Marie Louise, Ferdinand's wife, is fascinated by them and being an amateur aquarelle painter, she depicts them in her watercolours as they pass by her palace windows. However, he prophesizes that *"in a few years more these picturesque varieties in the market- places of Sofia will be civilised beyond recognition. The Sofia crowds are becoming as monotonous in appearance as crowds in London. Even the policeman of Sofia resembles, in his air of civic benignity, his London brother."*

The Bulgarians wanted a clear break with the past, but

sometimes they didn't know where to stop. In 1905 Hagia Sofia's basilica, the symbol of the city, was scheduled for demolition, but happily, it was saved in extremis by a group of young architects, pupils of the German architect and art historian, Professor Cornelius Gurlitt, well renowned at the time; they took advantage of his visit and implored him to use his influence with King Ferdinand of Bulgaria for the preservation of the monument, then in ruins. With this last minute intervention the church became the subject of renewed interest, research was carried out to determine the exact plan of the edifice and to throw more light on its history. The church was then gradually restored to its original state and started to attract visitors once again.

At about the same time (1904) the building works for the cathedral Alexander Nevski were started, although its foundation stone had been laid in 1879. Interestingly, when the work was underway, the foundations of an extensive building, stretching all the way to Paris Street and maybe even to Rakovski Street, were uncovered: the remains of the old caravanserai Siyavus Pasha, the biggest in the city, that we have already spoken about.

Arch. Tangarov believes that this edifice was initially built to house the Turkish cavalry in those earlier times, when Sofia was the main base for the military campaigns in the west. In a later period of the Ottoman rule, this caravanserai was turned into caserns, which were still in existence at the time of the Liberation. However in 1879 they were destroyed by an explosion that occurred in the artillery warehouse. So the cathedral was to be built over the remains of an ancient caravanserai, which in turn had been erected over the remains of a Christian monastery, that of St. *Elijah*, as some believe, for the foundations of two more churches were discovered underground between St. Sofia and the Parliament.

St. Alexander Nevski was to be a monument, dedicated to those who gave their lives for the Liberation from Ottoman rule and was financed by a nationwide subscription. It's named after a Russian saint – the patron-saint of the Russian Emperor Alexander II. The building, the work of the Russian architect Alexander

Pomerantsev, was finished in 1912 and cost 5.5 million Bulgarian levs (1 lev at the time was the equivalent of 1 French franc). It is a five-nave basilica in a neo-byzantine style with a big central dome and numerous smaller domes and half-domes, a few of them covered with gold leaf. The bell tower is 53 metres high and houses 12 church bells, cast and brought from Moscow. There is an extensive crypt underneath the cathedral which is now a museum.

Another iconic landmark, dating from that time, is the building of the Central Mineral Baths that came to replace the old Turkish baths, demolished previously. The winning design by the architects Petko Momchilov, Yordan Milanov and Friedrich Grünanger (1906) was in Vienna Secession style with Bulgarian, Byzantine and Eastern Orthodox elements, and to quote again the art historian we met at the beginning of the book, comes across as a *"cheerful image completed as a persuasive-paradoxical synthesis between a temple, a hammam and a public palace"*. The baths opened on 13 May 1913, but it took 2 more years to finish the work off and for a garden to be laid out in front of the baths. The baths are mentioned in a guide book of Sofia from 1910. They are located *"opposite the Central Market Hall"*, also an imposing building which opened its doors in 1911 (work of the Bulgarian architect Naum Torbov in the Bulgarian neo-Byzantine style, popular at the time). There is mention of *"the small baths, already raised by the large baths that are in a process of building"*. Then there is an explanation that these baths are *"the best in the kingdom. The water is crystal clear, its taste is a bit unpleasant with a hint of hydrogen sulfide, showing a weak alkaline reaction; its temperature is 47.2^0C."* A schedule is also included in the guide; it states that on Mondays the baths were intended for the exclusive use of the soldiers; Tuesdays, Thursdays and Saturdays (5:00 am – 22:00) – for men; Wednesdays and Fridays (same time) – for women; Sunday morning – for men again – 1st class, while Sunday afternoons (at a much cheaper rate) were specifically for the poor. And if somebody didn't fancy the public hammam, they could've asked for a bath for their personal use – 1st or 2nd class, paid accordingly (the rates are indicated).

While these developments were going on in Sofia, King Ferdinand was occupied with his own housing projects. He had bought an old farm with extensive grounds (80 hectars) on the outskirts of Sofia and was busy transforming it into a palace which was to become known as Vrana. Initially a two-storey hunting lodge was constructed, followed later by a much larger building, the Palace. The hunting lodge is the work of Bulgarian architect George Fingov and *"the architectural design combines an exquisite interpretation of the Plovdiv baroque with Viennese decorative elements, and is considered one of the masterpieces of Bulgarian architecture from the beginning of the 20th century"* (from the webpage of Simeon, the grandson of King Ferdinand I).

The Palace itself is the work of Bulgarian architect Nicola Lazarov and it took two years to build – from 1912 to 1914. From the same web page we learn that *"its architecture is an interpretation of Byzantine and 19-century Bulgarian revival-style influences, combined with art nouveau and French classicism. This sophisticated architectural language is subject to a consistently executed baroque composition, extrapolated to the park surroundings with ponds and floral decorative compositions"*. Czech landscape designer Anton Kraus was commissioned to transform the park, aided by a few more foreign specialists, brought in for this venture: Jochen Kelerer, Austrian rock-garden specialist and botanist, Joul Lochot, French landscape architect and Wilhelm Schacht, German landscape architect. There were already ponds and rock gardens and the team worked to create an outstanding 19th century style English park, come botanical gardens, to the liking of Ferdinand, an enthusiastic botanist and gardener.

Back in the centre of the capital city, construction on a new theatre building was well *underway,* the work of the renowned Viennese architects Ferdinand Fellner and Hermann Gottlieb Helmer, both specialised in this field. This splendid neoclassical building in red, white and gold, situated in the heart of the city, took the place of an old wooden structure that had also housed a theatre. The 40 metre high façade comprises a large triangular pediment, supported on six white marble columns, depicting Apollo and reclining muses. Two towers rise behind, each one topped by a sculpture of the goddess Nike, portrayed as a trumpeter in a chariot.

The National Theatre opened its doors on 3rd January 1907 with a special presentation. Prince Ferdinand, who attended this first spectacle, was booed and jeered at by a crowd of students, who were protesting, not just because only the ruling elite and the rich upper class were invited to the special event, but also against the overall politics of the Prince. Ferdinand retaliated the very next day by closing the University for 6 months and dismissing the professors and lecturers. This did not go down well. The Minister of Education, Ivan Shishmanov, after trying in vain to reinstate them back and finding no remedy for the situation, decided to resign. His successor brought in 70 foreign lecturers and high school educators to teach at the University, but most students were not interested to pursue their education in such conditions; only 7 students subscribed to the courses and eventually, this absurd situation came to an end with the new government of the Democratic Party which brought the former professors back.

The University of Sofia was expanding. It did not have a campus and was spread all over the place. In 1906 there was a competition for the design of a new building (in fact initially a group of 10 or so buildings). It was won by the French architect Henri Bréançon. The project was very ambitious and the building plans were not finalised before the start of the First World War. Bulgaria fought on the losing side, so after the war, the University's governing body had to abandon the pricey project. However, the University needed a building, therefore in 1920 Jordan Milanov, a Bulgarian architect, was charged with the alteration of the existing project and it was he who scaled it down to one single building.

The First World War marked the end of an era as much in Bulgaria as elsewhere. In the aftermath of the Bulgarian defeat, in

1918, King Ferdinand abdicated in favour of his son, who reigned under the name Boris III. One year after Boris's accession, Alexander Stamboliyski, the leader of the Bulgarian People's Agrarian Union, was elected Prime Minister. Though popular with the large peasant class, Stamboliyski earned the animosity of both the middle class and of the military. The political situation in the country in the early inter-war years was very unstable, but Stamboliyski made concerted efforts to improve relations with the rest of Europe and as a result, Bulgaria became the first of the defeated countries to join the League of Nations in 1920.

Meanwhile in the beginning of 1923, there was a festival presented in the National Theatre under the pompous title of "Apotheosis of our National Dramatic Art", to mark both the 65th Jubilee of the first theatre presentation in the country and also 15 years since the inauguration of the building. But this Jubilee didn't start well. The very first evening, 4th February, during the performance a bomb attack was carried out against the Prime Minister, Alexander Stamboliyski. Luckily, no one was hurt and the performance went on.

A few days later on 10th February 1923, was the presentation of a well loved play, based on *Christoph von Schmid*'s "Genoveva", the most popular theatrical production during the Bulgarian Revival. The story of Genoveva (or Geneviève) originates from a German legend, similar to the tale of Griselda, Desdemona and so many other heroines, whose unwavering loyalty was severely tested by suspicious and jealous husbands. While this melodrama was going on, another real life drama was about to unfold. It was during the fifth act of this sentimental drama that fire erupted in the theatre. Talk about an electric atmosphere!

We might see the funny side of it today, but at the time it wasn't a laughing matter – the outcome was truly disastrous. What caused the fire? An electrical short circuit or a gas lamp? It was never ascertained. But a lot went wrong that night. The safety curtain didn't work properly - it got stuck a metre or so above the stage - and the fire propagated from the stage to the auditorium. Panic spread amongst the spectators. The main exits were closed, following a directive, given in the aftermath of the bomb attack, so people got out of the windows or ran onto the terrace. While the audience and even the police were getting away, actors, musicians, some members of the public and even school kids were trying to salvage whatever they could as the fire spread towards the back, where the offices and the storerooms were. Costumes, fixtures, furnishings, manuscripts – a desperate race with time took place amongst the flames and the smoke. The press reported the tragic accident in detail: *"The National Theatre, the pride and glory of Bulgaria, burnt down. Huge blazing flames engulfed it in a moment and destroyed it. Today there are just ruins left. Forlorn, the festive flags, left from the Jubilee, are blown by the wind, as are the laurel leaves, torn from the wreaths, presented to the theatre... Pain is twisting the heart, sorrow seizes the soul. Young and old alike cried when they watched how the flames were destroying the only national temple of art. Fate! Inaugurated in 1907 amidst scandals, after 15-years existence, its Jubilee celebrations were darkened by the bomb attack that took place in it. A week later it was destroyed."*

In spite of this the theatre building, like a Phoenix, rose from the ashes. It was restored six years later, in 1929, based on the design of the German architect Martin Duelfer. As well as the new reinforced concrete framework, the theatre's seating capacity was increased to over 1000. Sophisticated new stage mechanics, similar to those used in the best theatres in Europe, were imported from Germany. They work to this day and are used for all the performances on the big stage of the theatre.

On the other hand, the work on the University building, supervised by Milanov (who was charged with modifying the design of the winning French entry as we saw earlier), didn't start till the summer of 1924. The same year, the French architect Bréançon, not pleased with how things developed, started and won a judiciary procedure against the University's governing body for infringement of his author's rights. But the building work continued with a very committed architect Milanov in charge, doing his best. But he had been burning the candle at both ends for a long time; overcome by a nasty cold in the winter of 1932, he died at the building site on 8th February, before the end of the works. The building was finally inaugurated in December 1934. Additional wings were added later on, till the building took its present day appearance. The University library was housed in a separate building, dating from the same period, the work of two Bulgarian architects, Ivan Vasilyov and Dimiter Tsolov.

There was also an international competition for the monument of the so called King-Liberator (The Russian Tsar Alexander II) in 1900 and the winning project was that of Arnoldo Zocchi, a prominent Italian sculptor, author of numerous works commissioned in both Italy and around the world (Garibaldi in Bologna, Christopher Columbus in Buenos Aires etc). The King-Liberator monument was inaugurated in August 1907 and stands to this day opposite the Parliament building. According to an urban myth, when the monument was about to be finished in the winter of 1905, and already stood on its base, protected by wooden planks, there was a heavy storm, that wrecked the palisade and broke the sword of the Goddess of Victory. According to another version, the monument, made in Vienna, was then shipped down the Danube to the port of Lom and from there - on an ox drawn carriage to Sofia city, at which time, the sword was broken.

The prominent Bulgarian poet, Pencho Slaveikov, apparently was not at all impressed with that Goddess Nike. Her provenance did not appeal to his patriotic (or even nationalistic) ideas, judging by what he had to say about the new monument: *"Ahead of these troops with her wings wide open, flies some Goddess, whose name should've been indicated, so to become clear to us, the mere mortals, who the hell is she! A modern Bulgarian monument doesn't need such ancient Greek allegories..."* Pity, he should've known better! In fact Nike was highly regarded in these lands since Antiquity – the Thracians, who inhabited this area, were formidable warriors and worshiped the winged Goddess; judging by numerous archaeological finds, her image is depicted on a great many artefacts, especially on their armour, on rings or on coins.

A NEW WORLD OF TECHNOLOGICAL DEVELOPMENTS

The first tram went up boulevard Vitosha on the 30 November 1900: *"A big crowd was enjoying the view of the speeding tram and the sparkles appearing under its wheels and at the wire above. The tram goes fast and smoothly, is electrically lit and is furnished elegantly."* That's how the event was described by a local newspaper. According to Dimo Kazasov though, an eyewitness, who later described it in a memoir: *"The speed was 15 km/h, and the stylish furnishings consist of two long red velvet cushions, laid over the rough wooden benches in the first class compartment of the narrow short tram cars."*

It wasn't till 15 January 1901 when a permanent service was assured and even then just for two of the 6 tramlines ready at the time, in order, so the Municipality insisted, to allow the population to get used to the high speeds of the new traffic...

The renowned Bulgarian writer, Ivan Vazov is not particularly impressed by this new means of transport (*"In the Electrical Tram"*), not only on account of this *"netting of the air with a web of wires"*, but also he finds the experience unpleasant, the passengers *"packed like sardines or maybe like in Noah's Ark, choose whichever of the two comparisons you like, with travellers from both sexes and all ages."*

He wasn't very excited with the bicycle either. In one of his short stories (*"Inhospitable Village"*) he talks about an enthusiastic Russian cyclist, riding *"his two-wheel machine"* in a cloud of dust on a very hot day somewhere in the extensive Sofia plain, who stops in a village and talks to the peasants, who jokingly refer to his bike as *"devils wheels"*.

The motorcar had already made its appearance before the start of the new century. In 1907 a private firm, "Dundov&co" started a public transport service, transporting passengers from Sofia to the town of Samokov and back in a 6-seater "De Dion Bouton". But the first car dealerships in Sofia date from 1910. "Shpeter&Luskov" were the first official representatives of the

Ford Motor Company in Bulgaria, while the Sofia-based dealer Alexander Kirov started to import the German made Benz and NAG and the American Studebaker. The same year the Bulgarian Automobile Club was founded.

Another exciting event that also happened in that year, but in Brussels, was that King Ferdinand of Bulgaria *"established a record of being the first monarch to go aloft in a heavier- than-air machine when he went for a flight in a biplane with M. Delaminne at the aerodrome of Kiewiet. Prince Boris, the heir apparent of the Bulgarian throne, and Prince Cyril, the King's second son, also flew."* The New York Times, July 16, 1910

The King appeared to be very pleased and announced that he would open an aerodrome in Bulgaria. He kept his word. The air field was to be at Bojurishte, just outside Sofia and its first wooden buildings were erected in 1912, together with a railway station, by the Bulgarian Royal Engineers directed by German specialists. The hangar and office buildings were added in 1913. King Ferdinand and his sons would go flying from there and they remain in history as some of the few Royals to take such risks at that time.

In 1912 at that same aerodrome is flown a glider, work of Assen Jordanoff, a 16-year old boy from Sofia, who later went on to become an inventor, avionics engineer, aviator and author of bestselling aviation books (that apparently even Neil Armstrong used to consult). A leading light on the international aeronautics stage, he was ultimately based in America. Back in 1912 he was something of a child-prodigy: *"In the last few days, on the field between the infantry camp and the pioneer barracks, a very young Bulgarian aviator-to-be practices with his glider built by himself. He is a high school schoolboy, Assen Jordanoff, the son of the Administrator of the Bank of Agriculture. He is fifteen, passionately keen on aviation and as a child, fashioned toys that could fly. Last year, when visiting France and Italy, he saw the biplane of Maslennykov and Tchernyak, and from then on thought seriously to conquer the air himself. His glider is a very simple, light affair, based on the constructions of the Wright brothers and*

of Farman. It is 7 meters long, 1.20 m wide, with a surface area of 14 m2 and weighs 23 kg. Yesterday he flew for over 12 minutes and reached an altitude of 10 to 12 meters. This young man's glider deserves praise, especially from aviation specialists."
Newspaper "Utro" ("Morning"), 16 February 1912

Three years later, in 1915, Assen, who had gained more experience, designed and built the first Bulgarian-made airplane. He came up with an ingenious idea, to add a third, flap-like wing, which prevents the plane from losing altitude. He test flew it in the summer of the same year. The plane was named after him *Diplane (biplane) Yordanov-1* and in the space of only one year Bulgaria produced 23 planes. August 10, 1915 is considered as the launch date of the Bulgarian aircraft industry.

Meanwhile the Grand Bioscope arrived in the Bulgarian capital; in the autumn of 1904 a new shed (or rather a tent) appeared near the Lions' Bridge in Sofia and the Sofianites were introduced to the 7th art for the first time. In fact, it was another Czech, Jan Prohaska, who lived in Sofia that is connected with the dawn of the cinema in the country (*kino* in Bulgarian). Prohaska sold a kinematoscope (magic lantern) to Vladimir Petkov, a Bulgarian circus actor turned entrepreneur, who then started the whole thing.

This first improvised movie theatre would show short films and comedy sketches. But the location was not well chosen, a bit to one side, and the "cinema" was not a big success. It had to be moved nearer the city centre.

However, a 12-year old boy, Vasil Gendov, who saw a film there called "Smuggler Dogs", was so impressed that after completing his studies abroad (Vienna and Berlin), on his return home, about 10 years later, he made the first ever Bulgarian feature film titled "*Bulgaran is a Gallant*". The film was a black and white silent movie, a short comedy. Gendov was not just the scriptwriter and the producer of the film, but also starred in it as the main protagonist, Balgaran. Balgaran, a courteous young bloke, meets a pretty young lady in the street and tries to impress her with flowers; she decides to teach him a lesson and asks him to accompany her to the market place and to help her with carrying her purchases. They go to a restaurant where he pays the bill and then they go to her place where they meet her husband. The woman then asks her husband to pay her "bag carrier" and Balgaran is given a coin for his efforts. The movie was shown in the Modern Theatre – a purpose built cinema that had opened in 1907 on Marie-Louise Street.

There was already another cinema in Sofia at the time, the Apollo Theatre, showing films and newsreels. On 21st November 1908 a short documentary was shown there, featuring King Ferdinand returning to Sofia from the city of Turnovo after proclaiming the independence of Bulgaria and the foundation of the 3rd Bulgarian Kingdom on 22nd September 1908.

FOREIGN VISITORS TO THE CAPITAL

Harry De Windt, a Special Correspondent of the "Westminster Gazette", an explorer and author of many books, is very favourably impressed with the Bulgarian capital in 1907 and doesn't have any reservations about its transport system (he refers to the trams as "street cars"). He remains in Sofia for awhile and describes his experiences in his book "Through Savage Europe": *"...at this point the journey ended and the "Orient-Express" clattered into the handsome Gare at Sofia having accomplished the journey from Paris in under 48 hours. The capital of Bulgaria occupies the same site as the squalid poverty-stricken town once governed by the Porte. No mushroom city in Western America ever sprang so quickly into a prosperous being from the ashes of filth and a corrupt administration. Twenty years ago the mean looking buildings and foul dark streets of Sofia rendered the place a nest of filth and disease and its rapid conversion into a modern city of fine buildings broad, well-paved streets, and pleasant parks and gardens, is one of which Bulgarians may well feel proud."*

"The new Palace and "Sobranie" or House of Parliament, he goes on to say, *would grace any European capital and so would the hotels, theatres, restaurants, street cars, and electric light.*

Everything here is more up-to-date than in Belgrade; French and German are spoken in shops and hotels and you might walk on smooth asphalt instead of painful cobbles." De Windt finds the cost of living *"absurdly cheap – a leg of mutton costs tenpence, meat is only threepence a pound and 12 delicious apples can be bought for one penny and other fruit in season as cheaply."*

De Windt goes on to state that he would happily live in Sofia were it not for the political unrest that reigns in the city: *"For the close connection between politics and bloodshed is anything but agreeable to the peaceful stranger from Western Europe."* He then sombrely describes the horrific assassination of Stambolov, the Prime Minister in 1895, while he was driving home with a friend from the Union Club. He also explains that *"political executions" are of weekly occurrence in Sofia though you may walk through the darkest and loneliest streets in the small hours without fear of molestation"*. He reckons that people are so used to them that when a member of the Macedonian Committee was shot dead in broad daylight in the public gardens, *"the incident created less excitement than a cab accident in Piccadilly"*.

De Windt doesn't mince his words while writing about Prince Ferdinand. He says that the prince is not very popular with his people, partly because he hardly stays in the country (probably from fear of assassination), but also on account of his extravagant lifestyle; he quotes that his marriage cost £ 130 000 and while on his journeys the prince may run up expenses of as much as £100 per day!

De Windt also shares his impressions of the local people, who, he finds, *"if less hospitable, more serious and better read than the Servians"* (Serbs). The Bulgarians are also *"more up to date as regards the treatment of the Jews, who in Sofia, at any rate enjoy the same privileges as in that earthly paradise of the modern Israelite – England."* He adds that the remainder of the population *"is very mixed and you hear German, Russian, Italian and Greek spoken on all sides as well as the native language."* There were less than 2000 Turks left and only one active mosque, the others being used *"for secular purposes"*. These Turks were happy enough with their lot for *"the Mahometans (Muslims) in Sofia are treated exactly like Bulgarian subjects"* and *"nothing in the world,* he says, *would induce them to return to their own distressful country."*

The Englishman stayed at hotel Bulgaria (*hotel de Bulgarie*), an *"excellent establishment"*, adjoining the Palace, *"a fine building in the style of Tuileries"* and overlooking the public gardens *"and when a military band was the attraction I frequently saw Christian and Muslim strolling about on the friendliest terms"*.

A Bulgarian friend of his, also a journalist, whose name he withholds and just calls him B, told him that the Palace only needs a *"to let sign"*, for it always looks so deserted with its blinds lowered for two thirds of the year. This same friend also took him to see *"the House of Parliament which cost over £70 000 and which is indeed a contrast to the ramshackle Skupshtina at Belgrade."* B lived *"in a pretty villa"* but he and his *"beautiful wife (pretty women are as numerous here as they are rare in Servia) had to lay the cloth for super, their domestic having left the house at a moment's notice."* Apparently it was not easy to get servants in Sofia at the time and the Bulgarian girls were known for their character, this one in question having left *"in a huff"*, because her mistress failed to formally introduce her to some visitors during that day! To get round this problem, an agency saw its chance and started to recruit *"German girls much to the delight of the ladies of Sofia"*.

William Miller, the English journalist, concurs: *"no Bulgarian will ever enter domestic service unless absolutely driven to it by extreme poverty."* He then adds that *"the servants consider themselves on an absolute equality with their employers and insist on being introduced to, and shaking hands with, the visitors."* He even reveals that *"the cleverest Bulgarian novelist of the day, Mr Ivan Vazoff – whose best work "Under the Yoke", has been translated into English, has made this subject the theme of one of his amusing sketches of life in the Bulgarian capital."*

Now let's go back to Mr De Windt - there was just one thing that this gentleman was not so happy about during his time in

Sofia – the lack of night life. The Bulgarians, too engrossed in politics, seemed not that bothered about theatres and the *"Bulgarian is made of sterner stuff than his frivolous pleasure loving neighbour. This is partly shown by the proportion of schools and educational establishments throughout the country, which even now number more than twice those of Servia. Sofia had hitherto lacked a University, but a fine building is now being erected for that purpose."*

He then adds that the schools and "gymnasia" (high schools) are intended mostly for the middle and lower classes, while the rich send their children to be educated in Western Europe…Times change, people don't – the well to do Bulgarians nowadays still tend to send their offspring to study abroad, even if this means that they have to tighten their belts and work very hard.

De Windt is happy with the climate, saying that at any time of year, except summer and early autumn it's *"healthy and exhilarating"*, but then complains about the *"deplorable"* drainage system, which, he hopes would be sorted out before too long.

De Windt left Sofia on a winter's day to pursue his journeys. From his bedroom window he looked at a wintry scene *"a Christmas card, designed by nature. The previous day had resembled Calcutta in July; but I noticed that the shady spot in the public gardens where we had then discussed cool drinks was now concealed by a carpet of snow."* Climate change one hundred years ago?

Arthur Douglas Howden Smith, an American journalist, arrived in Sofia that very same year. He stayed there for a time before joining a Bulgarian-Macedonian troop, a remarkable experience which he describes in his vibrant memoir *"Fighting the Turk in the Balkans; An American's Adventures with the Macedonian Revolutionists"*.

His impressions of Sofia are not that dissimilar from De Windt's. He also arrives by train to the *"clean, yellow station at Sofia"*. And although a friend had advised him to carry a gun, he finds that *"a stranger is perfectly safe in Bulgaria and Sofia is regarded by foreigners who have visited it, as the best policed city* on the Continent". He remarks on the street lighting, the trolley-cars, the telephones, but notes that *"Sofia has not been entirely civilized as to lose its Old-World charm, its spicy aroma of the East."*

To be sure some of his comments might sound a touch patronising; but that should be forgiven for Smith means well - he definitely likes the Bulgarians, he considers *"the sturdy, sober, industrious peasantry"* as the *"back-bone"* of Bulgaria. However, he finds it ludicrous to watch these same peasants from the neighbouring villages of Sofia, climbing onto the tram in Sofia (that he calls a street car) in a *"Brooklyn-like style"* (whatever that style might be), while wearing their quaint, lavishly embroidered traditional dress. And although he is amused by their sartorial choice, he perceives them as the *"most picturesque"*. Unlike some other visitors to Sofia, that we mentioned, Smith is impressed with the setting of the Bulgarian capital at the foot of Vitosha (which he calls Vitoshak) and likes the climate: *"Sofia is beautifully situated on a plateau 1800 feet above the sea, surrounded on all sides by mountains. Rising sheer above the town to the west and south, towering upward like a wall is the mountain of Vitoshak. It feels chilly in the early morning hours, one looks up at Vitoshak. If his top is white with snow it is a bad sign, but if the snow has disappeared or is melting, then people know that the sun's warmth is increasing. In the evening the inhabitants look toward the gap on the right flank of Vitoshak, known as "The Barometer". When a clear sky shows through, so the tradition goes, the next day will be pleasant. There are few times of the year, indeed, when the climate is not delightful, and it is always healthful."*

Smith sneers at the pomp of Prince Ferdinand, as he tries to outdo his English cousin, King Edward. He is amused when a coachman, who takes him for a rather bumpy ride *"over a rocky way full of ruts a cat could hardly climb out of"*, declares it to be Levsky Boulevard. But then he is quick to explain that this boulevard was a waste ground during the time of the Turks but now *"is lighted with electricity and planted with shade trees"*. The American is surprised by the large military presence in such a poor country and deems the buildings of the Officers' Club and the Ministry of War as rather large, while at the same time the city hall, that was supposed to be *"as big if not bigger than that in New York"*, is left unfinished due to lack of funds. When Smith investigates he discovers that nobody resents the fact that a third of the annual budget goes to the War Department, this being seen as *"a necessary evil"*.

But the peasants, Smith says, have also given donations for the building of *"a cathedral, which will be the largest in the Balkans, and lined with marble"*. The cathedral in question is Alexander Nevski, which was finished in 1912. Sienna and Carrera marble in the entrance, Venetian mosaics, Brazilian onyx and African alabaster elements, no money was spared to embellish the edifice. The golden domes of Alexander Nevski have since become a distinct landmark on the urban landscape of the Bulgarian capital.

Neither Smith, nor de Windt mention the "yellow brick road", probably not so surprising having in mind that the paving of the centre of Sofia starts that very year, 1907 and goes on till 1909. Still, the paving stone used, being so unusual, undoubtedly must've raised the curiosity of the visitor. The Bulgarian King Ferdinand is quoted in various sources as being the benefactor of this street embellishment; his extravagant taste being the reason for getting the expensive ceramic paving bricks on the occasion of his wedding to Princess Marie-Louise. In fact the marriage took place in 1893 and the Princess died in 1899 after dutifully giving birth to a fourth royal child. However there is documentation in the archives, to show the involvement of the mayor of Sofia, Martin Todorov; he manages to obtain a loan from German banks, sets a budget; a Bulgarian firm wins the contract and arranges for the ceramic paving bricks to be imported from the Austro-Hungarian Empire (the material used is a limestone from that region, known as mergel/marga, extracted from a mine in the vicinity of Budapest). One whole part of the city centre is thus covered with yellow paving stones – very impressive but lethal when it's wet or icy!

The French geologist and writer Louis de Launay published a book on Bulgaria in 1907, *"Bulgaria of Yesterday and Tomorrow"*. Although he is not so enthusiastic about the capital of new Bulgaria, he has some interesting observations to share. Like so many other visitors, Launay is definitely taken with the *"lofty Vitosha, towering above Sofia, its granite summit, enveloped by clouds"*; *"this picture of Vitosha in the background, makes for all the beauty of Sofia's panorama..."*

Launay only mentions some of the buildings he has caught sight of on his way from the station to the centre of town – European style houses, *"the last mosque standing"*, *"an imposing yellow rendered building with a bit of a garden and a grille, representing the palace of the Prince"*, the Parliament building, a public garden, the beginning of an elegant district, in the style of the "West End", at the finish of which a sort of a "Bois de Boulogne" spreads out into the countryside. *"The impression I have of Sofia on the whole,* says Launay, *with its spaced houses, surrounded with gardens, sort of fine airy cottages on wide avenues, is of a nice country suburb near London or of an English colonial town. This impression is due to the fact that the modern city is entirely built out anew into rectangles, firstly framed by straight roads at right angles, before even having the houses constructed, like in the new cities in Australia, America or South Africa."*

Launay is mostly interested in the geological resources, of course, especially in the thermal springs. He underlines the fact that the Turks were particularly fond of hot baths, as much as the Byzantines and the Romans before them; *"their rudimentary installations are still very popular with the Bulgarian people."* However Launay reckons that *"these abundant, salutary waters could be put to a better use."* He has high hopes that something would be done, because for years, a very distinguished man has been working on this, the head of the Mining Department in person, a Mr. Michailovsky, a fellow graduate of the Ecole des Mines de Paris, who has already implemented some excellent water collection systems. The future looked bright in those pre-war years, but wasn't it the same elsewhere in Europe?

WARS, TERRORIST ACTS AND CIVIL UNREST IN THE FIRST HALF OF THE 20TH CENTURY

On 22 September 1908, taking advantage of the chaos that ensued in the Ottoman Empire following the Young Turk revolution, Prince Ferdinand proclaimed Bulgaria's *de jure* independence from the Turkish overlordship. On top of that, he also proclaimed the country a kingdom (known in history books as the Third Bulgarian Kingdom) and himself a king – taking the traditional Bulgarian title Tsar.

This was yet another breach in the 1878 Treaty which the Great Powers did not appreciate. The Bulgarian Independence Crisis caused rising tensions in Europe. The British diplomats were wondering whether the Coburger on the Sofia throne was "going off his head" and what course of action was he going to pursue afterwards. "Bad Coburg blood", understood to imply mental deficiency, was an allusion frequently made in those times, applied to various European Royals of this illustrious dynasty.

Ferdinand's deed brought a rash of activity on the European diplomatic stage. In the early days of 1909 there is talk of *"a sort of political duel"* between St. Petersburg and Vienna for dominance in Sofia. The Turks, usually playing off the Powers against each other, must've rubbed their hands in glee. Still, Bulgaria's independence was finally internationally recognised in the spring of that year.

From 1912 onwards Bulgaria got involved in various armed conflicts, starting with the Balkan wars, then the First World War, followed by some more or less peaceful years till the beginning of WW II, when once again the country ended up on the wrong side of the conflict. The result was yet another defeat and 45 years under the Soviet sphere of influence.

If the Balkan wars were truly disastrous, WW I is seen to have been "a national catastrophe" for Bulgaria. In the aftermath of the war King Ferdinand was forced to abdicate on 3/10/1918 in favour of his son, who became king under the name Boris III.

WW I

The turn of the century is a period of prosperity and growth for the newly liberated Bulgarian state. Sadly this period comes to an end with the outbreak of the Balkan Wars, which end in catastrophe for the country and then soon afterwards, just when it's on its way to recovery, World War I starts and, although belatedly, Bulgaria can't do anything else but to join in.

The headlines of the Anglo-Saxon press of that period (Times Sydney Sun Services, October 4th) declare: *'Definite agreement concluded* (between Bulgaria and the Central Powers) *Fears overcome'* (The Duke of Mecklenburg is said to have succeeded in overcoming Bulgaria's fears). At the same time the French Le Temps (October 4th) asserts: *Sofia under Martial Law – Teutonising signs apparent – Fooling the public,* then explaining that *"the price of bread has been fixed, and all meetings have been prohibited. The Municipal Council decided to name the three principal Sofia squares 'Berlin', 'Budapest' and 'Vienna', while German and Bulgarian songs are being sung in the cafes, payments are made in marks and many other Teutonising signs are apparent."* Le Petit Parisian quotes *'a traveller from Bulgaria'* as having said that *"their rulers in Sofia are fooling the public, one day issuing proclamations that the army is going to march against Turkey, and next day proclaiming that the mobilisation is against Vienna. The soldiers declare that they will not fight against their old Russian comrades, and most of the troops lack enthusiasm."* On 5th October the headlines are already forewarning of impending disaster, quite prophetic in fact (Times Sydney Services, quoting a leading article from The London Times): *Bulgaria's Path Spells Suicide. Mournful and Tragic Sight:* "Russia has taken the only possible course by issuing her ultimatum. The paper fears that the stern protest will not deter Bulgaria's ruler and pliant Ministers from pursuing their course and violating the whole spirit of the brief history of modern Bulgaria in the Balkans. It is a sad story. There has been no sight more mournful or more tragic than the preparations by Bulgaria to shatter every prospect of Balkan unity by marching to battle beside the Turks, who oppressed the Bulgarians for 500 years. The path Bulgaria has taken spells suicide."

Then Bulgaria attacked Serbia.

The New York Times (31st October 1915) reports:
"BULGARS WON HEIGHTS, CLIMBING ON ALL FOURS; Storming of Zaiecar Puts Serbian Army in Peril, Says Sofia.

SOFIA, Wednesday, Oct. 27, (Delayed.) -- The fall of Pirot this morning was a severe blow to the Serbian Army, since the reduction of this strong position leaves open the road to Nish and invites a strong Bulgarian advance toward the centre of Old Serbia. "

Extract from Raemaekers' cartoon History of The War: "At the same moment the Bulgarians in great force attacked the Serbians on their right flank and by the 28th joined forces with the Teutonic troops."

Meanwhile, on 28th October, the inhabitants of the Bulgarian capital were witness to the arrival of the first German Zeppelin in the skies of Sofia. In its issue of October 28, 1915 the Bulgarian newspaper "New Age" wrote: "Yesterday, around 10 a.m., the citizens of Sofia admired the wonderful sight that was the arrival of the first German Zeppelin. The pleasant autumn day allowed this air monster to fly round several times over the city. The citizens of the capital emerged out on the streets to watch the huge oval object in the air, from the front boat-car of which flew the Bulgarian flag. Many citizens were greeting it by taking their hats off and loudly shouting "Hurrah". The Zeppelin, 174 meters long, flew at a height of about 150 meters. At about 12 a.m. it had to go down in the field of the Sugar factory."

King Ferdinand and other dignitaries were already waiting there along with "thousands of people come to see the wonderful work of the German genius." The King was particularly impressed. This is what was reported in a New York Times article of November 11th 1915: "'This is one of the great moments of my life!' King Ferdinand exclaimed as he welcomed the crew of the *airship and its distinguished passenger. The Zeppelin, after virtually all Sofia had visited and admired it, started on its return voyage."* The distinguished visitor in question was said to have been Duke Adolf Friedrich of Mecklenburg.

Another newspaper (The Mercury - from Rome 12th November) in an article with a headline *"Bulgaria and Germany Celebration at Sofia"* reports that: *"Yesterday King Ferdinand of Sofia gave a banquet in honour of the arrival at Sofia of a Zeppelin airship. The Duke of Mecklenburg, Prince Hohenlohe and General Liman Von Sanders attended. King Ferdinand proposed the health of the Kaiser and the Alliance with Germany and smashed his glass after drinking the contents. Everybody present imitated the example."*

A very different article appeared in the Daily Mail under the title *"Why the Zeppelin went to Sofia"*; said to be from its Parisian correspondent, it was a piss-take of the Bulgarian monarch. For those who appreciate English humour – enjoy it in full!

"The King of Bulgaria according to Balkan advices has an exaggerated fear of aeroplanes. When he learned that English and French airmen were cooperating with the Serbian Army, he became very anxious and was reduced to a state of terror on hearing that aircraft had been landed at Salonica.

He immediately summoned a Ministerial Council and, declaring that it was necessary to protect Sofia from hostile raids, ordered all the Bulgarian airmen to be recalled from the front. A bomb-proof roof was erected over the royal palace and at night search lights swept the sky ceaselessly. The trembling monarch even asked the Kaiser to send a Zeppelin and dispatched feverish telegrams to hasten its voyage. When it arrived at Sofia King Ferdinand conferred decorations on all its officers. The Zeppelin commander asked the Sovereign when he was to leave for the front. 'I don't know,' was the reply. 'You had better pass the winter at Sofia.' From that day the airship has not gone beyond the outskirts of the capital."

The Zeppelin arrived only one more time in Bulgaria, after the war, in 1929. It caused a big furore, flying over Alexander Nevski

Cathedral to the sound of the church bells. Even the Council of Ministers interrupted a meeting, so its members were able to admire the view from the balcony of the building. This time the Zeppelin did not land and after about 20 minutes or so, the big airship flew away. A popular, humorous song from that time goes as follows:

"The zeppelin arrived in our country
No visa, no formality - what an audacity!"

The first appearance of the Zeppelin over Sofia however had been in direct connection with the Great War in which these "flying boats" were actively used for reconnaissance and bombing of the enemy, and their menacing appearance caused confusion and fear among ordinary people.

Despite Bulgaria's initial military success, the war was becoming increasingly unpopular in the country and various mutinies broke out in the ranks of the army, inspired by the Russian revolution (February 1917); these escalated into the so called "Soldiers uprising" (September 1918), quashed by the authorities. By this time the country is on its knees. On 30th September 1918 the Armistice of Thessalonica is signed and Bulgaria, along with its allies, will have a high price to pay. On 3rd October Ferdinand abdicates in favour of his son, who reigns under the name Boris III.

The Treaty of Neuilly-sur-Seine, signed on 27th November 1919 required Bulgaria to cede certain territories to its neighbours (including most of Macedonia to the newly established Yugoslavia), to reduce its army to 20 000 men, to pay reparations of £100 million, but also to disband its air force. The military aircraft are to be destroyed and so the Bulgarian military aviation, renowned after the Balkan war, ceased to be. Even the airfield at Bozhurishte, just outside Sofia, narrowly escaped destruction and was turned into a civil airfield. Later on, in 1930, the first airport was built there. Then in 1937, disregarding the clauses of the Neuilly Peace Treaty, King Boris formally handed the military flags to the newly formed air forces at the airport of Bozhurishte which once again became military.

THE COUP D'ETAT OF 9TH JUNE 1923

Meanwhile, in the interwar period, the country had to recover from the scars of the war and to deal with the post-war crisis. In 1920 the Agrarian Party, led by Alexander Stamboliyski, came to power. Stamboliyski had challenging times ahead. Although popular with the peasant class, he had some very powerful adversaries amongst the land owners, the Military and even the intelligentsia. He didn't make friends with the Macedonians in Bulgaria either and was hostile towards The Internal Revolutionary Macedonian Organisation (VMRO). The latter preferred an armed conflict in order either to reclaim Macedonia for Bulgaria or to gain its independence. There was also a lot of infighting amongst the various factions within the organisation which did not help their cause at all. At any rate Stamboliyski was not having any of it. He favoured the idea of a Federation of the southern Slavs. He pushed for various reforms and effectively established a dictatorship by the Agrarian party, backed by the so called Orange Guard Corps, recruited from amongst the peasants.

In 1923 Stamboliyski, whose government was becoming more and more autocratic, signed an agreement with the newly founded Yugoslavia, concerning the border between the two countries and suppressing VMRO. This did not go down well amongst his fellow citizens and the Bulgarian Macedonians in particular, and so gave his enemies the motive to act. The retaliation was quick and merciless - a coup d'état (9th June 1923), the assassination of Stamboliyski and the coming to power of a very right wing government under the leadership of Professor Alexander Tsankov, that instigated the so called "white terror" against the Agrarians and the Communists.

The coup, of course, was organised by the military, for Stamboliyski had never managed to obtain their support – since the end of the war they had had no representation in the cabinet. A group of officers had formed the Military Union, an organisation that de facto, was commanding the army.

The opposition parties had conspired with the Military Union and together they had decided on the course of action. The preparations for the coup went ahead without a hitch. Long before the crack of dawn on 9th June 1923, an order was given for the garrisons at Sofia to block the roads, cut the telephone lines and to take control of key positions such as police stations, post offices and train stations, while the Agrarian ministers and deputies were arrested. Three hours were sufficient for this deed and by 5 a.m. the new government of Alexander Tsankov was installed in the capital; so far no casualties.

The next morning the initiators of the coup had an audience with the King, at his palace at Vrana, which lasted hours. Finally he agreed to ratify the new cabinet, on the condition that the new government should include Agrarians and that no repressions were to follow. Both conditions were disregarded.

Meanwhile Stamboliyski, who was not in Sofia at the time of these crucial events, nevertheless tried to gather the Agrarians from the provinces, who were not going to give in without a fight, and started an uprising, known as the June uprising, which, badly organised and carried out by mostly inexperienced peasants, was quickly crushed. Stamboliyski himself was apprehended and allegedly executed by a bunch of extremists from VMRO.

The communists, who had a military organisation of their own, did not support the Agrarians, seeing it as *"a power struggle between rural and urban bourgeoisie"*, but came to regret it soon afterwards, especially when told off by Comintern (The Communist International, initiated in Moscow in 1919). Their insurrection, staged in September 1923 was too little, too late and was also brutally crushed by the army who had got wind of its preparation. And then the terror started in earnest. Both Agrarians and communists were persecuted and forced into hiding.

THE TERRORIST ATTACK AT ST NEDELIA CHURCH APRIL 1925

The repressive regime that was now in power was provoking civil unrest and the communist movement was gaining more supporters. The repressions against the communists were not going to continue without retaliation and an extreme left wing group decided to resort to violence and to wipe out the whole ruling elite in one go. They hoped to facilitate a Bolshevik invasion in the anarchy and chaos that would follow. The outcome is the bloodiest terrorist act in the history of Bulgaria.

The conspirators enlisted the cooperation of the verger of St. Nedelia cathedral who let them into the building, where they brought explosives, placed them under the roof above a pillar supporting the main dome at the south entrance of the church and got the bomb ready – it was to be detonated by a 15 m-long cord to allow the terrorists the chance to escape. The plan envisaged the assassination of a high ranking official, for whose funeral service all the leaders would flock to the cathedral St. Nedelia, making them an easy target. That was duly accomplished – General Constantine Georgiev was assassinated in front of St. Sedmochislenitsi church, as he was going to the evening service, accompanied by his granddaughter.

The date for the funeral service was set on the Maundy Thursday of the Holy Week, 16th April 1925. The funeral procession arrived at 15:00 h at the church and initially the coffin was placed exactly at the foot of the pillar where the explosive was installed. However it was later moved forward, due to the great confluence of people who had come for the ceremony. It was fortuitous for the country's leaders, who also moved along to be near the deceased. At 15:20 the bomb exploded, the main dome collapsed, burying a large number of people underneath. Around 500 people were injured and 150 people died, amongst them women and children, quite a few officers and 3 deputies. But all the government members survived, getting away with only slight injuries. The King was not present – he had narrowly escaped another kidnapping attempt, during which two other people were killed and so he was attending their funeral.

The shock was immense. It's not surprising that martial law was declared immediately afterwards and it lasted till 24th October. And while the country, in mourning, had to deal with the devastation wreaked in the aftermath of the terrorist act, the foreign press was full of sensationalist headlines decrying the violence in the Balkans. Meanwhile the government took repressive measures against the communists, and these came to be known as the April events.

The church itself had to be restored yet again. This was done in the period between 1927-1933 (by arch. Vasiliov and arch. Tsolov who more or less rebuilt it anew) and it was then that it took on its present day appearance. The gold plated iconostasis which had survived the assault was returned to the church, which was then inaugurated in April 1933.

THE COUP D'ETAT OF 19TH MAY 1934

"Last June a politician's coup made Bulgaria a virtual dictatorship under the leadership of one-eyed, Hitler-lipped Kimon Gueorguieff whose favorite cry was "Our government is neither Right nor Left, but STRAIGHT THROUGH THE MIDDLE" (TIME, June 4). First reports were that this Gueorguieff dictatorship had the full approval of Little Tsar Boris. But royalists in Austria and Hungary, trying hard to recoup their own fortunes through the restoration of downy-lipped Archduke Otto, learned almost immediately that Boris was practically a prisoner of the dictatorship."(Time, 4th February 1935, Bulgaria, Tzar's coup)

This coup d'état was also carried out by 800 officers from the Zveno Military organization and the Military Union led by colonel Damyan Velchev, who set out to overthrow the government of the so called Popular block and succeeded, just ahead of their rivals from the Popular Social Movement, who supported Alexander Tsankov.

On 19th May at 2:30 am all four entrances of the royal palace were blocked by a squad of officer-conspirators. Meanwhile other military units spread out around Sofia city and took over the major establishments, the Post Office, the railway station etc. The password was "sabre". Kimon Georgiev, chum of Damyan Velchev, marched into the palace accompanied by General Zlatev, with a decree for the new cabinet in his right pocket and an announcement of the tsar's abdication – in his left one. Boris III was not a fool. Realising that he didn't have much choice in the matter, he met the duo in his parade uniform and signed the decree. If you can't beat them, join them, as they say! The coup ended without a single shot being fired.

The conspirators installed a government under Kimon Georgiev and this government (despite its unpopularity) abolished the Turnovo Constitution (the Constitution of Bulgaria, adopted in 1879), disbanded the National Assembly and banned political parties, organizations and trade unions. Some economic measures were adopted, a state monopoly was introduced and as for a new foreign policy, Bulgaria established diplomatic relations with the USSR and moved closer to France.

However the King did not stay *"a prisoner of the dictatorship"* for long; he was just biding his time. And as the conspirators did not get on well and were not very united, the King managed eventually to oust Kimon Georgiev in a counter-coup in January 1935 and in April of the same year he appointed Andrey Toshev, a civilian whose loyalty he could trust, as his Prime Minister.

The King would've been in good spirits then, when on 3rd March 1935, the national holiday, he and his wife Giovanna hosted a Luncheon in the Royal Palace to commemorate the Liberation of Bulgaria from the Ottoman rule. Usually menus at the table of the Bulgarian Royal family were in French, but the celebration of 3rd March by its nature had to be an exception, so the menu, a copy of which is preserved, is in Bulgarian. It features *banitsa* as a starter; a Bulgarian national dish, a pastry stuffed with lamb's brains mixed with a sauce of white (feta) cheese, mushrooms and onion. This was followed by trout; fished from the lakes of Rila Mountain, baked in Champagne, then roast saddle of lamb with roasted vegetables and peas in butter. For dessert there was Crème Nadejda – baked custard (similar to *crème brûlée*), named after the King's sister, and fruits.

WW II, BOMBARDMENTS AND THE AFTERMATH

Despite its attempt to stay neutral, in March 1941 Bulgaria was embroiled willy-nilly in WW II and suffered the consequences.

The German invasion of the Soviet Union (22 June 1941) caused a wave of protests and triggered off a mass guerrilla movement led by the underground Communist Party. Bulgaria did not participate in the invasion neither did it declare war on the Soviet Union. However in December 1941 it was forced to declare a token war on both the United States and the United Kingdom. No wonder that the British and American Air Forces heavily bombarded Sofia, causing much death and destruction.

Meanwhile, after a visit to Germany on 28th August 1943, King Boris III, a popular monarch, suddenly died (possibly from a heart attack) at the age of 49. His son Simeon II was only 6 at the time, so a council of regents was set up. The untimely death of the Bulgarian king gave rise to all sorts of conspiracy theories. It appears that Hitler was furious with him for not joining in the attack on the Soviets and also on his refusal to deport the Jews within his realm. Reportedly, after his visit to the Fuehrer's headquarters, just a couple of weeks before his untimely death, the King had confided to his adviser Strashimir Dobrovitch (on 16th August): *"Hitler went into a rage when I refused his demands [...] Screaming like a madman, he attacked me and Bulgaria in a torrent of accusations and threats. It was horrible. But I didn't give in one inch! He tried to frighten me, but, instead, I calmly explained the situation, saying what I had to say, clearly and unequivocally, i.e., that I have decided that we should follow our own road. My hands are now free. [...] I saved you. Even if I have to pay for it!"*

Was he really poisoned? The two German doctors who attended him both believed that he had been administered a slow poison that takes weeks to work and which causes blotches on the skin of the sufferer before death occurs. In the wake of the grand state funeral in Alexander Nevski Cathedral the country was left in complete disarray - to mourn and to fight a war that nobody wanted.

And then the Americans and the British decided it was the moment to strike. From 14th November 1943 to 17th April 1944 eleven air strikes took place on Sofia. About 2000 civilians perished during that time. Lots of civic buildings were hit; some totally destroyed like the State Printing House, the District Court of Justice, the Odeon Theatre, the City Library (40 000 books burned), the Catholic Cathedral St. Joseph and also thousands of residential buildings, about 12 500 edifices in total. Other buildings, including the National Theatre, St. Spas church (9th century), the Theological Academy, The Parliament, the Bulgarian Agricultural Bank, the Bulgarian Academy of Science, the Central Mineral Baths, were all heavily damaged.

On 20th December 1943 at Bozhurishte, Lieutenant Dimitar Spisarevski on board of his Messerschmitt BF 109 Gustav was to take off, together with 35 other fighter pilots, to intercept 150 American military airplanes heading for Sofia. Did he have the premonition that this was going to be his ultimate mission? When his plane didn't start, the Bulgarian aviator had to take off in another one and arrived, somewhat belatedly, at the battle scene. Lieutenant Spisarevski aimed his aircraft at the group of 16 American B-24 Liberator bombers and crashed it into the leader of the formation. The American bomber split in the air and fell, never reaching Sofia, while the Messerschmitt of Spisarevski crashed near Pasarel. His body was found amongst the smoking debris of his plane. For his heroism he was promoted posthumously to the rank of Captain.

The worst bombardment was on 10th January 1944. It started at noon when the capital was attacked by 143 American bombers – "Flying Fortress" and 37 B-24 Liberators. Sofia Air Defence sent 39 interceptor aircraft to counteract them. They were backed up by a German group of 30 Messerschmitt Me 109 (Jagdgeschwader "Eismeer"). Their commander Captain Gerhard Wengel was shot down at Radomir, the only foreign pilot to lose his life defending the city of Sofia. He was only 4 days short of his 29th birthday.

But the worst was yet to come. For the civil population there was no respite - the bombardments continued throughout the night when 44 RAF Wellingtons arrived at the scene. General Stoyan Stoyanov, a fighter pilot who took part in numerous air combats remembers clearly that time. *"There was chaos in the* city, it looked like a picture of hell. Demolished houses and ploughed up streets, smouldering fires and ruins, damaged electric grid and burst water mains, cold and confusion, frightened populace furtively returning home – this is what Sofia was like at about 22:00 h. People were looking for their loved ones or just for a warm place to spend the night, when all of a sudden, without any warning from the sirens, they heard the sound of the artillery, saw the enemy aircraft and the bombs falling above them accompanied by the rumble of machine guns and cannon fire. The whole city was lit by fires and parachutes and lanterns were seen to slowly descend from the skies. Each and every one of us hid wherever we could, surprised by the bombardment."

Another heavy bombardment occured on 30th March 1944 when 370 American "Flying Fortresses" came, not for any military targets, but released their bombs above the historic centre of Sofia. 3575 buildings were demolished and 139 civilians lost their lives that day. An eyewitness, Krikor Aslanian, just a young kid at the time, clearly remembers that night: *"In the evening, can't remember what time it was we heard on the radio the chilling 'Achtung, achtung!' The American bombers were approaching Sofia again and soon after that the glowing orbs were released above the city. We were 25 km away, but could see them clearly as if they were above our heads. If one didn't know their destructive intention, one might think that there was a fête. Big, multicoloured, they fell above Sofia like a rain of toy balloons and illuminated the sky so in the dark night the capital was lit by thousands of suns. And then again bombs, again destruction, again fires. During this fatal night the capital of Bulgaria was subjected to the worst bombardment in its history. The old historic centre of the magnificent centuries old town was entirely destroyed. There were again lots of civil casualties, peaceful citizens – men, women, children, old folks. There were curiosities too. In front of the Bulgarian National Bank the bomb had flung a whole tramway rail up and had driven it vertically into the ground. On the corner of Clementina Street and Lege Street the blast had hurled a whole motor-car on the roof of the 4-storey building."*

The "glowing balloons" must have been incendiary devices, they are not explosives, but weapons designed to start fires.

One of the edifices demolished during the air raid, was the ancient 3-nave basilica "St. Nicholas of Myra, the Miracle-Maker", one of the most loved churches in the capital. However, miracles do happen, for there, amongst the ruins, a part of the iconostasis still stood intact and the icon of the patron saint was on it with a candle burning in front, as if to honour those who had perished and as a token of God's mercy.

The bombing that took place on 17th April 1944 became known as "Black Easter" for it fell on the second day of the celebrations. The raid was carried out by 350 bombers (B-17 and B-24) with an escort of 100 fighter planes – Mustangs and Lightnings. 749 buildings were totally destroyed. Casualties were 128 people killed and 69 wounded.

THE COUP D'ETAT OF 9TH SEPTEMBER 1944 AND THE RED ARMY IN SOFIA

On 26th August, concerned about the advance of the Red Army, the Bulgarian government hurriedly declared neutrality and ordered the German forces out of the country. It also opened peace talks with the USA and England. Meanwhile the Bulgarian communists, supported by Moscow, started preparations for an armed insurrection. On the 2nd September the German troops began to leave the country. The Soviet Union declared war on Bulgaria on 5th September and invaded its territory. The Bulgarian armed forces did not offer any resistance. On 8th September Bulgaria declared war on Germany and found itself at war with everyone!

Such was the situation when, during the following night, the Fatherland Front accomplished the coup d'état. The Fatherland Front was a coalition of antifascist leftwing parties founded in 1942. Kimon Georgiev, an officer who had had his fair share of coups, (having participated in both the June 1923 and the May 1934 coups, which earn him the nickname *"the old coup-maker"*), took control of this one as well and soon afterwards became

Prime Minister for a second time.

This coup d'état, subsequently called the "armed popular insurrection" against the monarchic-fascist dictatorship and the Nazi occupiers, and the subsequent triumphal arrival of the Red Army became the turning point for Bulgaria. It wasn't just a question of changing sides and joining the Allied Forces in the war with Nazi Germany, but cutting ties with its entire monarchic past and moving into the Soviet sphere of influence.

So on 9th September, Sofia awoke to find itself painted red and entered into a new age. The citizens of Sofia welcomed the Red Army with banners and flowers as they marched into the city. After months of heavy bombardment from the Allied Air Forces, the Bulgarian capital breathed a sigh of relief. Peace at last! But the rejoicing was cut short for now was the moment to settle scores, between the new political powers and the old ones. And this was going to last some time.

As the armed forces went on to the front, the city was left to lick its wounds.

POSTWAR PERIOD AND THE BEGINNING OF THE NEW MILLENNIUM

"Sofia is a model city no drunks, no disorderly gangs, the gardens around that pillared and pink-washed National Theatre, the ache of respectability. Banks of red roses, symbol of Bulgaria; colored fountains; the evening promenade of citizens. New international hotels spring up like dragon's teeth and your old-fashioned Sofianits mourns the elbowing-aside of the rusty old Thracian settlement, its Roman pavements and black-bricked Byzantine churches, its labyrinthine streets where you press yourself against a wall to let the tramcar squeeze through, its little shops such as you would find in a village. They are still there, but you have to poke about to find them. Much of cultural Sofia is semi-subterranean the Aleksander Nevsky full of medieval icons, the sunken church of St. Petka of the Saddlers. But Europe's second-highest city remains tightly-knit and you can be out of it and

halfway up Vitosha mountain, 6,000 feet, in half an hour, ' among deer, foxes and an alpine botany. It is a mandatory excursion, a good summit from which to plan your Bulgarian itinerary."

Sofia: it aches of respectability By Leslie Gardiner London Daily Telegraph, Sofia, Bulgaria, June 1979

This more recent period of the existence of the city is well documented and some of the people, instrumental in rebuilding it after the ravages of WW II, are still alive. The war had not only destroyed the old city centre, but had put an end to Musman's town plan (completed in 1938) and had opened the space for Stalinist type edifices that became the new face of Sofia. As Bulgaria ended-up in the Eastern bloc and therefore in the Soviet sphere of influence, it's not surprising that the style of architecture in its capital city Sofia tended to emulate that of its powerful ally.

The renowned archaeologist Magdalina Stancheva explains in one of her last interviews: *"What did they do? Five huge buildings in the city centre – The Home of the Party, flanked on each side by two more buildings. They put there the Central Department Store and Hotel Balkan – an inn for the official visitors and a shop, favoured by the entire country because it was stocked with merchandise not available elsewhere. The other two were enclosed Ministries – the Ministry of Heavy Industry (now Council of Ministers) and the Ministry of Electrification (now the Presidency). That's because they wanted to transform Bulgaria into a centre of heavy industry. According to the initial project, to the west, on the other side of the tramline, was to be the Council Hall, so the Largo to be entirely bounded. Thanks God, things changed. People realised that such architecture is old fashioned, that it's too heavy for Sofia, not for our scale and architectural traditions. So the building of the Council Hall was renounced."*

The largo was then called Lenin and a large white stone statue of him was erected there, facing St. Petka Church and the Home of the Party, although there is no connection whatsoever between the Soviet leader and the city of Sofia.

Here, to avoid confusion, lets clarify the term "largo"(from the point of view of town planning and not music): the noun "*largo*", which just derives from the Italian adjective "*largo*"('wide', 'spacious', 'ample', 'large'), is used in the sense of an *"open area in a city that is bordered by buildings or streets"*; though apparently smaller than a *"piazza"*. Sadly, instead of a nice place for walks, where one goes to see and to be seen, the Largo appears to have lost its soul. Says Architect Tangarov :
"The so called 'Largo' or central promenade, which stretches eastward from the Sheraton [now Balkan] *Hotel, is reduced to the absurd by the Stalinist monument-type buildings that surround it. Without any shops or restaurants, the "Largo" and also the space around the Rotunda "St. George" are deserted. Only from time to time do curious tourists come to have a look and take pictures of the ruins and the rubbish bins that surround them."*

In the mid 80s Tangarov and his team had a concept plan to develop the area behind the recently refurbished hotel: *"In the first instance, our idea for restoring the space of the 'apodyterium' in a contemporary style and to realise the winter-summer cafe-bar on the rooftop terrace above the restaurant, was accepted as being economical and very effective. But surprisingly the designer of the building and the investor categorically refused to discuss our proposal. The main reason which was given, during the Communist era, was that the terrace looks towards the office of the First Secretary and the Security Service would not allow such a thing."*

It was at about the same time that Tangarov ventured into one of the dark tunnels stretching exactly under St. Nedelia church (on the other side of the above mentioned hotel). That tunnel had been discovered during the building of St. Nedelia Church (1856 – 1865), but hadn't been explored at the time. More exploration was conducted in 1935 when speleologists penetrated it at the time of the building of the N 5 tramway stop. It became clear then that it was part of a Roman construction. They discovered a two storey tunnel, 6 m below ground level.

Down in this underground world, known only to the

speleologists, Tangarov has been the only architect to go in search of answers and that's how he discovered for himself the vast and really unique Roman emperors' *thermae*. It's easy to imagine Constantine the Great taking the waters there. The covered swimming pool, *natatio*, *"the largest and the best of all those discovered in Bulgaria",* makes Sofia the only capital in Europe to boast of so many antique mineral spas in such close proximity. *"The tunnels are high enough for the tallest basketball player to be able to walk in there;* Tangarov explains, *the lowest point of the 'Constantine's Baths' is 2.40 m. The swimming pool was in the central part, and the other three areas where Constantine might have had an enjoyable time, have got floor and wall heating – something unique for its time.*

Architect Tangarov came up with a quite daring, new wave idea of how to expose some of those antique relics and make them a focal point for the city centre. He and his team produced a model on four levels demonstrating the potential to display the treasures of the Forum of Roman Serdica. This project, quite revolutionary for its time, was hailed as a star project by many interested parties but never got off the ground, as frequently happened to undertakings that lacked Communist party support.

It is inevitable that the Communist era, architecturally, should leave its mark. Like it or not, you can't just cross-out 45 years of history. Besides, along with certain really ugly buildings of that era, some real gems were to be found that stood out and marked the urban landscape:

Mausoleum – now gone, was a simple neo-classical building, erected in a hurry – for just 6 days in 1949 to accommodate the mummified body of the late George Dimitrov, the Bulgarian communist "leader and teacher", following the example of Soviet Russia. This communist temple also doubled as a platform for subsequent country leaders to greet the crowd during the so called manifestations, commemorating important historical events or national holidays. 50 years later the new regime decided to get rid of it and for the remains of the late communist leader to be buried in the cemetery amongst the mere mortals.

Interestingly the demolition of the edifice took a day longer than the building work – a good week despite the modern machinery employed. It was a pity to destroy such an emblematic building, it could've been put to good use – to house the museum for example.

NDK – Palace of Culture with its surrounding gardens and soaring skyward Monument, dedicated to the 1300th anniversary of Bulgaria, a phallic symbol of ideological propaganda, now obsolete. Back in the 80s when it was built, NDK was a symbol of revival and progress, a showpiece, meant to impress the visitor. At the time there were not enough residential buildings to house the then 1 million or so Sofianites, but the Government carried on anyway, splashing-out on this sumptuous modern structure, which quickly became a focal point for young and old. It is certainly a well thought out complex, the striking Palace itself, the design of Alexander Barov, a prominent architect of the communist era, with its gardens, water features, subways, underground transport connections; making it accessible from any direction.

Only the huge monument, situated somewhat to one side, meant to illustrate the epic past of the country, spoils the effect. The work of a then famous sculptor, it's now just a ruin, its stone tiles, once there to embellish it, are gradually falling like autumn leaves, which has necessitated fencing it off for safety reasons. Its metal skeleton still remains there, in such a lamentable state that it only but adds to the overall feeling of sadness at the view of this whole grandiose project, once so vibrant, now left to rack and ruin, like so many of the creations of the old regime. At least NDK is still standing and there is some hope that someday, someone might restore it to its former glory. For it seems that an euro project of several billions, to be financed by the European Union, aims to rejuvenate the gardens around the Palace with the likelihood to pull down the Monument, while the fate of the Palace itself remains still very uncertain.

Whatever the outcome, one thing is sure – demolishing the monuments of an oppressive old regime is not going to erase 45 years of history. Worst, those who forget the past, are doomed to repeat it, so they say.

Back to the early post-war years, unlike the time at the turn of the century, most of the architects toiling after WW II were Bulgarians, educated in Sofia. By that time the city had expanded a great deal. And a real accommodation crisis was upon it. For the authorities the way to deal with it was to restrict the residency permits for Sofia.

As early as July 1942, during the war years, a new regulation was issued in order to prevent a housing crisis in the capital, stating that "the settlement and registration of new citizens of Sofia is prohibited." This did not apply to persons employed in Sofia and holding positions of state, municipal or other office of public authority. Temporary stays were possible, with police authorization, in case of illness, visit or business trip. Exceptions were made for students.

The authorities also obliged owners of properties in Sofia with available living space in their dwellings to let it out for residential use. Later on it was stipulated what the living space per resident should be: 2 people to share 1 room, while 1 family or household wasn't allowed to have more than 1 accommodation in the capital. This regulation underwent various changes as time went by and was in force till 1990! What happened was that in practice two, sometimes even three generations of one family were obliged to live for years under the same roof, sharing one bathroom/WC and one kitchen.

During the early years of the socialist era, there were even cases where some had to share their accommodation with complete strangers. An acquaintance of mine recounted how after years and years of co-existence with an unwanted lodger in their flat, situated in the very centre of the city, they found out that he actually owned a property in the suburbs and were finally able to kick him out.

After the changes of the 90s, things reached the other extreme – Sofia became once again a huge building site and its citizens, eager to make up for all the years they were crammed together, started to increase their property holdings. The careful planning of the previous regime was over and done with and new constructions went on unchecked. With corruption thriving, that meant that building permits were easily granted for the right amount of money and no consideration was given neither to ecological issues, nor to archaeological treasures. Nobody really cared; that is nobody except a handful of idealists who were fighting a losing battle.

Architect Tangarov, a leading Bulgarian architect, was frequently in conflict with the establishment and with some of his colleagues over such issues. In 2000, when the remains of a 4th century monastery, very likely connected with the notorious Ecclesiastical Council of Serdica, were discovered in the capital, as a coordinator of the Friends of Sofia Committee, Tangarov tried hard to save the ruins threatened with destruction by construction work. He published an article in Arch – Art, a Bulgarian publication (9th August 2000) and yours truly got involved, writing a letter to UNESCO on his behalf. All was in vain. The building work went on regardless. *"The nonchalance of the institutions, responsible for the city memory, is incredible,* says Tangarov, *after three letters from the National Institute of Monuments of Culture to halt the project and an order to stop from the States Building Control, the construction work still continues."* He goes on to emotionally conclude: *"2000 years ago Christ was crucified and later he rose from the dead. Today we are witnesses to a long awaited rising, only to see it concreted over with the 'three crosses' of the new Golgotha in the holy altar of the oldest monastery in Sofia."* UNESCO's administration didn't even take the trouble to respond to the letter.

The results of this rampant construction work in Sofia are there to be seen – lots of new, unfinished high rise buildings, erected without planning permission, are scattered all over the capital and are falling already into rack and ruin, along with many beautiful houses, built at the end of the 19th century, which need some investment and TLC to be brought back to their former glory. There is a plenitude of empty flats, bought just "as an investment", while a growing number of people live on their own, in accommodations designed for big families.

Lots of new churches also saw the light of day in the post-Communist era. While in other European cities churches fall into disuse and are often converted into secular buildings, the churches in Sofia have multiplied. And, it should be noted, places of worship for other religions besides Orthodox co-exist peacefully side by side in the very centre of the Bulgarian capital. One can find here the Synagogue, the Banya Bashi Mosque and the newly restored St Joseph Catholic Church in very close proximity to the Christian Orthodox churches of St. Petka and St. Nedelia.

One other area, we have to say, remains unchanged – Sofia was and still is a very green city; literally. Parks and gardens still dominate its territory and hopefully it will stay that way. This is important, because in some other respects things look, well, a bit grim.

Despite the new and fancy developments, the city infrastructure is not up to much, the roads can't cope with the increasing traffic, the streets, beyond the main traffic arteries, are not properly maintained, pitted with potholes and the luxury vehicles that circulate about, just park on the pavement, forcing the pedestrians onto the road, because there is a shortage of parking spaces in the city.

Most Sofianites today seem to go about their affairs, quite oblivious of their surroundings. Well, not exactly – they do concentrate their efforts on beautifying their homes – and on acquiring the best vehicles that money can buy, even if they have to drive them through the mud and the potholes – what the hell – out-doing the Joneses is all that matters!

The 70s *"model city that aches of respectability"* of Leslie Gardiner has been transformed into something completely different in the new Millennium – a city of contrasts – more exciting, more daring, definitely, but also rather harsh, with the old charm – lost somewhere on the way.

However, those who don't know Sofia of old, might have a

more favourable opinion. The Lonely Planet sees it as a *"pleasingly laid-back capital often overlooked by tourists"* and appreciates its modern appearance with *"its old east-meets-west atmosphere"* where *"onion-domed churches, Ottoman mosques and stubborn Red Army monuments share the skyline with vast shopping malls and glassy five-star hotels"*. Sounds enticing; however, it's one thing to come as a tourist and to potter about, enjoying a carefree vacation and quite another to live here permanently.

And one other thing, just for the record: the onion-domed churches are in fact Russian; there is only one of them in the centre of Sofia, the splendid St. Nicholas church, built as the official church of the Russian Embassy, which used to be next door at the end of the 19th century. The Bulgarian Christian Orthodox Churches are influenced by the Byzantine style and the domes are not onion-shaped. Even the Alexander Nevski Cathedral, built in honour of the Russian troops who perished during the Russian–Turkish war, named after a Russian Saint and designed by the Russian architect Pomerantsev, has got traditional, albeit gold-plated, domes. As for the *"stubborn Red Army monument"* – it has to be singular, for there is just one, becoming now a very controversial monument. Lots of people want to get rid of it – in fact since 2010 there is a "Citizens Initiative Committee" in existence, aiming at *"the removal and the displacement of the Soviet army monument"*. The reasons for this initiative are all valid, although they omitted one important consideration – no lives were lost during the Soviet invasion of Bulgaria, because it was unthinkable that the Bulgarians would ever fight the Russians. The Nazis knew it and withdrew without much ado before the Red Army's arrival. So a monument like that is not appropriate to say the least. Yet, demolishing it is not going to change a thing. It should be left where it is as a warning – to quote Levski: *"Whoever liberates us, will also enslave us."*

However, there is another monument from the Communist era, very similar in style, dedicated to those who fell for the freedom of their country, meaning here the Communists, the five-pointed star indicating the Communist connection. It was inaugurated on 2nd June 1956, the anniversary of Hristo Botev's death, whose name is dear to every patriotic Bulgarian – a revolutionary from a completely different time, who fought for the liberation from Ottoman rule. The monument, an imposing feature, whose central part is a 41 m high obelisk, is situated in the park which was then known as "The Park of Freedom", but today has reverted to its previous name Boris' Garden (after King Boris III). At that time the monument was a place of "pilgrimage" for the Communist elite and the stage for many commemorations. Now it looks rather forlorn and abandoned. Some of its bronze figures, frozen in their heroic postures, have either been maimed or have lost their weapons as a result of the vagaries of time or the attacks of protesters. The words engraved in the granite – only just visible – are a quote from Botev's famous poem, but look out of place here; written at a different time; *"The one, who falls in battle for freedom, will never die"*. Those lines do apply to the charismatic Bulgarian revolutionary poet, who indeed sacrificed his life for his country's freedom, in joining belatedly the doomed April uprising, following the Radetzki ship exploit. However, the monument of freedom itself, as a relic of the previous regime and a burial ground for pre-war Communist martyrs, has been largely forgotten.

    On the other hand, getting rid of the monument of Comrade Lenin, facing St. Petka's church and the former Home of the Party, although not an easy task, was a very popular idea. Moving this communist colossus that weighted some 45 tons to the Museum of Socialist Art, where it rightfully belongs, must have been quite a challenge. And although not everyone likes the modern statue of St. Sofia erected in its place, it is eye-catching enough and in a way it embodies the spirit of the city. Perhaps with time people will appreciate it more. Even the Eiffel Tower had its detractors at the time, including Maupassant, Dumas, Gounod and many more, yet it has now become the symbol of Paris.

    Meanwhile, Peter Dikov, the chief architect of Sofia, sees a bright future for the city. The new vision for Sofia includes more pedestrian zones, more areas for sport and recreation, improving the traffic in the city centre. The areas around Sveti Sedmochislenitsi Church, along Graf Ignatiev Street and from there - the stretch along the river Perlovska, all the way to Eagles Bridge, are to receive a makeover, with the aim to transform the city centre into an "attractive, ecological and beautiful" place. These plans are yet to be approved; the Sofianites are invited to get involved in the discussions and then – it would be decision time and a question of financing the project. We should watch this space!

So there we are – Sofia today is struggling to come to terms with its communist past and to keep pace with the ever more demanding present day. The city that doesn't age has to run just to stay in one place. Time flows faster than the water from its numerous springs. Even so, it's time to finish with another quote of Levski: *"Time is in us and we are in time, it turns us and we turn it."*

CONCLUSION

The Sofia of today is well and truly a 21st century city. But should you care to look past the modern facades, you'll still find the remains of the ancient metropolis. While I was writing this book, the city has undergone a metamorphosis. The diggers we saw in the beginning, are now gone to a new site, another metroline is to run through the centre and who knows what treasures might be discovered? However, at long last and for the time being at least, the tiny St. Petka church is left in peace. The metro station nearby is already in service and the metro runs through the ancient city, buried for millennia underneath the later urban layers. Parts of *Decumanus Maximus* and *Cardo Maximus*, at their intersection, are once again exposed to the elements, just a few metres beneath the present street level, showing us the open heart of Roman Serdica. So we can literally walk in the footsteps of Constantine the Great!

Some treasures of this ancient world, discovered during the excavation process, have now been brought up to the light of day and displayed in a museum in situ for everyone to see and admire. They could have been better presented of course. The Roman capitals for example should be seen from underneath to be appreciated; as it is they don't look that impressive in the glass cases in which they are placed.

But still! The gods of the underworld have allowed us to recuperate what was once ours. Let's hope that we recognize its value and preserve it. In one other respect they have been generous; the thermal mineral water still flows as freely as it ever did. Come, cup your hands underneath and drink as much as you like – its delicious, this undervalued treasure of Sofia the wise!

My story comes to an end. I rest my pen. Or shall I say – I am about to switch off my computer – it's just not the same! Anyway – end of story – but not the end of Sofia's story! Hope, you liked it! And if it has awoken your curiosity and you decide to find out more, to go to the city, to explore, to roam the streets that Constantine the Great once roamed – my task will be done, my wish would have been granted.

BIBLIOGRAPHY

Sofia Municipality, Old Sofia Municipal Enterprise with Historical Museum of Sofia , Cultural Heritage of Sofia. Problems and perspectives, 2010 (Bulgarian language)

Historical Museum of Sofia, Sofia History Society, Serdica – Sredets – Sofia, Publishing of the Fatherland Front, Sofia, 1976 (Bulgarian language)

John Boardman, I. E. S. Edwards, E. Sollberger, and N. G. L. Hammond, The Cambridge Ancient History, Volume 3, Part 2: The Assyrian and Babylonian Empires and Other States of the Near East, from the Eighth to the Sixth Centuries BC, 1992

Norman Davis, Europe A History (Pimlico, 1997)

R. P. Guérin Songeon, Histoire de la Bulgarie depuis les origines jusqu'à nos jours, 485-1913; avec une préface de Gustave Schlumberger

Leon Ruzicka, The Coinage Of Serdica, 1915, translated from German by Darte Kurth (English translation of Ruzicka's 1915 catalog of the Roman Provincial coinage of Serdica. Including plates and enhanced with photographs of coins with permission of the owners)

Howard Hayes Scullard, From the Gracchi to Nero: A History of Rome from 133 BC to AD 68

Watson, Alaric, Aurelian and the Third Century, London: Routledge (1999)

J.F. Knipfing, The edict of Galerius 311 AD – re-considered

Joan Mervyn Hussey, The Cambridge Medieval History, Cambridge University Press, 1957

Ovidiu Albert, The Council from (sic) Serdica (343) – A Crossing Point between West and East, Studia Antiqua et Archaeologica, XII, Iaşi, 2006

George Sale, George Psalmanazar, Archibald Bower, George Shelvocke, John Campbell, John Swinton, An universal history: from the earliest accounts to the to the present time, Part 1, Volume 14, (Printed for C. Bathurst, 1780)

John Anthony Cramer, A geographical and historical description of ancient Greece, (Section V, Thracia, page 284) Oxford at the Clarendon Press MDCCCXXVIII

J. B. Bury, A history of the later Roman Empire from Arcadius to Irene, 395 AD to 800 A.D. (1889).

J. B. Bury, History of the Eastern Empire from the Fall of Irene to the Accession of Basil: A.D. 802-867

J.B. Bury, The Cambridge Medieval History, volumes 1-5

Ammianus Marcellinus. With An English Translation. John C. Rolfe, Ph.D., Litt.D. Cambridge. Cambridge, Mass., Harvard University Press; London, William Heinemann, Ltd. 1935-1940.

The Roman History of Ammianus Marcellinus. During the Reigns of the Emperors Constantius, Julian, Jovianus, Valentinian, and Valens, translated By C.D. Yonge, M.A

Jonathan Bardill, Constantine, Divine Emperor of the Christian Golden Age, 2012, Cambridge University Press

Charles Matson Odahl, Constantine and the Christian empire, 2004, Routledge

Noel Emmanuel Lenski, Failure of empire: Valens and the Roman state in the fourth century A.D., 2002 by the Regents of the University of California

Thomas S. Burns, Barbarians within the gates of Rome, a study of Roman military policy and the Barbarians ca 375-425 AD (1994)

Peter J. Heather, The fall of the Roman Empire a new history of Rome and the Barbarians, Oxford University Press 2006

Amédée Simon Thierry, Histoire d'Attila et de ses successeurs, 1864

Thompson, Edward Arthur, The Huns, Blackwell Publishing, 1996

Alan K. Bowman, Peter Garnsey, Averil Cameron, The Cambridge Ancient History: The Crisis of Empire, A.D. 193-337, Cambridge University Press 2005

Sidonius, Poems and letters. With an English translation, introd., and notes by W.B. Anderson. Published 1936 by Harvard University Press in Cambridge. Written in English.

Priscus, fr. 8 in *Fragmenta Historicorum Graecorum* (Priscus at the court of Attila, translation by J.B. Bury)

Penny MacGeorge, Late Roman Warlords, 2002 Oxford University Press

Procopius, De aedificiis, IV, I, ed. Haury,III, 2

Constantine VII, 10th century Eastern Roman Emperor, *De Administrando Imperio* ("On the Governance of the Empire")

Panos Sophoulis, Byzantium and Bulgaria, 775-831, 1974

M. Meško, Pecheneg Groups in the Balkans (ca. 1053-1091) according to the Byzantine Sources. The Steppe Lands and the World Beyond Them, 2013

Paul Stephenson, Byzantium's Balkan Frontier: A Political Study of the Northern Balkans, 900-1204

Choniates 434 (trans. 238)

John V. A. Fine, The Early Medieval Balkans: A Critical Survey from the Sixth to the Late Twelve Century, 1991, published by the University of Michigan Press

István Vásáry, Cumans and Tatars: Oriental Military in the Pre-Ottoman Balkans, 1185–1365, Cambridge University Press, 24 September 2009

Kiril Petkov ,The Voices of Medieval Bulgaria, Seventh-Fifteenth Century: The Records of a Bygone Culture, 2008

Alexandru Madgearu, Byzantine Military Organization on the Danube, 10th-12th Centuries, Koninklijke Brill Leiden NV,The Netherlands, 2013

Steven Runciman, A History of the Crusades, Cambridge University Press, 1951

John Haldon,The Byzantine Wars, The History Press, 2008

Jeannette Miteva , Sofia, une ville à la croisée des chemins. Histoire et culture (in French)

Ward, Adolphus William, Sir, 1837-1924; Waller, Alfred Rayney, 1867-1922, The Cambridge history of English literature (1907), New York: G. P. Putnam's Sons, Cambridge, England : University Press

Colin Imber , The Crusade of Varna, 1443-45 (Crusade texts in translation), 2006, Ashgate publishing Ltd

Forbes, Nevill, Toynbee, Arnold Joseph, Hogarth, D. G., Mitrany, David , The Balkans: A History of Bulgaria, Serbia, Greece, Rumania, Turkey, 1915, Oxford Clarendon Press

Franz Babinger , Mehmed the Conqueror and His Time, 1978 published by Princeton University Press

Ogier Ghiselin de Busbecq, Imperial Ambassador at Constantinople, 1554-1562, The Turkish Letters: Translated from the Latin of the Elzevir Edition of 1663; LSU Press, 1927   Robert Dankoff, The Intimate Life of an Ottoman Statesman: Melek Ahmed Pasha (1588-1662): as Portrayed in Evliya Çelebi's Book of Travels (Seyahat-Name)

Nukhet Varlik , Disease and Empire: A History of Plague Epidemics in the Early Modern Ottoman Empire (1453-1600), University of Chicago, 2008

Encyclopaedia Britannica, 11th Edition, Volume 4, Part 4 "Bulgaria"

James Henderson, The travels of Bertrandon de La Brocqúière, to Palestine: and his return from Jersulem overland to France, during the years 1432 & 1433. Extracted and put into modern French from a manuscript in the National library at Paris; Translated by Thomas Jones Esq at Hafod Press MDCCCVII (1807)

Bertrandon de la Broquière, Le voyage d'outremer de Bertrandon de La Broquière, premier écuyer tranchant et conseiller de Philippe le Bon, duc de Bourgogne; publ. et annot. par Ch. Schefer, 1892, E. Leroux (Paris)

Mundy, Peter, The Travels of Peter Mundy, in Europe and Asia, 1608[-]1667, 5 vols, edited by Richard Carnac Temple, 1907[-]67

Spencer, Edmund, Travels in European Turkey in 1850, 2 vols, 1851

Jean Chesneau (Author), Charles Henri Auguste Schefer, Le Voyage De Monsieur D'Aramon Ambassadeur Pour Le Roy En Levant (1887) (French Edition)

Gédoyn "Le Turc", consul de France à Alep 1623-1625, Journal et correspondance, ouvrage publié pour la Société d'histoire diplomatique par A. Boppe. Published 1909 by Typ. Plon-Nourrit in Paris. (in French)

James Samuelson, Bulgaria, Past and Present: Historical, Political, and Descriptive, 1888, London Trübner

Cengiz Toraman, Sinan Yilmaz, Fatih Bayramoglu, Estate accounting as a public policy tool and its application in the ottoman empire in the 17th century, De Computis, Spanish Journal of Accounting History, 2006

Caroline Finkel, Osman's Dream: The Story of the Ottoman Empire 1300-1923, first published in Great Britain in 2005 by John Murray (publishers), an Hachette UK company

An Economic and Social History of the Ottoman Empire, edited by Halil İnalcık, Donald Quataert, Cambridge University Press, 1994

Ferrières-Sauvebœuf (comte de), Mémoires historiques, politiques et géographiques des voyages du comte de Ferrières-Sauvebœuf: faits en Turquie, en Perse et en Arabie, depuis 1782, jusqu'en 1789 : avec ses observations sur la religion, les mœurs, le caractere & le commerce de ces trois nations : suivies de détails très-exacts sur la guerre des Turcs avec les deux cours impériales, d'Autriche et de Russie, les dispositions des trois armées, & les résultats de leurs campagnes par Louis François]

Ami Boué, Recueil d'itinéraires dans la Turquie d'Europe (in French)

Milen V. Petrov, Everyday Forms of Compliance: Subaltern Commentaries on Ottoman Reform, 1864-1868, Cambridge University Press

Émile de Laveleye, La péninsule des Balkans: Vienne, Croatie, Bosnie, Serbie, Bulgarie, Roumélie, Turquie, Roumanie, published by C. Muquardt Bruxelles, 1888 (in French)

William Miller, Travels and Politics in the Near East, 1898

John LC Booth,Trouble in the Balkans (Experiences of a Special Correspondent in Macedonia in 1904), 1905

Frederick Moore, The Balkan Trail, New York, the Macmillan Company 1906

De Windt, Harry, Through Savage Europe, being the Narrative of a Journey, throughout the Balkan States and European Russia, 1907

M.A John Macdonald, Czar Ferdinand and his people, 1913, London, Edinburgh, T. C. & E. C. Jack

Mari Agop Firkatian, Diplomats and Dreamers: The Stancioff Family in Bulgarian History

Maude M. C. Ffoulkes, My own affairs, by the Princess Louise of Belgium, tr.

Forbes, Toynbee, Mitrany,Hogarth, The Balkans : a history of Bulgaria, Serbia, Greece, Rumania, Turkey, Oxford University Press, 1915

Robert de Bourboulon (Count), Bulgarian Diaries, Colibri, 2007

Will Seymour Monroe, Bulgaria and Her People: With an Account of the Balkan Wars Macedonia and the Macedonian Bulgars, 1914, Boston

Felix Kanitz Danubian Bulgaria and the Balkans(Leipzig, 1882)

Konstantin Josef Jireček ,Travels in Bulgaria(Czech, 1888)

Simeon Radev The Builders of Modern Bulgaria (in Bulgarian - Строителите на съвременна България. Том 1 (*Царуването на кн. Александра 1879-1886*) Симеон Радев)

Stefan Tsanev, Bulgarian Chronicles, (Bulgarian language; Български хроники: история на нашия народ от 2137 пр. Хр. до 1453 сл. Хр., Стефан Цанев, 2008)

Louis Launay, La Bulgarie d'hier et de demain, Hachette, 1907 (in French)

Raymond A. Jones The British Diplomatic Service, 1815-1914

Adolphe Laurent Joanne, Émile Isambert, Itinéraire descriptif, historique et archéologique de l'Orient, Librairie de L. Hachette, 1861

Svetlana Paunova From Ottoman to Western Infrastructure: Preliminary notes on Building the Waterworks of Sofia in the second half of the 19th century, Sofia University "St. Kliment Ohridsky"

Gancho Bakalov , People's Club "Slavic Discourse" (1880-2005) , Sofia, 2005 (in Bulgarian)

INDEX

Aaron, Governor of Sredets (65, 66)
Alexander Asen, Sebastocrator (84, 85)
Alexander Barov, Architect (222)
Alexander Battenberg, Prince (17, 165, 166)
Alexander Dondukov-Korsakov, Russian Commissioner (147)
Alexander the Great, Macedonian Ruler (19, 20)
Alexander Pomerantsev, Russian Architect (187)
Alexander Stamboliyski, Politician (191, 209, 210)
Alexander Tsankov, Politician (209, 212)
Aleko Konstantinov, Lawyer & Writer (176)
Alexius I Komnenos, Emperor (72)
Amcazade Huseyin, Grand Vizier (120)
Ami Boué, Physician, Scientist, Linguist, Travel Writer (126, 127, 128, 129,130, 172, 234)
André Lutken, Danish Traveller (161)
Andrew I, King of Hungary (70)
Anthemius, General/Emperor (4, 48, 49, 50)
Anton Toma Bezenšek, Slovenian Linguist (183)
Antonin Kolar, Czech Architect/Urbanist (181, 182)
Apollinaris Sidonius, Poet/Saint (49)
Arab Receb Pasha, Supreme Commander (119)
Arnoldo Zocchi, Italian Sculptor (193)
Arthur Douglas Howden Smith, American Journalist (200)
Asen I, King of Bulgaria (83)
Aspar, Master of the Soldiers (50, 51)
Assen Jordanoff, Bulgarian Inventor, Avionics Engineer (195, 196)
Attila the Hun, Ruler (4, 14, 47, 48, 50)
August Schedevi, Czech Entrepreneur (155)
Aurelian, Emperor (30, 32, 33)
Ban Yanuka, Commander (95, 96)
Barbarossa, Leader of the 3rd Crusade (5, 81, 82)
Bayezid II, Sultan (106)
Basil II, the Bulgar-Slayer, (Boulgaroktonos) Emperor (4, 65, 66, 67, 68)
Basileios Tzintziloukes, Military Commander (74)
Béla-Alexius, Despot/Kaiser/King of Hungary (76, 77, 81)
Bertrandon de Brocquiere, Councellor of the Duke of Burgundy (99, 233)
Bogomil /Bishop Domnio (54)
Boris I, King of Bulgaria (63, 64)
Boris II, King of Bulgaria (65, 66, 108)
Boris III, King of Bulgaria (28, 169, 170, 191, 212, 214, 227)
Botko, Governor (68)
Clémentine of Bourbon Orleans, Queen-Mother (166, 167)
Comentiolus, General (57)
Conrad III, Leader of German Crusaders (74)
Constans, Emperor (38, 39, 40, 41)
Constantine I the Great, Emperor (27, 33, 35, 36, 37, 113, 229, 231)
Constantine II Asen, King of Bulgaria (98)
Constantine X, Emperor (70)

Constantine Tikh, King of Bulgaria (86)
Constantius II, Emperor (4, 38, 39, 40, 41, 42)
Caracalla, Emperor (30, 31)
Czernin, Diplomat (110)
Damian, Bulgarian Patriarch (65)
David, Governor of Sredets (65, 66)
Denkoglu, Philanthropist (133, 135)
Desislava, Wife of Sebastocrator Kaloyan (86)
Dimitar Petkov, Mayor (148, 161)
Dimitar Spisarevski, Bulgarian Aviator (215)
Dimitar Traykovich, Philantropist (134)
Dimcho Debelianov, Bulgarian Poet (179, 180)
Diocletian, Emperor (8, 33, 35)
Dukas, Historian (104)
Edicon, Attila's Envoy (48)
Edmund Spencer, Captain, British Travel Writer (11, 92, 128, 129, 130, 131)
Elias Riggs, Dr., American Missionary (131)
Elmas Mehmed Pasha, Grand Vizier (120)
Emile De Laveleye, Belgian Economist (157, 158, 159, 160, 234)
Eudokia, Empress (71)
Eumène Queillé, French Financial Controller (158)
Evgenia Mars, Bulgarian Poet (174, 175)
Evliya Chelebi, (5, 116, 117, 118, 119)
Felix Kanitz, Austro-Hungarian Geographer (151, 157, 234)
Ferdinand Fellner, Viennese Architect (189)
Ferdinand of Saxe-Coburg Gotha, King of Bulgaria (12, 166, 167, 168, 169, 170, 171, 172, 186, 187, 189, 190, 191, 195, 197, 202, 204, 206, 207, 208)
Fife, Captain, British Military Attaché (144)
Frank Lascelles, British Ambassador (160)
Frederick Moore, Writer (185, 186, 234)
Friedrich Grünanger, Austro-Hungarian Architect (164)
Galerius, Emperor (27, 33, 34, 35)
Gallienus, Emperor (31)
Gerhard Wengel, German Aviator (215)
Germanus, General (4, 55)
George Scylitzes (80)
Gervase of Ebstorf , Cartographer (88)
Geza, Crusader, Brother of King Béla (81)
Giovanna, Queen-Consort of Boris III (213)
Godfrey of Bouillon, Leader of 1st Crusade (72)
Gratian, Emperor (44)
Gregory Antiochos, Civil Servant (77, 78)
Grenaud, Count, Marshal of the Palace to King Ferdinand (167)
Gurko, Russian General (144)
Hans Dernschwam, Diplomat (109)
Haralampi Tachev, Bulgarian Artist (184, 185)
Harry de Windt, Travel Writter (147, 197, 198, 234)
Henry II, Duke of Austria (76)
Henri Blount, Traveller (111)

Heraclius, Emperor (58)
Hermann Gottlieb Helmer, Viennese Architect (189)
Hormidac, Hun Leader (48, 50)
Hristo Botev, Bulgarian Poet (139, 143, 150, 227)
Irene, Queen of Bulgaria (86)
Isaac I Komnenos, Emperor (70, 72)
Isaac II Angelus, Emperor (81, 82)
Ivan Alexander, King of Bulgaria (92, 93, 94, 97, 98)
Ivan Asen , King of Bulgaria (83, 84)
Ivan Hadjienov, Mayor (160)
Ivan Mrkvička, Czech Artist (182)
Ivan Shishman, King of Bulgaria (86, 87, 119)
Ivan Stratsimir, King of Bulgaria (94)
Ivan Vazov, Poet-Laureate (138, 174, 175, 194)
James Samuelson, Writer (150, 157, 233)
Januarius MacGahan, American Journalist & War Correspondent (143, 144)
Jaroslav Věšín, Czech Artist (182)
JLC Booth, Special Correspondent (185)
John Hunyadi (5, 95, 99, 100, 102, 104)
John Kinnamos, Historian and Military Secretary (74, 75, 76)
John Macdonald, Writer (141, 166, 167, 186, 234)
John Mandeville, Travel Writer (89, 91)
Jordan Tangarov, Bulgarian Architect /Urbanist (16, 21, 29, 187, 220, 221, 224)
Josef Waldhart, Austro-Hungarian Consul (144, 146, 147)
Joseph Sebastian Oberbauer, Artist/Engineer (182, 183)
Julia Domna , Empress (10, 184)
Justinian I the Great, Emperor (4, 11, 12, 53, 54, 55, 113)
Kaloyan, Sebastocrator (84, 85, 86)
Kasim Pasha, Commander (100, 101)
Kegen, Pecheneg Leader (69, 70)
Kimon Georgiev, Politician (212, 217)
Klevit, Metropoliatan of Sofia (98)
Konstantin Jireček, Czech Historian, Bulgarian Minister (149, 151, 181)
Konstantin Jovanović, Architect (153, 163)
Krakra, Governor (67)
Krum the Terrible, (26, 59, 60, 61, 62)
Kyril, Bulgarian Prince (170)
Lala Şahin Pasha, Commander (95, 160)
Laura Karavelova, Socialite, Wife of Peyo Yavorov (178, 179)
Léandre François René le Gay, French Vice Consul (141, 142, 143, 144, 145, 147)
Leo I, Emperor (48, 50, 51)
Leo III, Emperor (59)
Leo V, Emperor (62)
Levski, Bulgarian National Hero (6, 139, 140, 226, 228)
Louis Deshayes, Baron de Courmemin (110)
Louis François de Ferrière, Count de Sauveboeuf (124, 125)
Louis Gédoyn, French Consul (111)
Louis de Launay, French Geologist/Writer (13, 202, 203, 235)
Louise of Belgium, Cousin of Ferdinand (170, 171, 172, 234)

Magdalina Stancheva, Bulgarian Archaeologist (9, 28, 219)
Malamir, Bulgarian Ruler (4, 62)
Manuel I Komnenos, Emperor (5, 74, 75, 76, 77, 80)
Marcus Aurelius, Emperor (24, 25)
Marcus Licinius Crassus (21)
Maria Thamara/Kera Tamara, Bulgarian Princess , Consort of Murad I (94)
Marie-Louise of Bourbon-Parma; Queen-Consort of Ferdinand (168, 169, 170)
Marin Drinov, Head of Education (132, 181)
Martin Todorov, Mayor (202)
Mary Emma Olliffe Lascelles, Ambassadors Wife (160, 161)
Mary Wortley Montagu, Ambassadors Wife (121)
Matasuntha, Wife of General Germanus (55)
Maurice, Emperor (4, 56)
Maximinus, Byzantine Official (47, 48)
Mehmed II, the Conqueror, Sultan (104, 105)
Mehmed Pasha, Grand Vizier (125)
Melek Ahmed Pasha, Governor (116, 232)
Michael Palaiologos, Commander (74)
Midhat Pasha, Statesman/Governor (137, 138)
Mina Todorova, Yavorov's Muse (178)
Moses, Governor of Sredets (65, 66)
Muhammad Al Idrisi, Geographer / Cartographer (88)
Murad I, Sultan (93, 94, 119)
Murad II, Sultan (100, 101)
Murad V, Sultan (142)
Mustapha II, Sultan (120)
Naum Torbov, Bulgarian Architect (188)
Nedelia Petkova, Educator (133, 134)
Neofit Bozveli, Cleric (128)
Nicephorus, Emperor (4, 61)
Nicola, Governor of Sredets (65)
Nicola Lazarov, Bulgarian Architect (189)
Odo of Deuil, Crusader (15, 73, 74)
Ogier Ghiselin de Busbecq, Ambassador (108, 232)
Omurtag, Bulgarian Ruler (4, 62, 63)
Orestes, Attila's Envoy (48)
Osman Nuri Pasha, Commander (144, 145, 146)
Pencho Slaveykov, Bulgarian Poet (176, 179)
Peter Dikov, Bulgarian Architect (227)
Peter, Sebastocrator (84)
Peter Bogdan, Bishop (113, 114, 115, 116)
Peter the Hermit, Leader of the People's Crusade (72, 73)
Peter Mundy, Writer (159, 233)
Petko Karavelov, Politician (153)
Petko Momchilov, Bulgarian Architect (188)
Peyo Yavorov, Bulgarian Poet & Playwright (177)
Philip the Macedon (19)
Priscus, Greek Historian (47, 48)
Prošeks, Czech Entrepreneurs (156)

Radivoy, Governor (98)
Radoslav Maver, Bulgarian Noble (106)
Rauch, Russian General (144, 145)
Romanos Diogenes, Duke of Serdica/Emperor (70, 71)
Samuel, Governor of Sredets/King of Bulgaria (65, 66, 67, 68)
Sava Filaretov, Educator (133, 135)
Shaw-Lefevre, British Statesman (129)
Simeon II, King/Prime Minister of Bulgaria (28, 189, 214)
Stanislava Karaivanova, Educator (134)
Stefan Stambolov, Politician (153, 162, 167)
Stefan Uroš II Milutin, King & Patron Saint (105)
Stephen III, King of Hungary (76, 77)
Stephen IV, King of Hungary (75)
St. John of Rila (Ivan Rilski), the Miracle-Maker, (4, 80, 81, 105)
St. Nicolas, Bishop/Saint (45)
St. Petka (Paraskeva), Martyr (8, 9, 85, 218, 219, 225, 228)
Stoimen Rilchanin, Educator (131)
Suleiman II, Sultan (119)
Theodoric Amal, the Great (51, 52)
Theodoric Strabo (51)
Theodosius I, Emperor (44, 45)
Theodosius II, Emperor (47)
Tiberius I Constantine (56)
Turakhan Bey, Commander (100, 101)
Trajan, Emperor (29, 57, 67)
Tyrach, Pecheneg Leader (70)
Valens, Emperor (43, 44)
Velyaminov, Russian General (145)
Vasil Gendov, Bulgarian Film-Producer (196)
Vetranio, Emperor (4, 40, 41, 42)
Vigilius, Interpreter (48)
Vincenzo Maria Coronelli, Geographer and Cartographer (113)
Vittorio (Vito) Positano, Consul (145, 146, 147)
Vladislav Gramatic, Chronicler (105)
Walter Sans-Avoir, Leader of French Crusaders (72, 73)
Will Monroe, Writer (158, 159, 177, 234)
William Miller, English Historian and Journalist (162, 199, 234)
Władysław III of Poland/Władysław of Varna, King (99, 100, 102, 103)
Yegen Osman Pasha, Supreme Commander (119)
Yordan Milanov, Bulgarian Architect (188)
Zachary Krusha, Educator (132, 133)
Zeno, Emperor (4, 50, 51, 52, 53)

ABOUT THE AUTHOR

After obtaining her engineering degree in Sofia and a French language degree in Nantes, Bistra Johnson embarked on a new career as a freelance translator and writer. Having travelled a lot and having lived in different European cities, she finally settled in Paris.

By the same author:

THRACIAN PRINCESS
TALES FROM THE FUTURE
DOWN THE LOIRE GRAPEVINE

www.ingramcontent.com/pod-product-compliance
Lightning Source LLC
Chambersburg PA
CBHW061429040426
42450CB00007B/965